DESIGN AND COLOR IN
ISLAMIC ARCHITECTURE

DESIGN AND COLOR IN ISLAMIC ARCHITECTURE

EIGHT CENTURIES OF THE TILE-MAKER'S ART

Photographs by
Roland and Sabrina Michaud

Text by
Michael Barry

With 158 color illustrations

THE VENDOME PRESS
New York · Paris

The transliterations of words and names used in this book reflect Persian rather than Arabic forms.

Published in the USA in 1996 by
The Vendome Press
1370 Avenue of the Americas
New York, NY 10019

Distributed in the USA and Canada by
Rizzoli International Publications
through St. Martin's Press
175 Fifth Avenue
New York, NY 10010

ISBN 0-86565-975-3

Printed and bound in France

Contents

Hanging Gardens and Trees of Life

A Journey to Afghan Central Asia

To the memory of my father

The yellow-brown mountains of the Hindu Kush folded shoulders and brooded over the high Central Asian desert. No colour moved over its hard baked mounds and spiked dry bushes except two gleams of blue, hovering through the dust mist.

AFGHAN TURKESTAN: MAZÂR-E SHARÎF

The gleams were a pair of domes, sheathed in azure tiles. Except for these domes, the little Afghan town, all blind earthwork walls and sandy alleys, was as colourless as its surrounding desert. Indeed, the mud of its flat-roofed houses was moulded from the very mounds of the desert mixed with straw. Even the trees screening the oasis – curtains of ashen poplar to shield the town from sand gusts and, when cut, provide its low houses with roof-beams – were drained of colour. The date-palm does not grow on the heights of Iran or Central Asia: a livid world, biting in winter, in summer bleached.

Except for its mosques.

In 1963 the northern Afghan oasis-town of Mazâr-e Sharîf had no other relief to offer the eye but this cobalt-blue structure, glaring in the sun over its main square. A fretwork of complicated mosaic patterns was drawn over its large flat arched façade like an elaborately ornamented architectural stage-set. The two main domes of the mosque, themselves surrounded by the smaller domes of the minarets likewise clothed in tiles, shifted from green through azure to ultramarine, following the time and mood of day. At dusk, the tiles turned purple, then darkened.

Neither Westernization nor modern warfare had yet much changed Mazâr-e Sharîf in 1963. At vespers, merchants shuttered up their booths with loud slaps, sending up flurries of the doves fed by the faithful around the shrine. (According to local lore, any pigeon that haunts this mosque turns white after 40 days.) Worshippers hurried for ritual washing around the ablution tank. Most of the men were cloaked in striped caftans with overlong sleeves, usually not worn but left dangling or thrown capewise over their backs. Many swung lanterns in these days before there was much electricity: the crowds of devotees, assembling for vespers under the arches of Mazâr-e Sharîf's mosque, glowed like fireflies in the gathering darkness. Women hooded in dull drapes, with netting across their eye-slits, flitted through the courtyard as silently as ghosts. Unlike most Middle Eastern mosques, the shrine of Mazâr-e Sharîf at this time had not yet been disfigured by loudspeakers: summonses to worship were still delivered by human voice alone. Six mullahs called to each other in liturgical Arabic from the platforms of their respective minarets under the darkening domes as the first stars blinked across a "green" sky, as it is locally perceived and called in the town's vernaculars – mainly Afghan-accented Persian, some Pashtô, also Uzbeki or Eastern Turkish.

The following morning allowed more detailed inspection of the decorative complication of the shrine's revetment. Two strains stood out within its dominant blue: turquoise and night-blue. These were outlined in turn with mosaic dots or stripes of white, black, green, yellow and red – the "Seven

AFGHAN MASONS WITH HANDBARROWS
AT THE SHRINE OF MAZÂR-E SHARÎF IN 1964

Colours" or *Haft Rang* according to the medieval Persian designation for the traditional palette of tileworkers throughout Eastern Islam.

In 1963, after matins the precincts of Mazâr-e Sharîf's mosque were thronged not only with pilgrims but with masons. The shrine was renewing its tiles. Labourers rolled their pyjama trousers knee-high to climb wooden scaffolds propped wherever old tiles had flaked off to reveal medieval yellow brickwork beneath. Other workers below unloaded donkeys to empty panniers of sand into the lime-pits, or heaped fresh clay atop archaic barrows without wheels, slung like stretchers from twin poles carried by two men, one leading, the other aft. The foremen might be recognized by their small white turbans – befitting their status as educated men. As they called orders for adjustments to the new ceramic plaques placed in fresh cement, their accents gave them away: an old-fashioned form of Persian with the full ancient range of lengthened vowels, the language of the old poets of medieval Central Asia. These foremen were craftsmen from Herât, a small town in the western reaches of what today is Afghanistan, near the present borders of Turkmenistan and Iran – and once the capital of two great medieval Central Asian Islamic Empires:

the 12th-century Ghôrid and the 15th-century Tîmûrid.

Herât preserves the most renowned workshop for architectural tiles in the region. Down to the Soviet invasion of 1979, Herâtî craftsmen supplied ceramic revetments for all of Afghanistan's major mosques. In 1480 Herâtî artists first erected the structure visible in Mazâr-e Sharîf today. In 1963, their direct successors were sheathing the same shrine in a fresh set of tiles – the mosque was sloughing its old skin – under the patronage of the royal Afghan government.

As late as 1963, many saddle horses from surrounding villages still stood picketed in the by-lanes of Mazâr-e Sharîf. When turbaned riders trotted past the mosque, kicking up dust in a crack of quirts, then the illusion of watching not mid-20th-century repair work but the initial 15th-century construction of the mosque itself became very strong. One-humped camels also padded through the square every morning and evening, loaded with thorn-bushes for kindling. The whole scene around Mazâr-e Sharîf's mosque powerfully suggested almost exactly the same vision of a building crew at work as that painted at the close of the 15th century by Master Behzâd of Herât, the most celebrated of medieval Islamic figurative illuminators. Nothing in the bustle around this mosque seemed to have changed in the half thousand years since Behzâd: the same yellow-brick archway awaiting revetment, roped wooden scaffold, lime-pit, barrow carried on poles, turbaned foremen and shaven-pated crews in rolled-up trousers.

Pre-Soviet Afghanistan, shut in by mountains and waste stretches (its paved roads came only after 1964), still evoked an Islamic Tibet. Abstract designs and calligraphic devices worked into the mosque's redecoration in 1963 were dictated by sanctioned medieval patterns alone. Even during the closing years of Afghan independence when the roads and tourists first came, Herât's traditional craftsmen had no notion of contemporary Western trends in art.

Not that many original tiles from the 15th

THE BUILDING OF CASTLE KHAWARNAQ
WHERE PRINCE BAHRÂM-GÛR WAS BROUGHT UP AS A CHILD
A SECRET HALL HID THE SEVEN EFFIGIES OF HIS FUTURE BRIDES
ILLUMINATION BY BEHZÂD, HERÂT, 1494
ILLUSTRATION TO THE ROMANCE OF KING BAHRÂM
BY THE POET NEZÂMÎ

century still clung to the walls of the shrine by 1963. Eastern Islamic ceramic revetments are only frail membranes of colour thrown over whole buildings, less than a half-millimetre thick to each brick. The mosque's initial medieval tiles had served over several centuries to shield the underlying brittleness of basically poor construction material – ultimately baked clay, which crumbles within years when exposed to the weather. Mazâr-e Sharîf's protective medieval revetment had itself worn off before the middle decades of this century under the combined effects of snow, spring showers and summer sand-gusts. Central Asia's extremes of temperature had thus cracked the tiling to reveal the bare and somewhat homely mass of baked brick beneath. Stripped to its clay core, the design of Mazâr-e Sharîf's mosque appeared heavy-set and undis-tinguished, not to be compared with bolder arches and domes seen elsewhere in the region such as at Esfahân (Isfahan), Samarkand or Herât. But its pellucid skin of tilework had helped to transfigure and lighten even this ponderous provincial shrine, too, under a fairy-spell.

Yet even in Esfahân, Samarkand and Herât, better-known but equally flimsy medieval tiled revetments were also cracking apart by the opening years of this century. The last two generations had therefore seen major efforts at consolidation, restoration and sometimes outright re-creation of coloured revetments bequeathed by the later Islamic Middle Ages to present-day Iran, Uzbekistan and Afghanistan.

Modern Iranian craftsmanship is usually – though not always – hard to fault. Some of Uzbekistan's mid-century repair work, as directed by Soviet archaeologists, is also very good, but some of it is poor even in strictly technical terms and much of it marked with an almost repellent academic coolness, possibly due in some subtle measure to former Soviet scorn for the religious symbolism of what was restored. Slipshod workmanship with no respect for the strengths and drawbacks of traditional materials (which swell or contract a little with the weather) when mixed with modern binders, caused new Soviet tiles on the tip of Tîmûr's (Tamerlane's) dome in Samarkand to fall off within 20 years. Afghan restorations are not necessarily always of a higher aesthetic quality than Uzbek or Iranian ones, but are perhaps more moving, for they are invariably carried out not only with traditional methods but also with something like medieval zeal – bequeathed intact to the country's tilemasters by an uninterrupted line of artists in the Herât Mosque Workshop since the 15th century.

However architecturally thick-set with its low domes and squat, rook-like minarets, the mosque at Mazâr-e Sharîf at least offered sober support for the re-created exuberance of the tiling, whose motifs only gradually disclose themselves to the eye.

TREES OF LIFE AND HANGING GARDENS. On either side of the shrine's ogival or pointed archways, slender columns, twisted into cable-mouldings, rose from plinths atop other larger, semi-circular mouldings representing jars. The stalk-like shafts wound themselves in torsion to meet over the archway, as if growing out of their stylized bowls. Such shafts depict Trees of Life, one of the more ancient cosmological symbols of the Near East, emblematic of the divine unity that underlies the multiplicity of created things. Within the blind ogival niches of the façade, more Trees of Life, drawn in mosaic, sprang from two-dimensional vases as if in response, branching out into curved tendrils that spiralled symmetrically into mirror-images of one another across blue fields. These vegetal scrolls budded into mixed foliage of fig and plane, then into blossoms, before meeting above in arcs echoing their ogival frames. After the yellow glare of the surrounding waste, the shrine's walls tendered a wide expanse of cool blue orchards like Hanging Gardens of Babylon petrified in mosaic but forever in leaf. Arabic technical terms describing such decoration are *tashjîr,* "what is tree-like", and *tawrîq,* "foliage". No human or animal figure enlivened these hanging gardens – any more than in any other Islamic place of worship. As is now too well known almost to bear repetition, traditional Islamic iconophobia normally tolerated figurative art only as flat illustrations inside manuscript books (save of course in the Koran). Hence vegetal tendrils yielded place, on Mazâr-e Sharîf's walls, only to geometric mazes, or to calligraphy.

STAR-MAZES. On shrine-panels throughout the Islamic world, geometric mazes are hardly static but are made vibrant through the jarring of their intersecting colours. Their basic design is stellar: from hexagonal or octagonal stars of "David" or "Solomon" – corresponding to the magic seals of these Prophets – to other stars showing four, five or many dozen points: thereby exploding into multiple spines known as "sun-bursts" (shamseh), in turn prolonged and interlaced with the radiating spikes of other stars into increasingly complex mazes: geometric reflections of the labyrinthine tendrils of the Tree of Life. While the blue of the domes is most emphatically intended both to mirror and to figure the sky – the classical Persian language in turn calls heaven the gombad-e mînâ, "the enamelled azure dome" – the spangled polygons correspond to its stars. Traditional Islamic tilework thus mingles twin motifs of a Garden of Life and a stylized image of the sky to form together the Heavenly Garden: Paradise.

KORANIC CALLIGRAPHY. The maze created by Arabic lettering conjures up another Tree of Life – an important 13th-century mystical treatise (to which we shall refer again) explicitly says so – stylized into further abstraction. Varied calligraphic styles were glazed into the walls of Mazâr-e Sharîf: geometrically angular kûfî (kufic), successively inscribed in simple, knotted, braided and interlaced forms; and several cursives, including upright naskh and slanted thuluth, particular to Arabic, and the "pendant cursive" or nasta'lîq more usually reserved for Persian verses. Except for a few Persian quotations, nearly all the inscriptions at Mazâr-e Sharîf, threaded through tendrils and star-mazes over white, azure or ultramarine grounds, repro-

duced texts from the Arabic Koran. As in the depictions of the Tree of Life, these linked calligrams expressed the notion of an ever-present, under-flowing Cosmic Unity lurking within many forms: made manifest by God to mankind by Self-Revelation through the multiple letters of His Scriptures, even as He discloses Himself within the manifold branches, leaves and blossoms of His Tree.

Mazâr-e Sharîf's wealth of decoration, both what little lingered from the 1480s and the many more new tiles dating from the 1960s, reflected a burning piety that had never ebbed down the centuries, nor has it even today after the shock of Soviet military invasion between 1979 and 1989. The shrine is still, paradoxically, the holiest in Islamic Central Asia, even though Muslims living farther west – in Iran, Turkey or the Arab world – are utterly unaware of its very existence. Yet Mazâr-e Sharîf owes its foundation to the chronicle of a medieval Spanish Moor, that is, to a "Western" or Arabic-speaking Muslim.

Down to the 12th century AD, the site of Mazâr-e Sharîf was occupied only by a small village named Khwâjeh-Khayrân in the Persian sources (or Al-Khayr in the Arabic). This little settlement stagnated in the shadow of a then far more prestigious and indeed venerable nearby city ten miles over the steppe to the west: Balkh, the ancient satrapy of Bactra as it was known to its Macedonian conquerors, where Alexander wedded his Persian bride and which medieval Muslims continued grandly to designate as Umm al-Bilâd, "Mother of Cities" (actually only the exact Arabic rendering of its old Hellenic title of mêtropolis). But in the year 1135, the peasants of the village of Khwâjeh-Khayrân became agitated by strange visions. According to the contemporary writings of the learned Spanish-Arab Abû-Hâmid of Granada, then travelling through the Eastern Islamic lands, at first a single holy man living in the little rural settlement, then 400 of his fellow-villagers, claimed to have seen an identical dream: the revered caliph 'Alî, son-in-law to the Prophet, had appeared to tell them that his true resting-place lay hidden under the soil of their own oasis. News of the villagers' vision unsettled neighbouring oases and troubled the authorities. Khwâjeh-Khayrân's temporal lord was the Emir of nearby Balkh, himself subject to Sultan Sanjar of the Eastern Turkish dynasty of the Great Seljuks, overlord of the region from his capital at Merv in present-day Turkmenistan. An urgent meeting of divines was called at the court of the Emir in Balkh. A sceptical cleric reminded the assembly of what all informed Muslims had been well aware of since the first century of Islam: 'Alî, "the Lion of God", lay buried at Najaf in Iraq. This was a famous shrine. Pilgrims flocked there from all parts of the world. The holy man from Khwâjeh-Khayrân was therefore an impostor, his vision a lie and his congregation deluded.

That same night, the doubting cleric suffered his own kind of "dream". He saw himself suddenly set upon in bed with cudgels by the outraged "ghosts" of holy personages clad in white. The "ghosts" announced themselves as the offended kin of the caliph 'Alî. Was it only a "dream"? The next morning, the cleric's back and ribs were black and blue. (Indignant peasants from Khwâjeh-Khayrân had obviously burst into his bedroom and given him a drubbing, with threats of more, for casting doubt on their story and the honour of the village.) That day, the chastened cleric publicly retracted before the Emir, agreeing that the mortal remains of the "Lion of God" might have been secretly conveyed by the faithful so far to the East to protect them from enemies (or so runs the argument in the 15th-century updating of Abû-Hâmid's story by the poet-theologian Jâmî of Herât). In any event, when the Emir ordered the villagers of Khwâjeh-Khayrân to dig up the ground in their oasis, they duly found a body, miraculously preserved in a shroud, beside an old brick bearing this inscription traced "with a finger": "This is he who loves the Prophet, 'Alî – may God honour him!" (R.D. McChesney tr.) As overlord, Sultan Sanjar ordered the building of a commemorative shrine. This initial structure was completely destroyed during the 13th-century Mongol invasion of Islamic Central Asia. The very

memory of where it had stood faded away, even in the immediate neighbourhood. The rest of the Islamic world never paid any attention and continues to pay respects at 'Alî's tomb in Iraq to this day.

But in the year 1480, scribes at the court of Sultan Hosayn Mîrzâ Bâyqarâ, ruler of Herât, chanced upon the old chronicle of the Spanish-Arab traveller and suggested to their master that the holy caliph 'Alî might indeed lie buried within his kingdom. The reverend Jâmî, the most esteemed and learned divine in late 15th-century Herât, endorsed the tradition and so clinched the issue. A middling warrior but splendid patron of the arts with a talent for poetry and calligraphy, Sultan Hosayn (ruled 1469–1506) was a direct descendant of the dread Turco-Mongol conquering emir of Samarkand, Tîmûr "the Lame" (Persian *Tîmûr-e Lang,* whence the English "Tamerlane", Christopher Marlowe's "Tamburlaine"). Tîmûr bequeathed to his sons an Islamic Empire kneaded with gore and stretched in pain from Anatolia to the approaches of China. His more peace-inclined successors, the refined "Tîmûrid" rulers, chose Herât in place of Samarkand as their capital after his death in 1405. By the close of the 15th century, under the aesthetically sensitive but militarily incompetent late Tîmûrid princes, the kingdom of Herât shrank under the blows of dynastic rivals to little more than what is now the northeast corner of Iran and the northwestern reaches of Afghanistan. Still, Herât under Sultan Hosayn remained a leading intellectual and artistic centre of the Islamic East until his own death in 1506.

If Sultan Hosayn chose to swallow the story and bade his artists raise a proper building, this was undoubtedly a deliberate ploy to help prop up the tottering prestige of his dying kingdom. The ruler bestowed on the village the new name of Mazâr-e Sharîf, the "Noble Shrine", which grew, in turn, into the regional metropolis – while the former capital, Balkh, decayed to a market village.

While no trace exists of the earlier shrine built under Sultan Sanjar, we do know enough about early 12th-century Central Asian architecture reasonably to conjecture that this first mosque bore no other decorative revetment but carved stucco. The structure raised for Sultan Hosayn, however, was different. Fifteenth-century Tîmûrid royal taste demanded that a major shrine be entirely cloaked in blue-dominant tiles, fired by master craftsmen from Samarkand or Herât.

As Donald Wilber pointed out in a seminal article in 1939, the complete sheathing of buildings in coloured tiles, however characteristic in our eyes of Persian-Islamic religious architecture (and though the craft admittedly drew on ceramic traditions handed down from the earlier Near East), nevertheless appears only relatively late in the history of the region's medieval art. From the 8th to the 13th century AD, most monumental revetment in Islamized Iran and Central Asia was restricted to stucco: carved, gilded and painted. The traditional motifs were already there of course – calligraphy, stars and tendrils of the Tree of Life. But only under the House of Tîmûr in the later 14th and 15th centuries did these motifs now appear fired in ceramics that utterly blanketed the structures they adorned – thereby proclaiming in gleaming blue, with no little ostentation, the piety but also peerless wealth and power of the ruling family. The splendour of Esfahân, the azure-tinted capital of the Safavid Royal House of Persia at the turn of the 16th and 17th centuries, was cast in a style largely derived from, indeed adopted in a deliberate retort to, the prestigious models of Herât and Samarkand in the East, whose imperial Tîmûrid heritage the Safavids explicitly claimed. Even so, while good 17th-century Safavid tilework in Esfahân represents the culmination of an artistic tradition, it rarely equals the finest earlier walls raised either in the Central Asian Tîmûrid capitals of Samarkand and Herât, or even in the western Iranian cities of Tabrîz and Esfahân itself under the patronage of the late 15th-century so-called "Turcoman" sultans.

By the early 16th century, the House of Tîmûr had crumbled like one of its own tiled façades. Sultan Hosayn's kingdom fell to pieces in 1507. His lands – and cultural legacy – were clawed over, and finally split, between the Shî'a (or heterodox) rulers of Safavid Iran, and their arch-enemies, the staunchly Sunnî (or orthodox) Uzbek Turks. The Uzbeks remained masters of Samarkand and also – for centuries to come down to the founding of the independent kingdom of Afghanistan in 1747 – of Mazâr-e Sharîf. Herât fell to the Safavids for the next 200 years, though not without hard skirmishing between Shî'a and Sunnî mailed cavalry. But while Safavids and Uzbeks thus struggled for control of the trade routes of Central Asia, Portuguese fleets groped their way to India around the Cape of Good Hope and so ultimately helped to ruin the very overland trail on which Central Asia's merchant prosperity rested. Caravan centres like not only Mazâr-e Sharîf but even Samarkand and Herât faded into obscurity and neglect, so that their very names were all but forgotten by the world at large until Anglo-Russian colonial rivalry in Asia in fairly recent times took a grim interest in them again. And no one outside modern Afghanistan believes that he knows who truly lies buried under one of Mazâr-e Sharîf's twin domes.

But even after the fall of the Tîmûrid kingdom, regional religious fervour continued unabated around the mosque itself. It is the earnestness of Afghan pilgrims at the site in 1963, or today, straining their foreheads against the brass railing surrounding the gravestone, which is beyond doubt. Honest worship by local devotees is what transmuted an arguable pious political fraud by a late medieval sultan into an ornamented shrine glowing with at least their own spiritual intensity.

Fresh visits to Mazâr-e Sharîf, during the two-year lull in killing which intervened between the collapse of Kabul's Communist régime in 1992 and the resumption of Afghanistan's civil war in 1994, confirmed the shrine's survival through the worst. Several important medieval structures nearby were also spared, such as the small but exquisite blue-tiled Tîmûrid oratory of Khwâjeh Mohammad Abû Nasr Pârsâ, dating from 1460–61, in the old oasis of Balkh.

Mazâr-e Sharîf itself had changed. Rows of electric pylons now mounted guard along rectilinear streets paved to allow swift passage to tanks, in what became the main Soviet stronghold in occupied northern Afghanistan. As with the Tîmûrid monuments in neighbouring ex-Soviet Samarkand (or, for that matter, like the case with so many European medieval churches today), the shrine now stood artificially isolated in a dull asphalt waste, cut from its traditional urban moorings: a statue-building. At dusk, harsh neon bulbs erased nostalgic memories. Even the morning's glare, to a better practised eye, now shed only cold light on the lack of mellowness, and worse, garish yellows, raw blues and the rigid designs of the mosque's motifs. Mazâr-e Sharîf's latter-day mosaics lack the subtlety and depth of true Tîmûrid tiles. To see the latter one had to return to Herât, where even modern mosaics, with so many original models at hand, are still wrought with much more of the old magic.

AFGHAN KHORÂSÂN: HERÂT

Herât lies within the Afghan wedge of a triangular borderland formed by the meeting-points of modern Iran, Afghanistan and Turkmenistan. Present-day Uzbekistan touches on Afghanistan only a few hundred miles beyond, just over the immediate brown ridges of the Paropamisus – as Alexander's Greeks called this western spur of the Hindu Kush – which walls off Herât's eastern horizon. This zone, now dissected by so many barbed international frontiers, in past ages made up a single cultural area, called by medieval Muslims *Khorâsân,* that is to say, the "Levant" of the Iranian world, and known as "Areia" or "Ariana" to Alexander. When approached from the west, Khorâsân appears as the true threshold of Central Asia.

The region is almost cut off from the western reaches of the Iranian plateau by a vast salt waste, the Dasht-e Kavîr. But a major caravan trail, now a paved road, avoids this desert by edging along its northern fringe from the area around modern Tehran, through a string of oases and Mashhad, as far as Herât. Here the arid mountains suddenly rise over the thorny flats and block an east-bound traveller's view of the rising sun, but through a cleft yield life to the desert below. Flowing down from these heights, the hitherto cliff-choked waters of the Harî Rûd or "River of Herât" spread wide through the plain, and so create the oasis that nurtured the great city that became the capital of the historic "Levant".

Khorâsân, as the 14th-century Persian geographer Hamdollâh Mostawfî rhetorically put it, is the world's precious conch, Herât its pearl. Time and again, its lustre was quenched with blood, then rekindled. Herât's fertility and convenient site at the western foot of the Hindu Kush guaranteed its rebirth after every bout of destruction as the crossroads of caravan communications along the ancient Silk Route between the Mediterranean and Persia, China and the Indian subcontinent. Herât's mountain wall blocked caravans moving due east. But easier trails leading from Herât afforded access either to Turkestan and on to China through passes over the lower heights to the northeast, or down to India through the arid southern flats. Conversely, pack-trains from both India and Chinese Turkestan bound westwards, by skirting these same mountains, met in Herât's bazaars and *kârawân-sarây-hâ,* its clay-walled inns for caravans or "caravanserais".

Sultan Hosayn's late 15th-century kingdom of Herât, after the loss of its outlying provinces, corresponded exactly to historic Khorâsân, as shrewdly noted by the Sultan's cousin, Prince Bâber of Kabul, in his famous memoirs written in Eastern Turkish: "His country was Khorâsân, with Balkh to the east, Bastâm and Dâmghân to the west, Khwârazm [present-day Turkmenistan] to the north, Qandahâr and Sîstân to the south." Bâber added acidly: "When he once had in his hands such a town as Herî [Herât], his only affair, by day and by night, was with comfort and pleasure; nor was there a man of his either who did not take his ease. It followed of course that, as he no longer tolerated the hardships and fatigue of conquest and soldiering, his retainers and his territories dwindled instead of increasing down to the time of his departure from this world." (A.S. Beveridge tr.)

Sultan Hosayn's departure from this world spelled Herât's political ruin, and the city's recent history has been as stormy as at any time in her tormented medieval past. In the 19th century imperial Britain and Russia, locked in colonial contest, vied to control Herât as the "key to India". The late 20th-century Soviets failed to bend her people to their will in the course of their failed push to the Gulf. Today Herât and her surrounding territories constitute an autonomous and relatively peaceful fiefdom on the margins of Afghanistan's protracted post-Soviet civil war, and sometimes still offer an acceptably safe commercial corridor – again as so often in the past – between what are now the states of Turkmenistan and Pakistan. Her central bazaar with straight streets, intersecting one another at right angles, has survived for centuries under the blue sheen of the Friday Mosque. The medieval and still current sobriquet of this market-crossing under the mosque's tiled façade, the *Châr-Sû,* Persian for the "Four Directions", points to the city's enduring vocation for trade and her stubbornness to survive.

The first Christian traveller to reach the oasis – or to claim he had – was the Italian merchant-adventurer (and spy) Ludovico di Varthema, in the service of the Portuguese in India in the opening years of the 16th century: "Every day", he reported of the city of "Eri" (Herât), "there may be found here for purchase three to four thousand camels loaded with bales of silk." The royal historiographer of the *Casa da Índia* or "India House" in Lisbon, the Renaissance humanist and pioneering Orientalist João de Barros (1496–1570), noted both from hearsay and from a Persian-language chronicle that he ordered to be rendered into Portuguese "that for her fertility the Persians call her Xàr Gulzàr [*Shahr-e Golzâr*], which is to say, the City of Roses", and gave an account of Herât from her glory under Sultan Hosayn down to her recent conquest by the Safavids in 1510.

Herât has existed since remote Achaemenid times. Her first recorded name was *Haraiva.* Her population is mostly of old Persian stock and still speaks her choice medieval form of Persian with rare purity. While Sunnî to a majority extent – hence the historical estrangement from neighbouring Iran – Herât also shelters a large Shî'a minority in her central bazaars. Alexander the Great took the oasis-satrapy of "Areia" in 330 BC and gave the city his own name: *Alexandria Areia.* The Arabs conquered Herât in AD 651.

Medieval Herât enjoyed a first brief golden age under the sultans of the Ghôrid dynasty between 1175 and 1206. For less than a generation she held sway over an empire reaching as far as Delhi, while her architecture influenced the first Islamic building in northern India, and Muslim princes throughout Western Asia sought the strange bronze vessels for which her 12th-century smiths became famous: bowls stamped with signs of the Zodiac and chased in silver calligraphy with vertical letters ending in young women's faces (like the Serpent Queens of the *Thousand and One Nights*). Mongol cavalry overran the oasis in 1221. She re-emerged as a trading centre under her petty Kart dynasty. The limping lord of Samarkand, Tîmûr, slaughtered Herât afresh when the city baulked at his rule in 1383.

The miracle is that she was reborn to even greater beauty with her second golden age: the so-called "Tîmûrid Renaissance" of 1405–1507. Better than Samarkand, Herât Castle provided a strategic vantage point from which to survey the Iranian and Central Asian empire lately hammered together with skull-cairns and impaling stakes by the ruthless Tîmûr. When the latter died in 1405, leaving his son Shâh Rokh to rule, the new, somewhat better-natured Emperor (save when it came to chastising rebellious kin) abandoned Samarkand to the governorship of his own chosen heir, the gifted Prince Ulugh Beg, and set up residence in Herât, whose castle walls he proceeded to line with tiles in unprecedented luxury.

Under the dual reign of Shâh Rokh ("King Rook") in Herât and his son Ulugh Beg ("Great

Lord") in Samarkand, the early 15th-century "Tîmûrid Renaissance" turned both capitals into brilliant academies for the visual arts and into centres for literature written not only in classically sanctioned Arabic and Persian, but also in Turkish: a new development. The Tîmûrids were Turkish-speakers and proud of it. Prince Ulugh Beg, a dedicated astronomer, lent perhaps a more scientific cast to the cultural atmosphere in Samarkand, while his bibliophile brother Prince Bâysonghor ("Lord Falcon") patronized in Herât what became the most famous workshop for manuscript illumination and calligraphy in the Islamic world. The buildings raised by the dynasty in either city were equally resplendent and their coloured walls set the tone, as we will see, for later imperial capitals in Islamic Asia: Tabrîz, Esfahân, Lahore.

But Tîmûrid imperial sway barely survived the dynastic wars that shook the ten-year regency of the dowager Empress Gôhar Shâd following the death of her spouse Shâh Rokh in 1447. The closing decades of the 15th century sheared the Kingdom of Herât of significant military and political power and territorially nearly reduced her to the size of a city-state – although one as cultured and artistically creative, under the 37 years of civilized rule (1469–1506) of Sultan Hosayn Mîrzâ Bâyqarâ, as contemporary Florence far to the west. After the capture of Herât in 1507 by the rival Uzbek Turks, masters of Samarkand itself since 1501, the Tîmûrid prince Bâber, writing in Kabul, rued the fall of the queenly city: "The whole habitable world has not such a town as Herî [Herât] had become under Sultan Hosayn Mîrzâ, whose orders and efforts had increased its splendour and beauty as ten to one, rather, as twenty to one." Bâber dwelt with nostalgia on the vanished days of Sultan Hosayn: "His was a wonderful Age; in it Khorâsân, and Herî above all, was full of learned and matchless men. Whatever the work a man took up, he aimed and aspired at bringing that work to perfection." Bâber further remembered his month of sightseeing in Herât after the Sultan's death in 1506, as a guest of his royal cousins then trying to organize efficient defence (to

no avail) against the conquering Uzbeks: "Every day of the time I was in Herî I rode out to see a new sight. ... Not one famous spot, maybe, was left unseen in those 40 days." Whereupon Prince Bâber enumerates 56 monuments, including one he missed.

After the tumultuous years of Uzbek occupation in 1507, Safavid recapture in 1510 and further clashes between the mounted archers of both Islamic powers for possession of the former royal oasis for another half-century (the Iranians secured Portuguese muskets and won), Herât under 17th-century Safavid governors quietly faded into a provincial town which passed to Afghan rule in 1747 because the Safavid shâhs finally entrusted her defence to an Afghan tribe. But not even utter remoteness could any longer protect her from the havoc of 19th-century Anglo–Russian imperial rivalry, still less from Soviet bombing in the 20th, which combined to destroy most of the buildings on Prince Bâber's list – though not all.

In the spring of 1992, a single northwest tower of Herât Castle, along 250 metres (820 feet) of battlements stripped bare, still shone through the city's swirling palls of dust with spots of Tîmûrid tilework: remnants of a mosaic of tall, bold white calligraphy topped by azure rhombi against a field of pale brick. Wreckage extended over ten kilometres (six miles) to the very base of the tower: shattered mud hovels interspersed with bomb craters. A desiccated, searing wind drove sand through the broken streets at more than 60 kilometres an hour (37 miles an hour). The raised dust, made worse by passers-by, animals and vehicles, created a yellow fog by late afternoon every day. To forbid approach, and camouflage, to resistance fighters, Soviet occupation forces in the 1980s cut down the screens of dark pines that protected the oasis from the blasts of the Wind-of-One-Hundred-and-Twenty-Days, as it is known because it blows all summer, and from the same direction – the western desert.

Lashes of hot dust sprinkled dry showers of multicoloured, fragmented tile-sherds from the damaged but still standing medieval structures on the outskirts.

Herât Castle, then held by government forces, was carefully avoided by the two Soviet bombing waves in 1979 and 1984 which annihilated the western sectors of the city in resistance hands. As if drawn with a ruler, the fort's ramparts mark the sharp divide between what survives of the city and all that was destroyed – everything up to the very base of its walls. To the east of the rubble and the battlements of the castle, the blue-green tiled façade of the spared Friday Mosque looms over the markets and turns, for a few minutes, into a sheet of silver under the morning sun.

To the nearby bazaar of the "Four Directions", the mosque's coloured minarets and pointed arches provide something of a theatrical backdrop, suggestive of Herât in all her 15th-century imperial glory. In 1992, in the trading streets below, lines of refugees in drab cast-off military coats, recently returned from Iran, mingled with turbaned local farmers – most of whom now also wear the same sort of military coats – selling melons and cucumbers from the panniers of their donkeys. Reminiscent of happier times, horse-drawn cabs drove through the crowds with sudden merry jingles of harness and flashes of red tassles.

As at Mazâr-e Sharîf, Herât's mosque mostly fosters a medieval illusion: while founded in 1200 and enlarged in 1498, it has undergone extensive and continuous re-tiling since 1943. The Mosque Workshop's craftsmen did not even interrupt their stubborn labour of restoration during the darkest years of foreign occupation. By the autumn of 1992, within months after Islamic resistance forces had entered Herât in triumph, and while thousands of returning exiled families were plastering fresh clay to the sides of their devastated homes, the craftsmen were back on their scaffolds embellishing the mosque's façades. Nor did Herâtî citizens regard their work as a luxury, but recognized, as it were, the very essence of their city's rebirth as being in this weaving of coloured walls endlessly resumed by her greatest living artists.

ALEXANDER VISITS A HOLY MAN
ILLUMINATION BY BEHZÂD, HERÂT, 1494
THE PAINTER DEPICTS THE FABLED CONQUEROR
WITH THE FEATURES OF HIS SULTAN, HOSAYN MÎRZÂ BÂYQARÂ
WITH THE FORTRESS OF HERÂT
AS IT APPEARED IN THE 15TH CENTURY
COVERED WITH TILES

Despite destruction, much of Khorâsân's medieval tiled architecture does survive, not only in and around Herât itself, but also immediately over the border – very close at hand – in present-day Iran. Along with the masterworks of Uzbekistan to the north, the shrines of northeastern Iran and northwestern Afghanistan together bear witness to the most significant stages in the development of the Islamic craft of architectural tiles, from the 12th century down to our own day, where it is still illustrated by the living, almost changeless tradition of the Herât Workshop.

Even where mutilated by war, Herât's surviving shrines preserve the ceramic revetments of their halls within. On a mound overlooking the city's western rubble, the Mausoleum of Prince 'Abdollâh, rebuilt in 1487 over the site of an older grave believed to be the resting-place of one of the first Arab holy warriors in the oasis, suffered its main arched gateway to be sliced clean off by a bomb, as if by a giant scythe. Yet inside, under the twilight of its preserved dome, exceptionally fine medieval mosaics sparkle with azure- and sandalwood-coloured tendrils inlaid on coal-black fields. To the west of the city, a small mosque known as the "Cistern of the Fuller's Mill" (*Hawz-e Karbâs*), where resistance fighters hid in the 1980s and which dates back to 1441, also shelters a large ogival prayer niche ablaze with azure and night-blue tiling – under a collapsed vault and across from a shelled wall. In 1978, British archaeologist Bernard O'Kane recorded – only just in time – the tiled calligraphy on this wall, Persian verses by the 13th-century poet Sa'dî. Given their location, they are even more cruelly ironic now than when they were first fired:

> For years let there abide this inlay work, and craft –
> When every dot and speck of us has fallen off.
> This limning's purpose? Something of us should last!
> To our abiding here, I see no permanence.

Soviet warfare around Herât caused the total collapse of the tomb-dome of the Tîmûrid princess Tômân Âghâ in the village of Kôhsân – also dated 1441, and bombed in 1984.

HERÂT CASTLE (1416)

Medieval Islamic tradition said Alexander built Herât Castle on its embankment as a guardian to the crossroads of trade in the "Four Directions" below: "When the throne of kingship and the crown of royalty became fixed unto Eskandar," wrote the 14th-century Persian chronicler of the city, Ya'qûb al-Harawî, "it was he who built Herât to completion and set up its towers, all in the shape of a four-pointed cross – *salîb-e morabba'*." While the Old City beneath still forms an intersected square, the castle surges on its embankment like an irregular oblong vessel nearly 200 metres (656 feet) in length, in places more than 30 metres (98 feet) wide, and crowned with 18 towers themselves rising 30 metres above the platform of the mound. The emir Ekhtiyâroddîn, of the petty House of Kart, raised the castle from its ruins at the end of the 13th century after the Mongol sack of 1221. The emperor Shâh Rokh enlarged and utterly transformed it in 1416 with a coat of many tiles so that the seat of royal power might glow with colour like a mosque. A manuscript illumination by the greatest painter of medieval Herât, Behzâd, affords us a highly idealized vision of the castle as it might have looked in the year 1494: guarded by archers with crenellations gemmed in mosaic, it also stands on a stylized mound of tormented rocks imitated by the artist from a Chinese model.

So dilapidated was Herât Castle in 1975 that UNESCO undertook emergency restoration before terminal ruin set in. The outbreak of war in 1979 interrupted work in progress – then almost complete – and caused only minor damage to the parapets of several shelled towers. As hinted above, only the northwest-corner tower looking towards the quarter of the former Royal Gate (*Darwâzeh-ye Malek*) to the Old City, now Herât's most devastated stretch, preserved its original Tîmûrid tiling into the 20th century. It was precisely this northwest angle from which Behzâd painted the castle in 1494 to transform it into his own fairy-vision. Elsewhere stripped of its erstwhile protective ceramics, the ship-like fortress was slowly sinking into a colourless ghost of itself before UNESCO consolidation, as if back into the formless clay from which it was first moulded. Its yellow embankment ebbed down into the bazaar's hovels below in petrified waves.

Behzâd depicted Herât Castle in the full majesty of its tiles. In the illumination, azure- and ultramarine-faced bricks, arranged in rhomboid patterns, appear on the walls encased among other bricks left purposely unclad, their tone a warm yellow, almost pink, and their bared value offering a stark contrast. Such a technique of alternating bare and coloured bricks was known as *bannâ'i,* "mason-like" or "masonwrought". The bands of white calligraphy on night-blue fields circling the towers may reflect underglaze painted work on the original castle. Behzâd's flowery friezes of *tashjîr* and *tawrîq,* "tree-like" and "foliage", perhaps represent mosaic work. The medieval manuscript illuminator here stands revealed as a fellow to the craftsman in tile-design, at any rate his equal in reproducing abstract patterns on the surface of a castle – insofar as Behzâd in his painting does not entirely re-create them, that is.

The chronicles inform us that the original castle bore calligrams of praise to the ruler Shâh Rokh, composed by his court historian Hâfez-e Abrû. But the single enamelled northwest tower surviving today displays a triumph in abstract art in the most absolute sense of the term: the high white vertical geometric letters, drawn in the archaic Arabic style known as kufic, here signify nothing at all. Nor are they even real letters, but truncated, stylized letter-shapes: a series of aesthetic variations on pure calligraphic motifs for sheer visual pleasure. In the Persian usage of the tileworkers, such visual games are known as *kûfî gong,* "mute kufic".

Far from being mute, however, Behzâd's own illumination is charged with visual allusions. While his scene is supposed to occur at night – so the torch held by a guard informs us – the castle shines forth as if at noon, following the convention that medieval Muslim illuminators should not represent shadows. The twisted Chinese-type rocks of Behzâd's castle-mound remind us of the pronounced taste of Herâtî artists for the pictorial models offered on silk rolls and painted porcelain, which came by caravan to their oasis from the capital of the Ming Emperors with whom Shâh Rokh's court exchanged embassies and enjoyed trade ties. Most important, the painting uses Herât Castle to illustrate a moral episode from the *Eskandar-Nâmeh* or "Alexander Romance" by the 12th-century Persian-language poet Nezâmî, one of the favourite classics of the Tîmûrid rulers.

In the foreground of the flamboyant castle, the Conqueror kneels before an ascetic depicted as a dervish, according to what is ultimately a medieval Islamic rendering of the ancient anecdote of Alexander and Diogenes. In the episode illustrated here, the ruler asks the sage for spiritual direction on how best to storm the fortress over the hill. Behzâd significantly represents the hero Eskandar or "Alexander" with the features of the ruling sultan of Herât, Hosayn Mîrzâ Bâyqarâ himself as he appeared in 1494, set against his own castle. The painter thereby expresses the idea that his Sultan is a symbolic successor to Alexander, the hero-prophet sanctioned by sûra 18 of the Koʼran – and moreover the founder of Herât Castle, as the city's medieval chroniclers liked to remember. Behzâd's portrait, of the barrelchested, bearded Tîmûrid Sultan with a hint of narrow Mongol eyes, drawn from life, closely tallies with Prince Bâber's sharp-penned description of the same ruler: "He was slant-eyed and lion-bodied, being slender from the waist downwards. Even when old and white-bearded, he wore silken garments of fine red and green. He used to wear either the black lambskin cap or the *qalpâq* [felt cap], but on a Feast-day would sometimes set up a little three-fold turban, wound broadly and badly, stick a heron's plume in it and go to Prayers."

The main concern of Behzâd's painting lies in a ritual admonition to royal humility, close here in spirit to Nezâmî's own text: it behoves the Sultan, ostentatiously and in the eyes of all, to turn his back upon his own castle, the emblem of earthly vainglory, in order to dwell upon the fate of his soul in earnest conversation with a holy man. In imitation the Moghol Emperors of India, who inherited possession of this manuscript in the 16th and 17th centuries, very often had themselves depicted just so, kneeling before some ascetic (even a Hindu yôgî) and turning away with an otherworldly air from their bejewelled courtiers while a groom held a splendidly caparisoned horse – their earthly pride – in check. This symbolism accorded with the Koranic warning of sûra 28, verse 88: "Everything perishes, save His Countenance."

Passing decades brought low the pride of Herât Castle after the dynasty fell in 1507 by stripping its guardian tiles. Untended ceramic revetments come loose with fluctuations in desert weather – though the full process of decay may take three or four centuries – and fall off. Once so stripped, Middle Eastern and Central Asian medieval monuments are gradually reduced, especially under the merciless buffeting of the spring rains, to shapeless brick hulks, then to heaps of clay, as happened to their architectural forebears in this same region, the *tells* of the ancient Mesopotamian and Persian cities. Such a fate befell the royal palaces of biblical Babylon and Susa. Their enamelled brick revetments turned them for a while into dream-castles and hanging gardens that awed contemporaries. Their glazed coats of colour, however, not only provided aesthetic pleasures, but also rainproof protection for the fired clay walls beneath. Just as in the case of the humblest jar, the clay from which even palaces and temples are moulded must owe its waterproof resistance to the fired triple wedding in the kiln of slip, frit and glaze.

Below the walls of Herât Castle, even before the sleet of Soviet bombs, city-dwellers had to repair their snow- or rain-damaged homes every spring with daubs of fresh clay while the rain-fed rivers of mud ran through their dirt streets. Then the summer wind dried out these streets and choked them with whirling pillars of dust. Herât's old-fashioned dwellings were therefore not so much really ancient – no more than those in traditional Samarkand, Shîrâz or Baghdad – as literally timeless,

in the sense that they needed to be built up afresh every year, and in exactly the same way.

Lack of good building stone, of course, constrained the architects of the ancient Mesopotamian lowlands and their Persian imitators, down to medieval and even modern Islamic times, to use clay bricks. Dearth of wood, also, in this arid zone forced the builders of humbler dwellings to be content with mere sun-dried brick, that is, daubed mud and straw: all too prone to crumble when untended. The luxury of fired brick, baked with that rarest and most precious of all fuels in the desert, trees, could only be afforded for structures of the highest religious or royal prestige. But even hardened in the kiln, the bricks of castles and shrines remained all too vulnerable and had to be glazed – again, in wood fire.

The Middle Eastern art of architectural tiling is an aesthetic transfiguration of desperately shoddy building materials. If there is magic in its ingenuity, it is there in the sense that magic remains the art of conjuring up illusion out of so little.

Through no longer being patted with fresh clay – or shielded with fresh glazed brick – and so renewed every spring, the ancient cities of Babylonia and Persia died and were erased from the earth, or rather, reverted to earth. Although their juniors by many centuries, the medieval Islamic cities of Iraq, Iran, Afghanistan, Turkmenistan and Uzbekistan would, and indeed do, suffer the same fate where not kept under constant repair. Their buildings survive only through endless self-perpetuation, especially through ceramic restoration. Tiles are both a beauty and a necessity. They delay, or stave off, decay. Those shrines that remain truly alive in today's Middle East and Central Asia, as at Mashhad, Mazâr-e Sharîf or Herât, are never-ending workshops for the master craftsmen in glazed brick.

The crumbling of tiles from the walls of castles inspired one of the most aesthetically poignant pictorial meditations in the history of Islamic art. This was a manuscript illumination dated to the years 1538–39 and painted jointly, as Stuart Cary Welch points out, by Âghâ Mîrak of Tabrîz and his fellow-illuminator Mîr Sayyed 'Alî, son to Mîr Mosawwer of Herât. This painting was created in Tabrîz, in Iranian Azerbaijan, then chief residence of the Shî'a rulers of the Safavid House of Persia. The Safavid shâhs were keen to further in their western Iranian capital the artistic impetus of eastern Herât, now fallen and annexed to their own realm. Behzâd was brought west in his old age to supervise the royal workshops in Tabrîz, whose native masters absorbed his lessons but in the meantime also drew on lively traditions of manuscript illumination from the preceding century in their own Western Iranian metropolis. Leading connoisseurs usually agree with Welch in considering the synthesis achieved under the early 16th-century Safavid shâhs of the traditions of the two great Persianate workshops for the arts of the book – those of eastern Herât and western Tabrîz – as marking the summit of medieval Islamic figurative painting.

The painting by Âghâ Mîrak and Mîr Sayyed 'Alî illustrates another story by the poet Nezâmî, from his collection of moral tales entitled the *Makhzan-ol-Asrâr* or "Treasury of Secrets". Nezâmî set in Persian verse a famous Iranian anecdote going back to pre-Islamic times and transmitted to early medieval Muslims by converted Iranian scribes in a variety of Arabized recensions (the great 14th-century Tunisian philosopher-historian Ibn Khaldûn, for example, quotes his version of the story from the 10th-century Egyptian chronicle of Mas'ûdî). As Nezâmî tells it, a king rides out to hunt in the desert, accompanied only by his wise vizier. He comes upon a ruined village where he discovers a brace of owlets nesting and hallooing in one of its crumbled buildings. The vizier pretends to understand and interpret their calls: owls like to nest in ruins, says the minister, therefore these birds are congratulating themselves on the tyranny of the reigning king, whose harsh rule has multiplied such abandoned villages throughout the realm as his subjects prefer to flee to kinder climes. The vizier's bitter words move the king, not to anger, but to repentance. The sovereign vows henceforth to rule with justice and mercy so that the dwellings of his

KING NÔSHERWÂN AND HIS VIZIER
LISTEN TO THE OWLS IN A RUINED BUILDING
ILLUMINATION BY ÂGHÂ MÎRAK AND MÎR SAYYED 'ALÎ
TABRÎZ, 1539–43
ILLUSTRATION TO THE *TREASURY OF SECRETS* BY NEZÂMÎ

kingdom may flourish once more. And he reflects upon the frailness of all earthly structures: piety and justice alone prepare the soul for the one everlasting dwelling beyond the grave.

Sixteenth-century painters commissioned to illustrate this story always rendered the poet's deserted settlement as a ruined palace rather than as a wasted village, the better to drive home the moral of Nezâmî's anecdote to whatever princely patron happened to have ordered the manuscript – in this case, the second Safavid ruler, Shâh Tahmâsp. Indeed, this particular ruler may have taken such admonitions all too seriously: Shâh Tahmâsp turned bigoted in later life and renounced all further patronage of figurative illumination and other artistic frivolities. But as long as he was content to sponsor the fine arts, never in the history of Islamic painting were the pathos and brittleness of these frail desert castles more movingly rendered than here. Spangled with "Seals of David" and "Seals of Solomon", drawn by both artists with the skill of master tileworkers, detached ceramics lie shattered upon the ground, leaving haggard brick walls for the monarch to ponder.

THE SHRINE OF GÂZOR-GÂH (1428)

Contrary to the case with Herât Castle, much 15th-century tilework survives at Gâzor-Gâh, the "Shrine of the Bleaching Ground" (it takes this name from its surrounding hamlet). This medieval sanctuary nestles by a covered cistern, in a fold of nettles and pines, on the flank of one of the desert foothills overlooking Herât to the northeast. Its tall ogival archway, rising among its dark pines and outlined against the backdrop of the tawny cliff, remains visible from many quarters of the city below. Gâzor-Gâh shelters the tomb of a cherished mystic and poet who wrote both in classical Arabic and in the city's own Persian dialect: Khwâjeh ("Master") 'Abdollâh Ansârî (1006–89), patron saint of Herât. The cleansed souls of pilgrims who worship at his grave are "bleached", according to local tradition. The 15th-century Tîmûrid family rebuilt his shrine with fitting grandeur. Many of its princes lie buried

around his tomb. The site is Herât's Westminster Abbey.

War left the building unscathed. Pilgrims congregate under its untouched ogival porch. No single place around Herât, or anywhere in Central Asia, better evokes the aesthetic, mystical and poetic mood of the Tîmûrid age. This is remarkable, because in fact war crept very close to this shrine. Beyond the immediate fold of hills rising just behind the sanctuary, lies an isolated ravine – out of earshot of the city – where the pro-Soviet régime in autumn 1979 executed more than 3000 individuals of both sexes by trucking them from Herât to this spot, lining them up blindfolded over a ditch, pistol-shooting them in the nape of the neck and then bulldozing them into the ground. Protruding bones with shreds of clothing – including men's shoes and bits of women's veils – betrayed the mass grave to a passing shepherd shortly after the fall of the Soviet-installed régime in April 1992. Today, the site – one of many execution grounds now coming to light throughout the country – has become a national Afghan shrine second only to Gâzor-Gâh in holiness. Current pilgrims pay their respects over the grey, barrow-like earthen mound of martyrs to modern repression, before walking down the stony hill to pray over the medieval tomb and return to a 15th-century burst of colour. All the remaining tiles at Gâzor-Gâh are Tîmûrid and rank among the most significant examples of this art.

While provided next to its gateway with a small covered oratory, the shrine at Gâzor-Gâh is not so much a mosque as a sort of cloister, for it faces not west towards Mecca, but east. Under its coating of tiles, its architecture is of the utmost simplicity: an enclosing wall rhythmically enlivened with ogee arches, some blank, others opening into dark recessed rooms, around an open courtyard paved in marble with the grave of the saint surrounded by the princely tombs. Before the entrance gate appears an architectural ornament absolutely unique in the lands of Islam: the sculpted marble figure of a dog, harshly stylized, lying prone before the threshold. Tradition holds that the architect of the shrine, master Qawâmoddîn son of Zaynoddîn of Shîrâz, thus symbolically chose to depict himself humbly prostrate. Although a beast normally considered impure by Muslims, this dog is without any doubt a visual quotation of sûra 18 of the Koran, which tells the Islam-sanctioned version of the famous story of the Seven Sleepers of Ephesus: seven pious young men who fled persecution and sought shelter in a cave with their faithful dog, who was in turn rewarded for his loyalty, according to traditional glosses, by transformation into human shape when the "companions of the cave" woke after their 199-year sleep ("or snorted we in the seven sleepers' den?" asks Donne in the Western Christian tradition).

Beyond representing himself as a dog, the bold architect found expression in the design of the shrine's two high ogival gateways, one true or real, the other blank, but both vastly recessed to the point of forming a pair of deep, vaulted porches. The true gate, at the entrance, is the lower, but also the more deeply recessed of the two. Its ogival vaulting shades two long marble bench-platforms running along the walls at either side of the door, where the shrine's guardians sit. The second is a blank pointed gate-shape, shallower but much higher, which over-shadows the entire building and closes off the eastern end of the courtyard while opening onto no other vista but the imaginary – and infinite – landscape of its own tilework.

Such a high-pointed recessed gateway – known in Persian as an *aywân* or *îwân,* whence Arabic borrowed the word – is the outstanding structural feature of all Iranian-influenced medieval Islamic architecture from Anatolia to India. While the visual impact of the Islamic pointed arch on the birth of European Gothic, though plausible in the course of the Crusading 12th century, remains a matter for debate, there is no doubt that the tradition of huge vaulted gateways goes back to pre-Islamic Persian times. The colossal 6th-century AD entrance arch to the ruins of the imperial Sasanian palace at Ctesiphon, now in Iraq, bears sufficient witness to this as a telling symbol of the dynasty's power. From the Sasanian shâhs, Islam in turn adopted towering gateways before its royal palaces as emblems of temporal rule. Such vaulted porches were deep enough to shelter the sessions of ministers. In Istanbul, the ʾÂlî Qâpı, the Sublime "Porte" or Gate under which the sultan's viziers sat, came to symbolize the Ottoman government itself, even in European languages. The palace-symbolism of the îwân was further religiously reinforced by a second feature of Islamic architecture: the *mihrâb* or blind pointed niche carved into the end wall of mosques, which indicates the direction of Mecca – an abstract gate opening only towards contemplation of the divine source, as it were. The entrance îwân of shrines thereby announces the farther, holier gate of the mihrâb: and as the earthly threshold to holy ground, itself receives rich, royal-style decoration. The twin portals of the tomb-shrine of Gâzor-Gâh, the earthly gate of initiation before, and the blank heavenly gate beyond (although not itself strictly a mihrâb in the particular case of this tomb-cloister since it points east), might almost be said perfectly to reflect this concept of the two succeeding doorways. Gâzor-Gâh's two gateways also neatly illustrate almost the entire evolution of architectural adornment in medieval Eastern Islam.

Over the door-lintel beneath the entrance porch, Tîmûrid craftsmen masked the bricks under a simple revetment of now colourless stucco, worked into relief incised with deep hollows, in order to create a design today decipherable only by its play of shadow and light: with two cypresses mounting guard on either side of a sculpted *shamseh* or "sunburst". Such revetment in carved stucco was already an archaic technique in the 15th century. Down to the 12th century, however, decorators in Iran and Central Asia normally resorted to carved stucco alone when they chose to hide their walls of bricks. Otherwise, they might set the bricks themselves into cunning geometric patterns or even into calligraphic bands. The technique of deliberately turning an intricately worked surface-maze of colourless bricks into a recognizable design, outlined by the sheer cast of grooved shadows under

– Mohammad – under a form recalling a starkly stylized human figure, head, trunk, two arms, two legs, composed of the Arabic letters corresponding to M-H-M-D worked into the pattern of an *Ensân-e Kâmel* or "Perfect Man", the prototypical Anthropos. (The 13th-century Spanish Muslim mystic, Ibn 'Arabî, refers to precisely such figurative calligraphic play on the Prophet's name in his treatise on the "Tree of Life".)

In slender bands framing the door run further bands of *tawrîq* or "foliage" set in mosaic faïence or, to use the Arabic term sanctioned by the craftsmen, in *mo'arraq,* "inlay". The 15th century saw the high point of inlaid tile-mosaic work. Each square tile, after firing, colouring and fresh firing, was chiselled into the shape of a stem, leaf or petal, then carefully set into its place in the mortar alongside the wall's other chiselled tiles. The ground of the band here is an intense ultramarine blue, highlighted with floral motifs not only in white and yellow but also "sandalwood" – to use the name by which the classical poet Nezâmî designated a glowing reddish-brown – on which Tîmûrid craftsmen were able to shed a soft autumnal lustre of such warmth and depth as has remained unmatched in ceramics before or since.

At the end of the courtyard, beyond the grave, the closing arch displays tiled calligraphic meditations pursued in fugues. Upon the twin bases of its inward-facing panels, bare ochre brick is incised by chisel into "stonewrought" work, or *hakkâkî,* in turn inlaid with enamelled constellations of floral sunbursts and star-seals "of David". Above rises imbricated work in the absolutely literal sense of patterned "masonwrought" bricks both enamelled and bare. The masters here so cunningly exploited the *bannâ'î* technique as to be able to write large, bold coloured calligraphic bands with little pieces of enamelled brickwork fine enough and set at small enough angles to be forced into a jagged but still almost semi-cursive script when read from afar, pulled around geometrically drawn coloured letters themselves composed into rigorous square mazes. Imbricated geometric play on lettering has been

strong sunlight, is known in Persian as *hazâr-bâf* or "Thousand Weavings". The finest example of this technique is the early 10th-century mausoleum of the Sâmânid emirs at Bokhârâ in present-day Uzbekistan; but the 13th-century panels of Herât's Friday Mosque display such workmanship as well.

The entrance-portal to Gâzor-Gâh, over the stucco lintel, refines the idea of a "Thousand Weavings", for here, within the pattern of warm sunlit ochre bricks left bare by design, the craftsmen have inset others enamelled in azure or deep blue, so forming fresh geometric labyrinths. Such interweaving of bare and enamelled brick receives the Arabic technical name of *bannâ'î,* "mason-like" or "masonwrought", which Behzâd, as we have seen, depicts on Herât Castle itself. Under the Gâzor-Gâh portal, dotted inlays of small square fragments of enamelled brick form a repeated calligraphic puzzle which may be resolved into the name of the Prophet carried here to the utmost limit where legibility and sheer abstraction meet, by turning architectural necessity to advantage through variations on Arabic's most archaic script – rigid kufic with its straight lines and right angles, woven upright or upside-down into azure and deep blue labyrinths which only slowly unfold their written message to the eye: cerebral toyings in script with the three names of Allâh, Mohammad and 'Alî.

While not themselves heterodox or Shî'a, Herât's formally orthodox Tîmûrid rulers did accord the greatest respect to the Shî'a figure of 'Alî, the Prophet's son-in-law, whom they considered the founder of their civilization's mystic and knightly brotherhoods. Nor were sectarian differences between Sunnî and Shî'a so bitter during the Tîmûrid age as they would become over the next century in the course of Islam's own Wars of Religion between orthodox Ottomans in the Levant, heterodox Safavids in Iran and orthodox Uzbeks in Central Asia. With a generosity of spirit unthinkable in the later hate-riven century, Herât's own Sunnî empress Gôhar Shâd, spouse to the Tîmûrid emperor Shâh Rokh, bestowed upon her Shî'a subjects in 1416–18 a splendidly redecorated shrine in honour of the remains of their imâm Rezâ in the nearby city of Mashhad – still a major pilgrimage centre in modern Iran. But even in Sunnî Herât, the name of 'Alî, emblazoned in brickwork on the lateral walls and closing portal of the sanctuary of Gâzor-Gâh, expressed the nostalgic messianic yearning – then still shared by nearly all trends of medieval Islam – that crystallized around the figure of the Prophet's martyred son-in-law.

Above the triple names of Allâh, Mohammad and 'Alî, the great closing ogee arch soars into a frieze of ultramarine mosaic work, inlaid with spidery white calligraphy curving in *thuluth* style and illuminated with a spot of azure tiling within the ring of every folding letter. Finally the vault's ornament yields at its summit to a night-blue field pricked with mosaic stars.

Nor were the artists yet content. The entire arch is framed within twin rising white calligraphic bands

on an ultramarine ground executed in the most technically difficult style of all: underglaze painting, a procedure invented at the turn of the 12th and 13th centuries at what was probably the zenith of Islamic technical creativity. While long and laborious to chisel, mosaic faïence at any rate neatly isolates each fragment of colour, fired separately, then fitted. But here, the artist brushed a portion of his white calligraphic curve directly onto the blue ground of one tile, then pursued this same curve over the blue ground of a second tile, then on over a third tile and so until the end of his frieze. On firing, an alkaline glazing covered and protected the several colours painted on successive single tiles and prevented them from overflowing and mingling. A single tile thus variously painted is known, in the Persian language of the workshop, as pertaining to the style of the *Haft Rang,* the "Seven Colours".

Once monarchs from the 15th century onwards wished to cover ever vaster architectural surfaces with colour, resulting in the completely sheathed shrines of 17th-century Esfahân, then craftsmen increasingly abandoned patient mosaic work to resort to tiles fired in the *Haft Rang* technique.

With its multiple decorative styles, Gâzor-Gâh is also the holiest place, if not in Central Asia, then at least in Herât. Barren women bind strips of cloth to the branches of the twisted olive-tree which springs from the ground by the tomb of the saint, begging him to grant them a child. Dervishes, locally known as *malang* and recognizable by their Arabian-style headcloths and headbands (worn by no one else in Central Asia), still observe around the tomb sessions of mystical *zekr,* or "Commemoration" of the love of God chanted in rasped tones, following the teachings of Sufism, the prevailingly pantheistic-minded school of Islamic quietism.

Regardless of their medium – tile, carpet, manuscript illumination or sculpture – Tîmûrid abstract designs remain of a type. Before the saint's tomb, itself surmounted by a chiselled marble pillar rising from its carved vase in the manner of a Tree of Life, several of the most intricately sculpted princely gravestones in Islamic art lie in showy humility.

Craftsmen carved the surface of the hard black marble sarcophagus known as *Haft Qalam,* "The Seven Pens", into lace-like overlapping depths of twined vegetal shoots and calligrams as delicately outlined as any underglaze painting in "Seven Colours" on the surrounding walls. (Originally commissioned by Sultan Hosayn for himself, the Stone of the Seven Pens covers the grave of one of his sons, prematurely deceased.)

For all its rich tiling, Gâzor-Gâh still left many bricks bare, as a contrast to the enamelled strips made in accordance with its predominant *bannâ'î* or "masonwrought" adornment. Complete revetment in *Haft Rang* or "Seven Colours" occurs at a monumental complex now known as the Mosallâ, which was begun by Empress Gôhar Shâd between 1417 and 1432, completed under Sultan Hosayn in 1498, more than half destroyed by Anglo-Indian officers in 1885, and nearly obliterated by Soviet bombing in 1984.

THE MOSALLÂ OR "PRAYER-GROUND" (1417–98)

The royal shrines and mausoleums on Herât's northwest edge have been collectively designated the "Mosallâ" since at least the early 19th century. Most of the monuments had disappeared by the early 20th, but what remains underscores the loss: a tomb-dome and nearby minarets. Close to her family sepulchre, Empress Gôhar Shâd raised a commemorative mosque. Sultan Hosayn added a religious university. His vizier Mîr 'Alî Shêr, an eminent poet in Eastern Turkish in his own right, put up still another college. Herât's nobility then built pavilions and laid out gardens in what became both the city's university and its fashionable suburb. Of all these buildings and pleasure-grounds, nothing beyond the tomb-dome and the minarets remains but a canal, partly silted, called *Enjîl* – literally, "The Evangel" (Islam recognizes the Gospel as one of the Holy Books). But much of the Mosallâ in its 15th-century splendour could still be seen by Europeans as late as the mid-19th. Russian officer Khanikov made good sketches in 1861. French officer Ferrier in British Indian service thus

described Sultan Hosayn's college in 1854: "Such as it is at the present day, it is still the most imposing and elegant structure that I saw in Asia. The mosque is completely covered with a mosaic of glazed bricks, in varied and beautiful patterns, and the cupola is of amazing dimensions. Several arcades, supported by pillars in brick, equal the proportions of the arch of Ctesiphon; and the seven magnificent minarets that surround it may be said to be intact, for the upper part of them only is slightly injured."

Within decades after Ferrier and Khanikov explored Herât, what they had reported as Islamic Asia's "most imposing and elegant structure" was rent to pieces. British imperial authorities feared that Herât, a strategic "key to India", might fall to swiftly advancing Russian colonial forces in Central Asia. In 1885, after the Russians overran what is now Turkmenistan and pushed to within 100 kilometres (60 miles) of Herât, British officers advised the Afghan emir 'Abd-or-Rahmân to dynamite the whole Mosallâ complex and so clear an artillery range to defend the city. The Emir, the shrewdest but also most brutal (and aesthetically indifferent) ruler in Afghanistan's pre-Soviet history, brushed aside the supplications of the city fathers – "I care for the defence of the living, not that of the dead" – and told his British advisers to proceed. It took an army of donkeys to clear the debris. Russian attack came: 94 years later. In 1911, Colonel Sir Thomas Hungerford Holdich (on "Herât" for the 11th edition of the *Encylopaedia Britannica*) remembered with regret, and perhaps remorse, what he had done: "The magnificent outlines of the Mosalla filled a wide space with the glorious curves of dome and gateway and the stately grace of tapering minars, but the impressive beauty of this, by far the finest architectural structure in all Afghanistan, could not be permitted to weigh against the fact that the position occupied by this pile of solid buildings was fatal to the interests of effective defence. ... But four minars standing at the corners of the wide plinth still remain to attest to the glorious proportions of the ancient structure, and to exhibit samples of that decorative tilework, which for intricate beauty of design and exquisite taste in the blending of colour still appeals to the memory as unique."

Empress Gôhar Shâd's dome survived, and of the whole complex nine minarets in all, five belonging to the Empress's monuments, the four others to Sultan Hosayn's college, their blue and white tiling still mostly intact as well as their balconies supported by typically Islamic, stalactite-like projecting corbel-work. So they were photographed in 1915 by the German Niedermayer expedition, then in Afghanistan to plead with Emir Habîbollâh in Kabul to break his treaty with the British in India and side with the Central Powers in World War I. It took the fall of one minaret to an earth tremor in 1931, followed by the collapse of two more in 1951, to convince the Royal Afghan Government to try to save the remaining six by planting a pine grove and so throwing up a protective tree-curtain for their surviving tiles against the desert wind. At long last, UNESCO in 1975 applied itself to consolidation – and it was high time that it should: tile fragments now fell in coloured drizzles from the minarets, the summit of the tomb-dome was already bare. The crowning disaster struck four years later. For those of us who reached Herât with humanitarian relief teams in 1992, care for the welfare of the living in no way precluded concern for what might remain of the artistic legacy of the dead – *pace* Emir 'Abd-or-Rahmân. A narrow path, summarily cleared by our *mojâhedîn* guides through the minefields, led us to the cratered wasteland of what had once been the Mosallâ. The two directors of the Herât Mosque Workshop, Ostâd ("Master") 'Abd-ol-Ahad Ahmadî and Ostâd Abû-Bakr, accompanied by Ostâd Sharîfî, superintendent to the city's monuments, and Ostâd Najîmî, one of Afghanistan's last surviving trained archaeological architects, confirmed our fears. Shelling had razed the pine grove. Only its stubs stood out among low mounds of yellow earth littered with shattered bricks, empty cartridge-cases and stacks of multicoloured, crumb-like particles of broken tilework. The mausoleum of the Empress was pocked with bullet holes, its eastern wall torn open by a shell. One minaret was reduced to a stump in a heap of rubble. The five surviving towers, now as bare and unsightly as factory chimneys, leaned at angles – threatening to fall – over the muddy waters of the "Evangel", with hills of tile-flakes around their respective bases. Scaffolding from UNESCO's 1975 restoration clung to one minaret, shot through its upper storey by a shell. Sultan Hosayn's now fissured black marble grave – almost as finely carved as the Stone of the Seven Pens at Gâzor-Gâh – lay exposed in a bomb crater: medieval Central Asia's greatest patron of the arts rested in the midst of the broken brick foundations of what had been his theological college – coming under archaeological excavation just before the Soviet invasion.

Pigeons flew under the dome of the mausoleum of the Empress through its eastern shell-hole. The inner face of the dome was intact: not tiled, but red-gilt. Multiple corbelling masked the squinches with stalactites in carved stucco, also red-gilt (the technical Arabic and Persian term for the architectural *tour de force* of such corbelled honeycombing being *moqarnas*). The resulting light of the chamber was both subdued and fiery, as of embers, with diffused sunlight gliding over the complicated red-gold fan-vaulting of the dome and honeycombed stalactites of the squinches – very similar in effect to the Alhambra (the "Red Castle" in Arabic, *Al-Hamrâ*), built, indeed, only a few generations earlier at the opposite end of the Islamic world. Carved gravestones, including that of the Empress, slept below the dome amidst the rubble on the floor. The tomb of the Empress's husband, Emperor Shâh Rokh, was however transferred, within a year of his death in 1447, to rest beside that of his father, Tîmûr, in Samarkand, as the dynastic wars began which wrecked the Tîmûrid Empire and reduced it to the city-state of Herât.

Not one but three superimposed domes shelter the mausoleum of Gôhar Shâd: an internal, seen by the faithful as a ceiling to the chamber; an external, visible to the passers-by outside; and an intermediate, serving to reinforce the other two, and visible to no one except through a narrow opening in the drum of the external dome. The external blue-tiled dome, bulbous with protruding ribbing in the characteristic fashion of late medieval Central Asia, made this mausoleum in Herât almost a twin to that in Samarkand, Tîmûr's Gûr-e Mîr or "Tomb of the Lord", completed some three decades before. Gunfire in the surrounding grove had now scattered almost the last of the dome's tiles, reducing its curve to a swollen hump of bullet-pocked naked yellow brick with the appearance of a rotten melon. Some coloured pieces still stuck to the base of its ribs and around its drum, however, although now brittle to the point where one could detach them by hand – fragments of a former beauty "that still appeals to the memory as unique", as Colonel Hungerford Holdich put it.

Although what the empress Gôhar Shâd built in Herât has suffered so much, we still have the shrine she raised in 1416–18 in neighbouring Mashhad as evidence of her taste in architecture: at least those original portions that survive beneath much modern Iranian restoration. Although always hidden in aristocratic purdah, Gôhar Shâd was feared as the proverbial power behind Shâh Rokh's throne; she wielded the regency herself for ten stormy years after her spouse's death; and made her occult presence felt firmly in the Empire's cities through the strong structures she ordered erected in them. Thus a visit to her shrine in present-day Mashhad helps conjure up what has vanished from Herât. The Mosque of Gôhar Shâd in the capital of Iranian Khorâsân still boasts its twin domes, one tiled azure, the other gilt. Its minarets of brick have been left purposely bare, ochre when sunlit, to provide the better *bannâ'î* or "masonwrought" foil for inlaid blue and white mosaic rhombi in staggered arrangement and each emblazoned with its own calligraphic motif – one of the 99 names of God which succeed one another in the ascent to the building's pinnacle. Its central portal is framed in a mosaic of perfect calligraphy, composed by the Empress's own son, Prince Bâysonghor, the "Lord Falcon", not only an earnest collector of other men's calligrams but himself a

superb scribe, in honour of "that Sun in the sky of chastity and continence, famed for her nobility and worship and piety, Gôhar Shâd, everlasting be her grandeur!"

The rulers of the House of Tîmûr, spawned by probably the most abysmally evil human being in pre-modern Islamic history, at the Conqueror's death in 1405 oddly turned into the Medici Princes of their own cultural zone: and this lasted for nearly five centuries, since the Indian Moghols themselves – down to the gifted poet-king Bahâdur Shâh deposed by the British in 1857 – descended through Prince Bâber of Kabul from the line of Tîmûr. Empress Gôhar Shâd – "Jewel of Joy" – appears as something like the family's Catherine de' Medici. Once regent, the Dowager Empress of Herât wove every plot, pulled every marriage string and crushed every conspiracy amongst her kin from the secret recesses of her purdah to hold on to the reality of power through the ten years of dynastic civil war that ended in her assassination in 1457 – at the age of 80 – at the hands of her own great-grandson, Prince Abû-Sa'îd – such was his fear of the dynasty's dam. She left her monuments in tile for later generations to destroy.

Those of us privileged to pick our way through the landmined ruins of her monument in Herât in 1992 suddenly stooped with a pious gesture to the memory of the Lady "Jewel of Joy". We began carefully to pick up a few of the thousands of tile fragments glistening in the dirt around her mausoleum, collecting them at first in the folds of our long Afghan tunics, to deposit them for safekeeping under her dome. Recovering all of them took several weeks. Those Western relief workers present in Herât that autumn who were sufficiently sensitive to the arts found words to convince three United Nations agencies on the spot – the World Food Programme, the High Commission for Refugees and the UN Office for the Coordination of Humanitarian Assistance to Afghanistan (UNOCHA) – to fund an emergency safeguard project for the mausoleum, supervised by the most qualified Afghans themselves: archaeologist Mr

Najîmî and the two head tileworkers of the Mosque Workshop, Masters 'Abd-ol-Ahad Ahmadî and Abû-Bakr, with their apprentices. By late 1994, with its shelled wall repaired, the mausoleum was sufficiently consolidated to allow a plan for the ultimate restoration upon the surface of the dome of its recovered fallen tiles. These were still being patiently reassembled like jigsaw-puzzles by the crews at the Mosque Workshop. Empress Gôhar-Shâd's monument, as the city's symbol, would thus be reborn.

As became obvious to all those involved in picking them off the ground, the fragments from the Empress's dome were not properly "mosaic", but tiles individually painted with varied colours in the *Haft Rang* technique. Several tiles had themselves been boldly moulded and fired into elaborately bent or staggered shapes to hug the stalactite-shaped corbels (now mostly shattered) around the dome's drum. A thin and rather dull black line – impossible to detect from any distance – divided the various bright hues (mainly white and sky-blue on night-blue) on most of these tiles. Such a separating line, in medieval times apparently composed (according to the most recent analysis in European museums) of manganese mixed with some sort of greasy substance which evaporated during firing, served to protect the sharpness of the different colours by preventing them from running into one another while baking. Contemporary Master Habîbollâh of the Herât Mosque Workshop, however, describes present-day ingredients for such a dividing line thus: "Slain copper [i.e. heated copper: *koshteh-ye mes*]; slain iron [*koshteh-ye chûdan*]; lead [*osrob*]; and some coal [or graphite]." (When referring to this last substance, Master Habîbollâh repeatedly used the word *maqn,* which I have been unable to trace in any Arabic, Persian or even Pashtô or Urdu dictionary, although the latter two languages increasingly influence the technical talk of modern Herâtî craftsmen.)

Technical resort to such a delimiting carbon-black line was introduced to late medieval European potters through the workshops of Moorish Spain, the prevailing Western shop term for this process remaining Spanish *cuerda seca,* "dry cord". But a closer look at some "dry cord" lines on Gôhar Shâd's dome shows added refinement: other lines traced, not in black, but in red – each to surround, and so smartly set off, a single, tiny, diamond-shaped dot of pure gold leaf. Even when sensibly reduced (as here) to the thinnest thread of colour, Tîmûrid ceramic red always remains disappointingly dull, not at all comparable to the glowing twin blues (azure and ultramarine), yellows, blacks, greens and "sandalwoods" otherwise available to 15th-century craftsmen. Bright red, in fact, is one of the most difficult colours to secure in tiling. Herât's medieval masters – like their modern successors – added tin and lead to iron-rust – which is volatile when fired, however, and mixes undesirably with white glazing. At long last, Ottoman Turkish potters in Iznik (ancient Nicaea) discovered, in about the middle of the 16th century, that a thick red clay found in Anatolia preserved its scarlet brightness in the kiln: this was "Armenian bole" (from Greek *bôlos,* "clay"), until then mostly sought by medieval apothecaries for its supposed medicinal properties (it is Chaucer's "Boole Armonyak"). Once aware of its real virtues, Ottoman potters applied it with a will on countless examples of "Iznik" ware.

For lack of "Armenian bole", Herât's 15th-century tilemasters restricted their dull iron red on Gôhar Shâd's dome to the rôle of humble foil for the gold dots around the drum. Now, each of these small gold splashes required a second firing of the piece it adorned. Difference in the melting temperature of various hues allowed the medieval Herâtî tilemaster to fire a piece in his kiln several times over to obtain the multiple colours he wanted. Thus he brushed one colour, to be baked at lower temperature, over a portion of his surface either left bare ("in reserve") or already painted with another colour sealed hard upon the tile by previous firing at higher temperature. Upon the blue baked into his piece over a high fire at, say, 800°C (or even 1000°C), and now dry and ready to receive application of another hue, the 15th-century artist added his spot of gold, whose melting point he obtained over a lower fire at no more than, say, 650°C – enough to seal his gold upon the blue without melting the latter. There was moreover a coquettish touch to his flecks of gold upon the dome's drum: for from the ground, they are absolutely invisible as such – but they cast their sheen. When intact, the dome sparkled in sunlight as if metalled with lustre so that "it might shine like unto the resplendence of the sun", to borrow an expression used by the early 14th-century Persian master potter and tileworker, Abo-l-Qâsem of Kâshân. Such secrets of the craft which caused Empress Gôhar Shâd's dome to glisten like the jewel in her name were the very stuff of a traditional Muslim tiler's workshop. The Workshop of the Friday Mosque in Herât is now one of the very last of its kind still in operation; its survival is a minor miracle.

THE FRIDAY MOSQUE OF HERÂT (1200–1498–1995)

With their narrow grey beards trimmed to a careful point, their fur caps or especially their turbans with the trailing liripipe-type scarf thrown over the right shoulder like a medieval European chaperon-hood, Master Sharîfî, superintendent of monuments, and Masters 'Abd-ol-Ahad Ahmadî, Abû-Bakr and Habîbollâh, the chief artists in tiles, might have stepped out of a 15th-century miniature by Behzâd. This impression they reinforced whenever they placed their right hands over their hearts to bow with a flourish of murmured courtesies – in Herât's medieval Persian accent – worthy of Tîmûrid noblemen. The illusion became fantastical seeing them gingerly progress with an air of preoccupied meditation over the flagstones of the immense mosque courtyard, still a little too cool to tread barefoot in comfort in the early morning, under vast blue-green panels alive with sunbursts and tendrils – motifs which they themselves had designed and set upon these walls over the last four decades. Mosaic blues emerged from their dawning purplish torpor to whiten in sudden sheens when the sun rose.

"This cursive writing around the two thick pillars is by Master Fekrî Saljûqî. See his fine Persian *nasta'lîq*. Master Saljûqî quotes verses from Sanâ'î and Jâmî. Over the gateway, the kufic composition in Arabic with knots and tresses was designed by Master Mohammad 'Alî Khattât, the Calligrapher. They are both dead now. Master Mohammad 'Alî passed away only last year. You did not know? He was still a refugee in Iran. Too old. Too weak. He was not able to return home. The pity, *afsôs!* ... All this war. The times are still bitter. Now, take those vases in *mo'arraq* [inlay]: Master Mash'al is old too, but still with us. Praise unto the Lord! No one knows as he does how to re-create the Tîmûrid manner – *sabk-e Tîmûrî*. You know him well. Your team of doctors looked after him properly. God bless you. Now, as for your help from the United Nations. Well and good. But it will not be enough to convince our younger apprentices to stay." Master Abû-Bakr sighed through his beard. But Master Sharîfî, who once studied archaeology for two years in Poland before returning to live among his people in the manner of his people, was tracing with his forefinger a design on one of the older panels along the southern edge of the courtyard to point out its more subtle beauties: an ultramarine-and-yellow stellar motif dating to the great restoration of the mosque carried out by the vizier and poet Mîr 'Alî Shêr in 1498–1500.

Without a word, Master Sharîfî led us deeper into the memory of the mosque, through the great ogee gateway that dominated the courtyard towards the inner mihrâb under a canopied forest of thick white pillars and arching vaults. This whitewash served to heighten the contrast with the luxuriant colour of the walls outside. Under one of these vaults, during the Soviet occupation, Master Sharîfî himself had ordered the workshop crews to haul to safety the great bronze cauldron that once stood in majesty in the middle of the courtyard. This famous vessel, whence sherbet was ladled to the faithful on feast days in medieval times, was cast in 1375. With its massive ringed handles and embossed Chinese-like tendrils and cloud formations, it ranks among the most distinguished pieces of medieval Islamic metalwork in the world. Tîmûr admired it in 1397 and ordered a replica for his shrine of Ahmad Yasawî in Turkestan. The imperial Chinese envoy to the court of Herât, Ch'en Ch'eng, mentioned it on his return in 1415: "In the middle of the city there is a great building erected of clay. This is a college, called *mo-de-rh-sai* [= Arabic *madrasa*, a theological school] in the language of the country. In it a large copper vessel has been placed, which is several fathoms in circumference, with letters engraved on it. It resembles in shape the ancient [Chinese] vessels called *ting*." (E. Bretschneider tr.) Experts abroad fretted over its possible disappearance during Soviet rule. Master Sharîfî had it pulled under the cover of an îwân after several rifle shots – for fighting did not even spare the courtyard of the mosque – had indented its bronze surface: these have become historic scars in turn.

The Friday or "congregational" Mosque goes back to the year 1200. It was founded by Sultan Ghiyâsoddîn of Ghôr, overlord to the Muslim conquerors of Delhi in 1192, who was buried in Herât in this very shrine. Whitewash on the western walls nearest the mihrâb was scratched in the 1960s to reveal sections of the building's primeval Ghôrid brickwork beneath, set into calligraphic *hazâr-bâf* or "Thousand Weavings" compositions. But it is the eastern face of the mosque which preserves an entire portal, crucially important for the history of Islamic art, dating from the days of Sultan Ghiyâsoddîn.

While the few surviving Ghôrid monuments are collapsing on their original Afghan soil from neglect or war-ravage, they were the models that inspired the design of the first masterpieces of Islamic architecture raised on Indian soil: the complex of shrines built up in Delhi from the turn of the 13th century around the colossal minaret of the emir Qotboddîn Aybak, at first viceroy to the Ghôrids, then independent sultan after 1206. As it happens, Ghôrid architects throughout the years 1150 to 1206 were among those Muslim artists chiefly responsible for the general aesthetic transformation of Central Asian and Middle Eastern buildings that saw stucco revetment begin to yield to tiling at this time. The earliest known specimen of turquoise tiled calligraphy inlaid on stucco has admittedly been identified on a minaret dated 1058 and found in Damghân in western or modern Iranian Khorâsân, hence before Ghôrid times and outside their domains. Dots of blue ceramic also occur from the earlier part of the 12th century at other Iranian sites such as Sanjan (again in Khorâsân) and, even farther to the west, at Qazwîn. Still, the most spectacular early manifestation of the new art of tile revetment appears on the late 12th- and early 13th-century architecture of the Ghôrids, as on Herât Mosque's Old Portal, which is both thickly spotted with, and framed in, turquoise faïence.

The oldest known structure of the Ghôrids, built even before their sultan Ghiyâsoddîn rode down from his mountain fastnesses in Central Afghanistan to annex Herât in 1175, is the splendid *madrasa* or theological college of Shâh-e Mashhad, hidden atop its isolated knoll above the high reaches of the River Morghâb, running here through a deep gorge near Jawand bazaar. This shrine was raised by a Ghôrid queen, still unidentified, in the year 561 of the Islamic era, corresponding to AD 1165 or 1166, according to the plaited kufic calligraphy. The very first foreign explorers to see its ruins, travelling on horseback, came in 1970 and over the following summers: German anthropologists Bernt and Ute Glatzer and Michael Casimir claim pride of discovery, then myself and French photographers Roland and Sabrina Michaud. Nor shall we ever forget its majestic ogee îwân rising over its desert mound as the surrounding cliffs of Morghâb Canyon rang only to the clatter of the stony torrent below. This îwân's adornment was still all brickwork and stucco, the prevailing style down to the mid-12th century. While medieval Islamic stucco decoration might indeed be very much picked out in paint – traces are still visible, for example, on several Ghôrid-period calligraphic bands of Herât Mosque – no hue remained on the fretted plasterwork of Shâh-e Mashhad's great portal except its own natural honey colour, gilded by morning

sunshine. Islamic plaster carvers anywhere have perhaps never attained, as they did in this forgotten Afghan canyon, such virtuoso flourishes of light-and-shadow play leaping into kufic and *thuluth* calligraphy, fields of stars and a wonderful lateral *shamseh* or sun-burst. Just before the age of tile revetment dawned in its turn, the art of stucco apparently reached its zenith under these cliffs. The site relapsed into impenetrable obscurity during the Soviet war; and Shâh-e Mashhad's tremendous îwân, left unattended, collapsed of itself at some sad unknown point of the dark 1980s.

So mysterious have the Ghôrids remained to history that we are not even certain whether their lost highland capital mentioned in literary sources, *Fêrôz Kôh* or "Mount of Victory", corresponds to this site of Shâh-e Mashhad – or to yet another site farther south, marked by the now famous solitary minaret of Jâm on the banks of the Harî Rûd, a week's ride on horseback through more steep gorges guarded by medieval clay watchtowers (I covered this stretch through Jawand Canyon in 1971). The minaret of Jâm itself was first made known to the world in 1957 by Belgian archaeologist André Mariq moving north, where he followed the Harî Rûd as it leaves the main dirt road to disappear through a then unknown canyon of its own. On the threshold of the aesthetic revolution from stucco to tile, Jâm's brickwork displays a first, precious ring of thickly studded turquoise dots and calligraphy, like a manifesto of the great art form to come. UNESCO's Andrea Bruno shored up this minaret, too, in the late 1970s. As I write, this priceless monument is also reported to be on the verge of collapse. My friend Bernt Glatzer tells me that "it leans like a stack of coins, held together by nothing but its own gravity; all its binding mortar has crumbled away."

If it falls, then, aside from some damaged mausoleums at Chesht-e Sharîf in the central highlands, the last great witness to Ghôrid architecture will be the Old Portal of the Herât Mosque, with its kufic calligraphy and scattered knobs of turquoise knotted into the fretworked honey-coloured stucco of the side panels – a harbinger of the blue-tiled blanket revetment to come with the shrine's Tîmûrid restoration in 1498–1500. In fact, the best Tîmûrid mosaic work left in the mosque – stars and tendrils on night-blue ground – occurs on the spandrels with which the late 15th-century craftsmen framed and partly hid the old Ghôrid Portal. In the 1960s Afghan achaeologists unfortunately had to cut away some of this Tîmûrid revetment to reveal more of the original Ghôrid work beneath, priceless because almost unique – so might flamboyant Gothic tracery fill a Romanesque archway, as in so many European cathedrals that are likewise palimpsests of succeeding styles.

The craftsmen busy every weekday morning under the Ghôrid Portal link the oldest moments of the mosque to its present facelift, for their workshop opens directly onto the Portal's court. Sitting on mats under the sun, the workers first hammer at blocks of white quartz. This is tiling's raw material. Initial rough work consists in so reducing, by mallet, the quartz to crumbs, but not yet to fine powder. Powdering is the next stage, today as in the past, as we are told not only by the present artists but also by the single surviving medieval Persian treatise on the craft, the *Book of Those Brides That Are Gems and Scents,* dated 1301, by Master Abo-l-Qâsem of Kâshân: "One must smash and crush these matters like unto atoms of eye-ointment, by pounding them and grinding them and so pulverizing them and sifting them and screening them."

Under the Workshop's vaults within, shaven-headed young apprentices pound the crumbs of quartz – now mixed with fragments of glass as further siliceous matter – until the required powder is produced. But this is still not fine enough. The powder is moistened and poured into a stone-carved mill that looks much like an ancient stove propped against the workshop's wall where it comes under the revolving wheel of the millstone for further grinding. The resulting paste escapes through a metal pipe into the receiving trough. This is the basic matter to which the various metallic oxides are added to create the "Seven Colours".

Persian usage imposed this traditional name of the "Seven Colours", or *Haft Rang,* because the number seven was held to correspond to that of the sanctified Seven Heavenly Bodies of determining importance so identified in all calendars stemming from Ancient Mesopotamian astronomy: Saturn, the Sun, the Moon, Mars, Mercury, Jupiter and Venus (whence, in the West, the Romance-language names of the weekdays and their Anglo-Germanic equivalents). According to the 12th-century Persian poet Nezâmî, the Seven Heavenly Spheres' matching Seven Colours were respectively black, yellow (or gold), green, red, blue, "sandalwood" (or brown) and white (or silver). The craftsmen of the Herât Workshop today give a slightly different list for their identified Seven Colours. Thus Master 'Abd-ol-Ahad Ahmadî:

1. YELLOW or BROWN (*zard*): Obtained by mixing lead (*osrob),* tin (*qal'î*) and flint (or "firestone", *sang-e âtesh-barq*). "We melt them together in the kiln. Then, in precise measure, we add a little pulverized essence of iron [*jawhar-e âhan*]."

2. TURQUOISE (*ferôzî*): Obtained by mixing lead (*osrob),* tin (*qal'î*), and powdered glass. To this is added "essence of slain copper [*jawhar-e mes-e koshteh,* that is, copper baked in the kiln] and by its means we secure the change in colour, *taghyîr-e rang*". In English, such a hue is commonly known,

although erroneously in view of the word's true etymology, as "azure".

3. WHITE (safèd): A mixture of lead, tin, flint and powdered glass.

4. BLACK (siyâh): Same basis as for white ("but with some mined lead, osrob-e ma'danî"), with added black of antimony (sormeh), then a "measure" (andâzeh) of graphite or soft carbon (maqn).

5. GREEN (sabz): Lead added to powdered glass and "slain" copper; then, "in precise measure, all this is mixed, and the colour green results."

6. RED (sorkh): A mixture of lead, tin, powdered glass and heated iron – or as Master 'Abd-ol-Ahad phrased it, "a precise measure of a flow of slain iron". Moreover, he added, "we can throw in some gold". Even nowadays? "Yes, even nowadays." As difficult to secure today by such traditional means as it was in medieval times, red is only used sparingly by Herât's modern masters.

7. NIGHT-BLUE (lâjward, literally "lapis lazuli"): a mixture of the same copper as used to produce turquoise: lead, tin, powdered glass, flint and finally "a measure of essence of lapis lazuli, or lâjward. But today we must use a certain German powder. It comes to us from abroad. We must buy it." Buy it? The paradox of this admitted dependency on a foreign product – to create what we think of as the most emblematic of traditional Islamic Central Asia's architectural hues – is already very old.

The fact is that material for the colour lâjward, "lazuli", has been reaching Persian markets from European mines since medieval times, as Master Abo-l-Qâsem of Kâshân testifies in his treatise of 1301: "And another sort they bring from the land of the Franks, Farângestân, ashen in colour, soft." To be sure, the initial source for "azure" is Oriental, in the sense that the English word derives, through medieval French azur, itself borrowed from medieval Spanish azul, from the medieval Hispanic Latin designation for the dark blue mineral itself: Lapis Lazuli, "Stone of Azure". The stone, however, gave its name to the colour, not the other way around. Originally, "azure" or rather Spanish azul does not describe a light, day-sky blue, but rather a dark,

intense, night-sky blue: that of the lapis. Christian Spain's term for "the Stone of Azure" came of course from Spain's Moors: it is lâjward in Arabic, in turn taken from Persian. Ultimately, Lâjward was the name of a small village near a mine in what is now the remote Afghan northeast, whence the stone was obtained for far-ranging trade not only during the Islamic Middle Ages but even in High Antiquity. Jewelry set with lapis lazuli has been found as far afield as Egyptian tombs.

While a favourite colour in Islamic art, the "Stone of Azure" itself could be used only by the illuminators working on paper, not by the potters, for lapis lazuli powder turns grey in the kiln. To adorn their margins and depict the domes of palaces and mosques, the manuscript painters for their part did apply heavy layers of powdered lapis lazuli, ground with mortar and pestle, cleansed through various washings and siftings, and moistened with olive oil into an appropriate paste. The tilemasters, however, had to be content with using only the name lâjward, which they transferred in the workshop to another ground mineral – cobalt. The "Stone of Azure", now, was held to possess magic properties and provide protection from the evil eye. Hence the wish of the tileworkers to keep the name "azure" for the mineral which they actually used – but by further adding another ennobling designation for cobalt alone, one which might be equally magical: the "Stone of Solomon" or Sang-e Solaymân.

In Islamic lore, "Solomon's Stone" initially referred to the most precious talisman of all, the seal-stone worn upon his signet ring by the biblical monarch whose Prophetic mission was further sanctioned by the Koran: Solomon, son of David, as human manifestation of the Royal Majesty bestowed by God. By this seal-stone, Solomon stamped the mark of his sway over all living creatures, faerie, demon, human, bird and beast (all of whose languages he understood). Muslim tileworkers might depict "Solomon's Seal" as an eight-pointed star or octagon; the six-pointed variety, identifiable in given contexts as

"Solomonic", could however also pertain to his father David. The stellar images of these seals were multiplied on walls. But had Solomon's Seal truly been carved of azure? Such at least was the professed belief of the tilemasters of the Iranian city of Kâshân at the turn of the 14th century.

In the Middle East, cobalt could be located, though in quantities far too limited for the tileworkers' demands, to the north of Esfahân, around just this oasis of Kâshân. Finds of kaolin in the area perhaps further explain why, from the 12th century onwards, Kâshân emerged, even before Samarkand and Herât, as a leading centre for ceramic firing in Eastern Islam, not only for pottery but even for wall decoration. Indeed, the very name of the city came to mean "architectural ceramics" in the region's languages. Persian thus says *kâshî*, "of Kâshân", to this day; medieval Eastern Arabic (with its usual harshening of a guttural) likewise referred to *qâshânî* work. (In 16th-century Europe, the name "faïence" – through French – derived in similar manner from the practice of the craft in the Italian city of Faenza.)

When listing his ingredients, Master Abo-l-Qâsem thus wrote in 1301 (we add a few words from the second known manuscript dated 1583): "The sixth stone is the Stone-of-Azure, Lâjward, and in the expression of the craftsmen, they say: the "Solomonic", *Solaymânî*. Its mine is at the village of Qamsar in the hills visible from Kâshân. And in their belief it is from this mine that Solomon the Prophet, upon whom peace!, extracted it. And it is like unto the white silver of Talqam, sparkling, in a matrix of black stone. And from it comes the colour of azure, Lâjward, like unto heaven-blue glaze [*âbgîneh*] and others still." But here Abo-l-Qâsem immediately adds: "And another sort they bring from the land of the Franks."

The blue used for the stained-glass windows at Chartres was likewise derived from cobalt, *bleu chartrain:* one of the many analogies, material and spiritual, between medieval European and Islamic craftsmanship. Indeed, Abo-l-Qâsem's treatise has only a single true equivalent in Western civilization:

the *Schedula diversum artium* by the 12th-century German monk Theophilus, the one surviving medieval key to stained glass.

After the mixing of colours remains the problem of transferring it to the surface of a brick. According to Master 'Abd-ol-Ahad today, the most prized flat tablets or bricks are moulded from "Chinese clay", *gel-e Chînî* or kaolin, which demand five hours' firing. Cut into a square of 16 x 16 cm, an ordinary flat clay brick destined to receive only a single coat of colour, for mosaic work, is fired for a total of three hours. First it is baked for 30 minutes. Then it is dip-coated or painted with the desired solution and returned to the kiln for two and half hours of further firing. By then it is glazed. A brick destined for multiple colouring or *Haft Rang,* however, requires five hours of firing. Preliminary baking lasts an entire hour. Once dry, its various colours are applied with each delimited by a black outline. Finally it comes under four full hours of firing and so emerges glazed with "Seven Colours".

Application of several colours may yet require successive bakings of the same brick, by playing on the different melting temperatures of each hue. According to Master Habîbollâh, glazing a polychrome brick might demand as many as three bakings in succession, or more. But his temperatures need not be too high, he adds: his black yields and melts at 200°C, his yellow at 150°C, his green at 130°C, and his white at only 100°C – this is the white mostly used to trace calligraphy on a soundly dried "lazuli" ground. Prior to firing, the painters dip their brushes into dishes full of grey pallid solutions, basins of shades incomprehensible to the uninitiated eye. The colours they want will emerge on firing. The fuel should be of soft wood: Herât's masters specify white willow "with its bark peeled that it should not emit smoke", as Master Abo-l-Qâsem already cautioned in the 14th century.

In Herât, the high kilns, reached by stairs beneath their blackened vaults, have not changed since the 15th century. The first kiln fires the raw clay bricks, stacked above one another on clay ledges against the kiln-walls in careful rows of 30 pieces, up to 1500 at a time. A second kiln seals in their colours. The main opening of the kiln-shaft, in appearance like a well dug into the platform top, is covered during firing. A peep-hole in the platform surface allows surveillance. The clear willow-wood fire burns in a hearth beneath the kiln and brings out the desired hues.

The next essential stage concerns design and carving. This is carried out in the oblong, well-lit and whitewashed central Workshop, its walls adorned with fragments of Tîmûrid tiling found on the premises and also with more recent pieces: a calligraphic specimen on a swath of paper by Master Fekrî Saljûqî, and two splendid mosaic panels representing Trees of Life, originally destined for the Great Mosque in Kabul – which will not be receiving them for some time since it was burned during a rocket attack in 1994. "The times are still bitter." Bent over his large sheet of oiled paper on a table, Master Abû-Bakr outlines with a ruler stellar motifs drawn into ever more complex mazes of interlacing points, while the cross-legged sculptors on the floor, at work on a mosaic, ply hammer, chisel and file to carve, polish and assemble or inlay their small sections of coloured brick. Then Master Abû-Bakr spreads his paper pattern over the flat wide piece of cardboard set upon a low platform in the middle of the room. He pricks the outlines of his drawing with a series of large needle points, then scatters over the holes of his paper a handful of very fine powdered charcoal. This charcoal dust runs through the holes and, when the oiled paper is removed, appears upon the cardboard beneath, reproducing the original drawing in shadowy outline. This traditional method of tracing – technically known in English as "pouncing" – was much used by medieval Muslim masters in the various arts, not only to multiply copies of tile-patterns, but also to furnish pupils with, say, set models of figurative design for manuscript illumination. The Herâtî sculptors now place their carved pieces of mosaic – face down – within the charcoal outlines upon the cardboard. This covered area has become a panel. The assembled backs of its

mosaic pieces are uniformly coated with cement. Once dry, the panel is raised – face up – and so reveals its completed mosaic. It is ready now for permanent cementing to its receiving wall.

It is instructive to compare tiling methods resorted to at the opposite edge of the Islamic world in Morocco – where some of the very last traditional workshops survive as they do in Afghanistan. Similarities in technique and design between the workshops in Fez and Herât are hardly surprising, given identical underlying Koranic symbolism, although the eastern work is far subtler and more varied. As much was recognized by the early 14th-century Moroccan traveller Ibn Battûta when noting his impressions of the shrine of the caliph 'Alî in Najaf upon his return from the east: "Its walls are [covered] with *qâshânî* which is similar to our *zalîj*, though it is of brighter colour and better workmanship." (Faris/Wilber tr.) For the history of architectural tile decoration in Islam, Ibn Battûta's remarks are key and were first pointed out as such by Donald Wilber in 1939. Ibn Battûta already knows, and cites, the Oriental epithet *qâshânî*, "that which pertains to the city of Kâshân", to designate architectural faïence. Here and elsewhere, he bears witness to the magnificence of revetments in the east even in the generation prior to their full, opulent flowering under the Tîmûrids. Moreover, where the Faris/Wilber translation says only that their colour was "brighter", Ibn Battûta's original uses a powerful comparative, *ashraq,* based on the root *sh-r-q* which may perhaps better be rendered as "more luminous" (with all the Arabic word's rich suggestions of a dawning sun or overpowering light arising in the east). Ibn Battûta's observation becomes all the keener on reflection that, in his own native Morocco, use of the ceramic tile or *zalîj* was then reaching its artistic apex on the shrine-walls of Fez, whereas the creative tile-centres of the east were hardly even close to their aesthetic zenith – attained only in the following century.

We should note that from the Western Arabic word used by Ibn Battûta for a wall-tile, *zalîj* – or in more properly classical form *zulayj* – derives the

PRESENT-DAY WORKSHOP IN THE FRIDAY MOSQUE, HERÂT
CRAFTSMEN CARVING MOSAICS UNDER TWO PANELS DEPICTING TREES OF LIFE

Spanish and Portuguese term *azulejo* (here as elsewhere, softer Portuguese pronunciation better reflects medieval Iberian usage and underlying Arabic loanwords). Resulting resemblance to Spanish *azul*, "azure", was sheer linguistic accident, though poetically very telling.

In Morocco as in the Moorish-derived Iberian architecture farther north, *zalîj*-tiles only line the lower parts of walls. French architectural historian André Paccard researched the mineral sources for the Seven Colours used by the living Moroccan *mu'allimîn* or masters, and found that their blue comes from "pebbles of Casablanca + lead + sand; yellow: a certain stone from around Fez only identifiable when it rains + rust from automobile radiators[!] + lead + sand; honey-colour [i.e. the clear brown equivalent to Persian "Sandalwood"]: red stones from the hills around Fez + lead + sand; white: zinc + lead + sand; black: *maghnâsiya* [magnesite] pebbles from the Sahara + lead + sand; red: a certain powder imported from France (over a little more than the last 20 years) + lead + sand." As for the flame in the kiln, Paccard verified it to be mainly fed with "ground olive pits". (André Paccard,

Le Maroc et l'artisanat traditionnel dans l'architecture islamique, 1979, vol. I, p. 350.)

For her part, leading American scholar on Afghanistan Nancy Dupree, in Herât in 1966, noted that the tilemasters of the mosque likewise then resorted to discarded automobile batteries, ground to powder, to help secure their yellow. Common to North Africa and Central Asia from medieval times to our own has been this transmutation of humble earthly materials into gem-like colours. It is hardly surprising, then, to read Abo-l-Qâsem proudly claim in the opening sentence to his treatise of 1301: "Concerning the art of tile-making, the which craft, in truth, is a branch of Alchemy" (*dar san'at-e kâshî, keh ân herfat, ba-haqîqat, naw'ê ast az Eksîr*). History fully confirms, although by turning it the other way around, the medieval Persian artist's conviction that what he did had something to do with alchemy, based not only on poetic suggestion or mystical intuition, but on sound technical knowledge of the groundwork of his craft.

The alchemical lore of medieval tradition, whether Islamic or European (the latter derived from the Spanish-Islamic), originated among the Hellenized Egyptian glass-blowers and faïence-makers of Alexandria around the beginning of our era. These craftsmen, reflecting on the way they wrought such dull materials as sand, lead, tin, quartz, manganese, cobalt or copper into jewelry and glassware that shone with the Seven Hues, allegorized their mystical correspondence to the Seven Heavenly spheres – as in the Greek treatises of a Zosimus of Panopolis or an Olympiodorus of Alexandria, the substance of whose thought was transmitted into Arabic in early medieval times as in the writings attributed to one Jâbir ibn Hayyân (the "Geber" of medieval Hispanic Latin renderings). The central issue at stake in alchemy was this: when would a practitioner's soul become sufficiently pure to effect the supreme transmutation, that of lead into gold? What added mineral powder, oxide, binding substance or specific flux for metallurgical fusion, hidden within some humble earthly matrix or under the guise of some vile ore and never yet found – save perhaps by the most sanctified souls – would prove to be the true Philosopher's Stone: the *Al-Iksîr* or *Eksîr* of the Arabs and Persians, whence the Elixir of the medieval Latin? For lack of ever actually finding it in matter, medieval Muslim mystics allegorized it into a metaphor for the transfiguration of the soul, as in Al-Ghazâlî's 12th-century treatise on the "Alchemy of Felicity". (Donne's poetry likewise – albeit playfully – moves from the despair of "no chymique yet th'Elixar got" to the metamorphosis of "I am every dead thing, in whom love wrought new Alchimie".)

Muslim craftsmen, for their part, approximated the desired effects of the elusive stone with whatever means they had to hand in the workshop. Hence the wistful expression to be found throughout Master Abo-l-Qâsem's writings, keen with unrequited yearning as he describes, for example, his technique for metallized lustreware (another art invented by medieval Muslim potters): "One removes them and rubs them with moist earth until there should come forth a hue like unto that of Gold [*sebghê mesl-e Zar bêrûn âyad*]!" And further: "And that which is brought forth from middling fire like unto Red Gold shall sparkle, and similar to the Refulgence of the Sun shall glow [*mesl-e Zar-e Sorkh derafshad, wa mânand-e Rôshanî-e Aftâb dorokhshad*]!"

THE REVETMENT OF SYMBOLS. Alchemical play with colours on a wall implies more than sheer delight in decoration. A traditional congregational or Friday Mosque – in Herât as in any other older Islamic city – rises clothed in no less visual symbolism than any Romanesque or Gothic church. Like the medieval European cathedral, a city's major mosque purports to be Holy Writ set forth in so many visible, decipherable signs. It affirms this purpose, to begin with, in the Koranic calligraphy running in white on night-blue ground around its walls, the underlying thrust of whose message is always a variation of the notion that there is no other god but God, nor any reality on earth or in the heavens but that of God occult or manifest. Every inscribed curve or vertical on a mosque's panels – at Mazâr-e

Sharîf, Herât, Mashhad or anywhere – is sacred in itself, since each letter, even the very smallest, amounts to a facet of the Book: that is, a portion of the Divine Multiplicity revealed in Scripture.

The aesthetic wedding of calligraphy and geometric design – as in the angular mazes composed of the repeated names of Allâh, Mohammad and 'Alî – often results in bold abstract patterns which remind many of us of, say, Piet Mondrian at his best. Nor is there any doubt that much in our modern way of looking at traditional Islamic non-figurative art – and of appreciating it at least in a formal outward sense – has been powerfully shaped by the West's own explorations in abstract painting over the last 90 years. At a later stage we may choose to enhance our enjoyment of Islamic abstract art by attempting to plumb its symbolic intent. As usually happens, such connoisseurship leads to further technical appreciation of formal qualities: the sureness of this calligraphic hand or brilliant intricacy of that geometric maze. What we sense in Islamic writing we find in Chinese and Japanese calligraphy also – no shaky lines, unnecessary flourishes, wavering patterns or messy blots, but only taut, disciplined, nervous penmanship (or brushwork), coupled with a rigorously self-instilled feel for balance and firm rejection of complacency even in the boldest abstract thrust. Here reverse comparison occasionally tells against a good deal of modern Western Abstract Expressionism, some of which (though by no means all) suddenly appears flabby and self-indulgent, and intellectually vacuous, when set against better Near or Far Eastern abstractions.

However abstract in form, a traditional mosque's adornments are anything but void of sense. Lettering and designs convey through knotted mazes the twin aspects of the Lord as made manifest to His creatures: Mercy (*Lotf*) and Wrath (*Qahr*). Islam's God is a Pantocrator or All-Ruler, He who Forgives and He who Scourges. The Signs written upon His walls are emblems to display His dual set of Names, one set gracious, the other stern: Beauty and Majesty; Lovingkindness and Wrath. By such

paired Words a wilfully ambiguous Universe expresses Its purpose, emblazoned as both Gentle and Cruel. The entire Universe is also displayed, and made known, through Writ. Indeed, it might be argued that in mosques, the Koran, quoted in calligraphy along the walls, takes the place of the all-present incarnate figure of Christ in churches. As is well known, in the eyes of orthodox Islam, no being wrought of flesh (even a Prophet) but only the Letters from the Book of Holy Writ may embody – at any rate on the panels of a mosque – the *Logos* or manifest "Word" of God. Through the recondite vessels of His Writ, the Lord reveals Himself and so gives Himself a visible aspect to His worshippers – if they have eyes to read, or ears to hear.

The complexity of medieval Islamic architectural decoration toys with another mystical idea. Mazes and vegetal tendrils pursued in fugues appear to mislead the eye at will. The beholder usually gives up attempts to follow a given pattern to its end. Such induced bewilderment may be deliberate. The Arabic word *iltibâs*, or *eltebâs* as pronounced in Persian, used in certain mystical glosses at the turn of the 12th and 13th centuries (the true high point of Islamic speculative writing), literally signifies "revetment" (insofar as it is derived from the Semitic root *l-b-s*, "to clothe") but takes on the further meaning of "ambiguity".

God, according to one of His Koranic Names, is As-Sattâr, He who Veils – and is often so invoked. The Iranian shaykh Rôzbehân of Shîrâz (1128–1209), a confirmed pantheist who pursued to its utmost logical conclusions the Neo-Platonic speculative trends in medieval Islam, and whose thought interestingly coincides with the Hindu notion of *mâyâ* (although he himself was probably utterly unaware of the resemblance), stressed that the lower visible world of multiple forms is a distracting illusion. It is caused by the *Eltebâs* or ambiguous "Revetment" or "Self-veiling" of God, according to Rôzbehân: a cruel game played by the Divinity to "cloak" Its own underlying Essence from the gaze of those too spiritually blind to recognize this very Essence (idolaters), while at the same revealing Itself by this very same "Revetment" to those souls capable of deciphering the manifest Signs of its all-pervading Unity through the multiple interlacing of Its infinite visible symbols. *Eltebâs* or Revetment thus both displays and distracts, reveals and hides – like polychromatic adornment on a mosque's wall. To show Itself to the believers through manifest Beauty: this is the Grace bestowed by the Divinity upon Its lovers. But to conceal Itself beneath the ambiguous mask created by Its very manifestation of Beauty is precisely the sign of the Divinity's Wrath, to overwhelm the polytheists and pagans dazed by the multiple appearances of the lower world.

Ideas of this sort are already very apparent in the writings of the poet who became the true creator, and indeed long remained the model, of mystical narrative verse in Islamized Persian: Sanâ'î of Ghaznî, born in what is now southeastern Afghanistan in the latter half of the 11th century. In his collection of didactic moral and spiritual anecdotes, the *Hadîqat-ol-Haqîqat* or "Garden of Truth", Sanâ'î lays particular stress on the Koran itself as the visible mirror of the Divine, indeed as the Universe itself made manifest in the form of a Book. To hear it recited is to listen to the most melodious of songs, and to look upon it in calligraphy – inscribed on a page or on a wall – is to behold the most beautiful image of the Cosmos. But this very Beauty, physical and external, of the Holy Book, weaves a Veil which diverts the awed beholder from piercing through its surface to grasp its inner meaning. As such, the Book's calligraphy and abstract illuminations – again, whether on paper or on the panel of a mosque – spin a maze as distracting as the beauty of the World itself, which the Writ mirrors:

> Fancy stands amazed by the show of its shapes
> And Intellect dazed by the core of its verse
> To the marrow – perfection its verb and its verse
> Heart-wrenching: heart-deceiving the shape of its show.

Further on, as he reflects upon the Majesty of the Koran (*fî Jalâl al-Qur'ân*) as the raiment of his feminized Beloved, Sanâ'î launches into untrans-posable word-play, verging on blasphemy, between the Arabic terms for "dialectical proof", *dalîl*, and "coquettishness", *dalâl*:

> Majestic She, by Veil of Majesty;
> Proof of it She, by Mask of Coquetry.

Later in date but no less important and influential a thinker on the subject-matters dealt with in Persian mystic verse, the early 16th-century Iranian divine Shamsoddîn Lâhîjî, commenting upon the crucially central 14th-century spiritual poem "The Rose Garden of Mystery" (*Golshan-e Râz*) by the shaykh Shabestarî, chose to summarize several hundred years of Islamic speculation along these lines in two neat Arabic hemistichs (I render them as two full lines). Lâhîjî plays on the classically paired contrast between God the Beautiful (*Jamâl*: the mirror of Grace) and God Awesome in Majesty (*Jalâl*: reflecting Divine Wrath):

> Your Beauty flows through all Realities
> And therein hides – within Your Majesty – no other Veil!

At the other end of the Islamic world, the very great Andalusian master, Ibn 'Arabî (1160–1240), bequeathed to later mystical schools, throughout the entire range of his civilization as far as Java, what became the last word on the closely related subject of the Tree of Life, or *Shajarat al-Kawn*. Ibn 'Arabî's treatise of this title is an aesthetic meditation on the visual ambiguity posed by the Tree. As it shoots, branches and flowers forth, the Tree is resolved into cosmic calligrams; it is God's own Writ. Bewildered before the external luxuriance of the Cosmic Tree, the Devil therein sees no more but its forbidding outer bark, and loses himself in trying to trace his way through the multiple branches and foliage inscribed with the Names of Wrath which are all that he may decipher. Only the Prophet may read, within the Tree as image of the Universe, the Divine Names of Grace along with those of Wrath emblazoned upon each leaf and discern the internal sap or all-unifying Flow of Life.

A further deliberately ambiguous cosmic image in medieval Islam conveys a notion of deliberately cruel

Divine beauty, not devoid of acid erotic flavour: the Spider's Web. Geometric mazes weave a spidery filigree across mosque walls. The metaphor of the Spider's Web – like Shelley's "web of being blindly wove" – carries constrasting meanings. In sûra 29 of the Koran, precisely entitled *'Ankabût* or "The Spider", the web symbolizes the utter frailness of all earthly dwellings, in whom one should no more put one's trust than in false gods (verse 41): "Like unto those who take, other than God, protectors, like unto them is the Spider that takes unto herself a dwelling, and truly the frailest of dwellings is the dwelling of the Spider, if they only knew!" The verse's sense is obvious, and even a medieval Koranic commentator as anxious to read the most esoteric meanings into the Holy Book as, for example, the 14th-century Iranian divine 'Abd-or-Razzâq of Kâshân, was content simply to gloss the contrast between upward-looking souls and those ensnared by lust in the world below. (The web as Devil's Snare occurs as well in Christian imagery, as in the 17th-century poetry of Edward Taylor.)

But the image of the Spider's Web is also granted far more favourable connotations in medieval Islam. According to tradition, the Prophet once hid in a cave to escape enemies, and a gentle spider immediately spun her web across the mouth of the grotto to make his persecutors think that no one had entered. The mystic Persian poet 'Attâr (1136–1220) praises the divine miracle of the Web – and its dual nature – in the prelude to his celebrated spiritual parable, the *Manteq-ot-Tayr* – medieval Islam's own "Parliament of Fowles":

> To the Spider in wisdom He granted a Snare:
> To the World's Prince He granted a Refuge thereby.

Sanâ'î had already seen through the paradox of the Spider's Snare as God-bestowed Shelter:

> Unto whom the help of God's Truth is a Castle,
> The Spider, to such, shall be his Curtain-Ward!

Thus the protective Web looms as a further guardian Veil to the Word. Mystic speculation seized upon the image as one more form of the Revetment which reveals, manifests, but at the same time conceals the Godhead from profane gazes. For the Web is a trap, and its multiple rings, in a chain of linked metaphors, even come to be assimilated in various spiritual poems and their glosses – notably those by Lâhîjî to the "Rose Garden of Mystery" – to the cascade of curls veiling the Countenance of the Beloved: rings not only to hinder and fend off the unworthy, but also to entice and so bind fast the Godhead's lovers. Who, then, is the Spider? The most illustrious 13th-century mystical poet in Persian, Rûmî (1207–73), was so bold as to lift a corner of this curtain, symbolized by the Arabic calligraphic woven maze of "My-Lord-the-Supreme" (R.A. Nicholson tr.):

> Since the spider seized prey so large,
> Behold what the snare of My Lord the Supreme will do!

Another Persian-language poet, Nezâmî of Ganjeh in Azerbaijan (1141–1209), with whom we will be especially concerned in these pages, dwells on the twin aspect of the Spider's Net as kind and cruel, shelter and snare, deadly trap and healing balm (for webs served to staunch blood in the traditional medicine of the time), as in this verse from his romance of courtly love, *Majnûn and Laylâ*:

> This should well be the Dwelling of the Spider:
> Which here binds up a wound: and thence, it claws!

In Nezâmî's masterpiece *The Brides of the Seven Climes* – the symbolic frame to the present work – Semnâr the Builder, to measure the sky, raises an astrolabe, whose reticulation was traditionally designated, in both the East and the West, as the "Spider's Web" (Chaucer's medieval English "Lopwebbe" in the *Descripcioun of the Astrelabie*):

> He glanced across the sky, his eye-beams weaving threads
> From forth the maw of the Spider in the Astrolabe.

It is as if the measuring instrument's web at once revealed, defined and caught in the trap of its own reticulation the very pattern of the visible universe, whose stylized reflection upon the walls of mosques both hides and mirrors the Image of the World and its Creator Manifest.

The verse romance of *The Brides of the Seven Climes,*

written in AD 1197

by the Persian poet Nezâmî of Ganjeh,

is the supreme narrative masterpiece

of medieval Islamic civilization.

According to the poet,

the ancient Persian king Bahrâm-Gûr

wedded seven brides from seven different lands.

The tales they tell him on seven successive nights

together yield the symbolic key

to the seven colours used by medieval Persian ceramists

on their walls and domes.

The seven colours when united

mirror the Cosmic Order.

Bahrâm-Gûr
Discovers
the Seven Portraits
of his
Future Brides

Central Asia

نُخراسان وخوارزم ماوَراءالنّهر

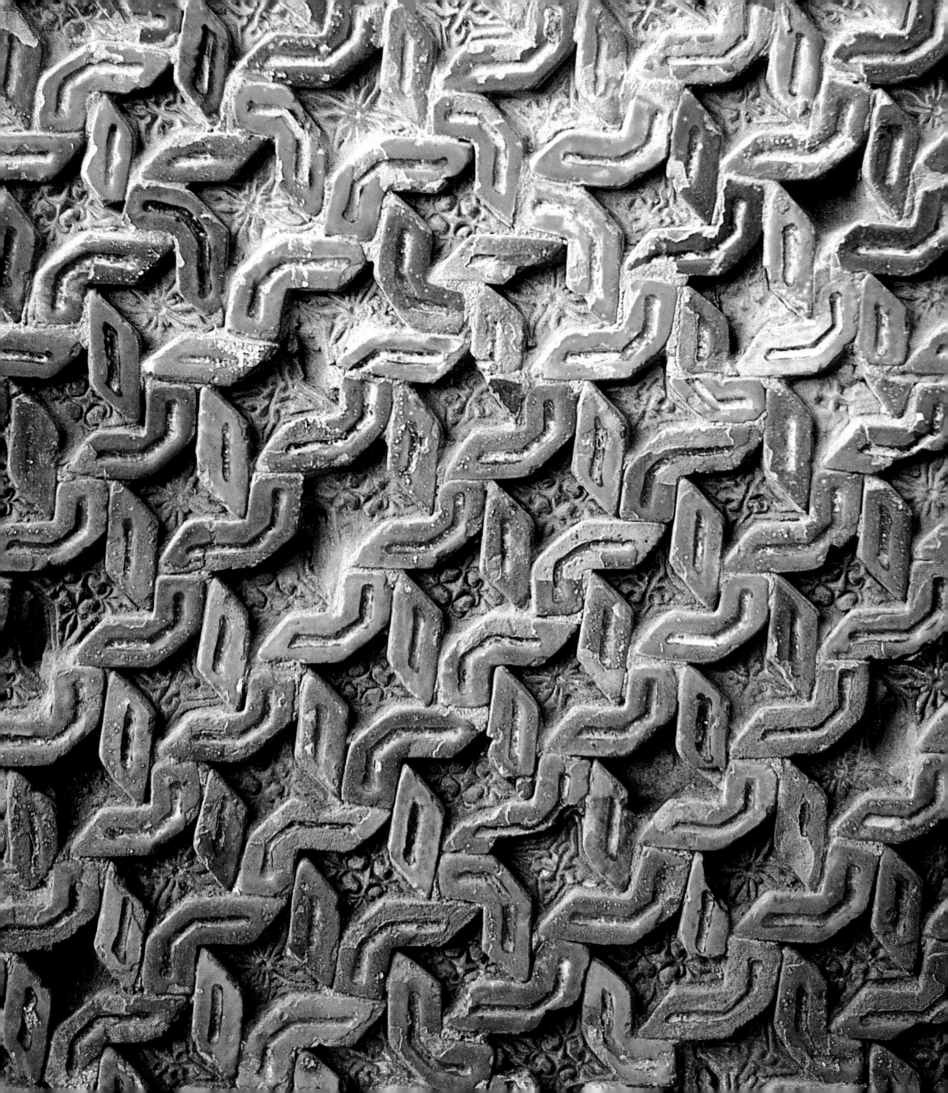

Under the Old Portal of Herât's Friday Mosque a modern Afghan craftsman paints calligraphy to be fired on a tile for the ongoing restoration of the shrine. Over his head, early 13th-century Ghôrid turquoise ceramic script – along with the turquoise knobs (below left) – mingles with carved stucco in one of the earliest major medieval Islamic examples of coloured architectural tiling. On the extreme upper right, a Tîmûrid spandrel from the mosque's late 15th-century restoration provides a glimpse of the art of tile revetment at its most polychromatic and complex at the close of the medieval age. Like the decoration of a European church combining Romanesque with later Gothic, Renaissance and Baroque, Herât's Old Portal, gateway to a living shrine, is a palimpsest of Eastern Islamic sacred architectural adornment, spanning three ages of achievement.

*PAGE 44: MAZÂR-E SHARÎF (AFGHANISTAN), 15TH-CENTURY TURRET,
POSSIBLY RESTORED IN THE 17TH CENTURY
PAGE 45: BASTÂM (IRAN), SHRINE OF SHAYKH BÂYEZÎD, 1313, TILING AND STUCCO
PAGES 46–47: HERÂT (AFGHANISTAN), FRIDAY MOSQUE, 1200–1498–1964*

46

SHĀH-E MASHHAD (AFGHANISTAN), MADRASEH, 1165–66
PAGES 50–51: HORSEMEN IN THE HIGHLANDS OF GHŌR

*M*onuments to the glory of the late 12th-century Ghôrid sultans, the minaret of Jâm (left) and the madraseh of Shâh-e Mashhad (preceding pages) lurked forgotten for the next 800 years in the most hidden folds of the central Afghan mountains; they were only rediscovered by chance, in 1957 and 1970 respectively.

Today they stand abandoned again and are rapidly deteriorating. The arch of Shâh-e Mashhad collapsed in the mid-1980s. Yet both monuments bear unique witness to a crucial turning-point in the adornment of Eastern Islamic architecture, when the art of revetment in carved stucco, then at its peak, began yielding to blue tiles. The ring of turquoise script and medallions around the minaret holds a portent of Eastern Islam's vast expanses of blue-toned tiling to come.

MAZĀR-E SHARĪF (AFGHANISTAN),
THE MOSQUE, 1480 AND 1963

The Chorasmian
Princess
beneath
the Green Dome

AHRÂM SITS ON MONDAY
BENEATH THE GREEN DOME
AND THE DAUGHTER OF THE KING OF THE THIRD CLIME
TELLS HIM HER STORY

نشستن بهرام روز دوشنبه در گنبد سبز

Monday came, and the SHÂH rose
Under the royal Green parasol, to the Moon raised happy omen:
The SHÂH rose like a green taper
Green upon green, like the Angel of the Garden,
Swept his robes towards the Green Dome
His heart set on mirth and cheer.
Then upon the emerald-green lawn
The garden of the stars scattered the stars in spring petals.
A cypress-form, she swayed there, Greenclad:
He wished her to open unto him her tight-locked sugarmouth,
A Faerie there; she raised invocation,
Unto this Solomon opened the curtain-web of her mystery,
Saying: "You by whom our souls rejoice, through your soul
All souls be sacrificed unto your soul:
The Abode of Prosperous Empire is your palace-pavilion:
Crown and Throne there but thresholds to your high palace:
The Crown rises exalted when worn upon your head:
The Throne sits in firmness beneath your arch-gate:
The encircling empire arches into its gem-key: your Crown,
And all the world lies needy before your arch-gate."
Thus she uttered invocation unto the high throne
And opened her mouth: coral fount of sugar.

According to the Chorasmian Princess, there lived once upon a time "in Rûm" a Byzantine Christian youth of noble line, wise and withal kind-hearted and chaste. His name was Bashr. One day, as Bashr was walking in a quiet lane, a strong wind by chance blew aside the face-veil of a passing woman to reveal a manifestation of the beauty of the full moon. Bashr was transfixed.

"Upon his way love played predatory Turk,
In confusion tossed up his intellect.
An image he saw muffled in raw silk –
Like through a dark cloud the Moon disclosed.
With no concern for Bashr she was wending her way
When the wind of a sudden stole off the Moon's veil,
To confusion the gust blew open a way
And the Moon from within a black cloud loomed forth.
Bashr saw; his knees weakened;
Her glance shot one arrow; it nailed him in place."

She was a married woman. Bashr was aghast. He loathed himself on account of the social, and moral, enormity of the sudden lust he felt. Seeking security in further continence, he left on pilgrimage to Jerusalem. On his way home from the shrine, he found for travelling-companion a learned rationalizing philosopher of rare arrogance, named Malîkhâ:

"Said he: 'You are Bashr, honour of men.
I am Malîkhâ, guide unto the learned.
All that lies in the sky, all that lies on the earth,
All that lies in the brain, and all in man's thoughts
I know altogether, by this my intellect.'"

The companions travelled on foot. They went astray in a patch of desert. By miracle, they stumbled upon a large earthenware jar buried to its neck in the ground, under a solitary tree, and filled to the brim with pure water. Of this they drank. Bashr, as was his wont, praised the Lord's bounty and the benevolence of those unknown men who had so thought to bury a water-jar in the desert: "Said Bashr, 'On account of heavenly reward, one has so done as so many have done, for fear that by a blow it might be shivered in two; therefore have they thus crammed it into the ground.'" Malîkhâ rejected such a simplistic explanation: the water-jar, he argued, had probably been thus dug into the sand as a decoy by hunters to lure thirsty game in the desert.

Malîkhâ announced his intention to bathe in the water and wash off his dust and sweat. Bashr was horrified by such blasphemy towards God, and lack of compassion, or even good manners, towards fellow men who might want to drink also. Neatly folding his clothes on the nearby sand, the philosopher dived naked into the jar – and sank into its depths! The jar had suddenly revealed itself to be an infinitely deep well. Bashr, alarmed by Malîkhâ's disappearance:

"Went unto the jar to search for him, looked to and fro,
Unaware that the master therein had drowned.
A drowned one he saw, a lost soul drifting therein,
And himself mirrored: head arched lid-like over the rim.
For a moment he lingered, in wonder what was best.
A stick from the branch of the tree he snapped,
A spear's length, somewhat more, perhaps less,
With fingers and nails he whittled it:
Like men who sound the depths of the sea
He measured the waters within the innermost jar –
Leave your jar! The deepest well he found
From brim to bottom wondrous wrought
With its top by a half-jar rimmed, lest wild game dive in.
Swiftly he raked the drowned one up
From the well's water – and down into a well of earth
Wherein he buried him with sand and stones;
Then by the gravehead sat, heart choked,
And said: 'Where be your wiles now, and wit?
Where is your cobbler's awl of wit to open riddled knots
And all your claim to solve whatever puzzle –
Beast's and devil's, man's or sprite's?
And then you said: "From the high Seven Spheres
To the zenith, their secret shall I coil into my noose!"
Where have gone all your claims to the Sciences Twelve
And bold show of manhood? You? Neither man now, nor woman!
All that flaunting of yours: "Ahead I see

All deeds, from subtlety of wit!"
The wellhead lay hidden even before you.
How came you saw it not, with all this foresight of yours?'"

Bashr collected the philosopher's clothes, searched them for his papers and found the pockets full of gold. This wealth the honest Byzantine chose to restore to Malîkhâ's family in his native city. When he found the right door and knocked, it was opened by the same woman whose face he had glimpsed unveiled in the street before going on his pilgrimage! The woman rejoiced to learn that she was now a widow well rid of an evil husband, praised Bashr for his honesty — and asked him to wed her. So, in the most roundabout way, the pious, chaste and scrupulous young man came to marry the woman he yearned for — and entered into all her husband's wealth:

"Seeing that she no longer dwelt far from the Heaven-dwellers,
He fashioned for her a Green garb like unto that of a houri.
To wear Green is better than the flaunting of Yellow.
Green came, and best befitted she of cypress-form.
The colour Green is welfare to the sown.
Greenness is raiment to the Angel.
To Green the soul is attracted above all things.
The eye is brightened too by Green.
All that grows inclines to Green.
All Green fertility is of such hue."

Thus she spoke her tale, the Moon, feast's adornment;
The SHÂH drew her close, and pressed her to his breast.

The technique of underglaze painting on tiles in "Seven Colours" reached perfection in the revetment of the complex, stalactite-like corbelling (moqarnas) around the drum. The work is highlighted with tiny spots of pure gold leaf so that the dome, to borrow the words of a Persian master ceramist of the early 14th century, "might shine like unto the resplendence of the sun".

A smaller sister to the shrines in Herât and Samarkand, this charming mosque in northern Afghanistan, raised over the tomb of a dervish of the Naqshbandî Order, has managed to preserve nearly intact – despite years of war – its typical Central Asian melon-like, ribbed dome:

Hark with the soul's ear to the sounds innumerable
In the hollow of the green dome, rising from lovers' passionate cry.

So sang the mystic poet Rûmî (in R.A. Nicholson's translation). Rûmî was born in this ancient oasis in 1207, two and a half centuries before he could have seen this shrine; but to the poet, all blue-green domes mirrored the curve of the sky.

Herât Castle was founded by Alexander in 330 BC, rebuilt by the emir Ekhtiyâroddîn at the close of the 13th century, restored and entirely sheathed in tiles by the Tîmûrid emperor Shâh Rokh in 1416 and photographed here shortly before it was saved from utter disintegration by UNESCO in 1975. Here, stripped of its protective tiling and exposed to centuries of winter rain and summer dust storms, Herât Castle, like a ghostly ship on a petrified wave, appears to be sinking slowly back into the sea of formless clay from which it was first moulded, to die like the ancient monuments of Babylon, almost without leaving a trace.

71

*C*rossed bare and enamelled bricks intersect according to the bannâ'î or "masonwrought" technique in maze-patterns of kufic calligraphy, offering abstract puzzles for the devotee to ponder and finally decipher after considerable difficulty. The patterns work themselves out into the following pious phrases: *"SUBHÂN ALLÂH AL-'AZÎM! Glory to God Supreme!"* (left and far right), and *"LÂ ILÂHA ILÂ-LLÂH WA MUHAMMAD RASÛL ALLÂH! There is no god but God and Mohammad is the Prophet of God!"* – surrounding the name of the holy caliph *'ALÎ* (right).

73

*L*ashed for five and a half centuries by Herât's searing, dust-laden "Wind-of-One-Hundred-and-Twenty-Days", the dome of the mausoleum of the Tîmûrid Princess Tômân Âghâ still preserved splendid fragments of tiling when this photograph was taken shortly before the human-wrought storm unleashed in 1978–79. This proved to be the last picture of this dome ever taken. Aimed at a suspected concentration of Afghan mojâhedîn, a Soviet bomb dropped in 1984 annihilated the cupola. On the left, a geometric pattern from the madraseh at Khargerd displays, at its centre, Solomon's Seal.

KHARGERD (IRAN), MADRASEH, 1445
KOHSÂN (AFGHANISTAN), MAUSOLEUM OF TÔMÂN ÂGHÂ, 1441,
STATE OF THE BUILDING BEFORE 1984

*This floral motif, cut in mosaic or "inlay-work"
(mo'arraq), is made up of carved ceramics fired white,
emerald green, turquoise, ultramarine and a rich reddish-
brown whose hue the poet Nezâmî once called "sandalwood"
– an amber-coloured tone the warmth and lustre of which
have never been equalled in tilework since the 15th century.
The design explodes with a* shamseh *or "sunburst"
surrounded by sparks which themselves turn into other stellar
planets: an image of the Divine Principle of Light emanating
into celestial hierarchies, according to the Islamic version of
Neo-Platonic mysticism. When viewed from afar, the panel
displays further spark-surrounded sunbursts and appears as
a field of stars.*

SAMARKAND (UZBEKISTAN),
CATHEDRAL MOSQUE OF "BĪBĪ KHĀNOM", 1399

The Slav Princess
beneath
the Red Dome

نشستن بهرام روز سه شنبه در گنبد سرخ

This day among all winter days
As short as a midsummer's night,
Of all the weekdays' days the finest:
The week's navel: Tuesday – third day after Sabbath –
This day belongs to Mars-Bahrâm: to Bahrâm-Mars's hue:
The SHÂH bore both their names
Red upon Red adorned
Dawn-riding towards the Red Dome.
Ruddy-cheeked, the Lady Slav,
Fiery her hair: and she, gracious like water
To pay him homage wound her sash:
A fine thing when a Moon so worships the Sun.
Then the night raised up the Crescent spearhead of its standard:
And therewith lacerated its curtain all across its archway.
The SHÂH, of this honey-apple red one
Requested a tale, to induce him to joy,
And she gracious, not to spurn his wish,
Scattered word-pearls from coralmouth, so:
"You! the sky lies as a threshold beneath your palace,
The sun-disc shines as a moon-pommel over your pavilion,
Higher than any pearl that might be pierced,
Better than any speech that might be uttered,
May none draw nigh you,
And blindness befall those who see not your glory!"

Such invocation to a close she drew,
Then a ruby-tale from the story-mine to the ruby-mine entrusted.

According to the tale of the Slav Princess, the ruler of a kremlin in Russia had a daughter whose beauty incarnated to perfection all the rose-red hue of the North:

"Heart-bewitching with magic glances,
Redrose-cheeked; tall cypress her stature;
To her face, comeliness that might tug hearts more than moontide;
And lips sweet-tasting, finer than cane-sugar,
She was hearts' Venus which Jupiter drew forth.
Sugar melted before her, candle-flame died."

This Princess of Russia moreover possessed subtle intellect and rare artistic talent: she mastered all magic sciences and painted icons with a refinement worthy not only of Byzantine masters but also of the Chinese: "She had read all the books of magic of the world, their sorceries and all things hidden therein."

Yet she rejected marriage, to her father's despair — although the ruler was content to humour all her whims. For what lover might claim truly to be worthy of her? Her father yielded to her conditions for wedlock. She would live henceforth on the mountaintops — of the Caucasus? — in a castle enclosed within walls of steel, its portal hidden to all, and defended by talismanic statues ranged along the narrow path winding thither:

"Then she shut herself up within the strong fortress,
Went in, Castlebound treasure, took her seat,
Her silver-limbed body into the stronghold went,
Her name became LADY OF THE CASTLE: *Dezh-Bânû* —
Who would steal her treasure? Her fort made them all helpless:
A STEEL CASTLE like to the BRAZEN HOLD: the *Rô'în-Dezh*.
And she in that Castle was LADY OF THE SLAVS: *Bânû-ye Saqlâb*:
No such LADY OF THE CASTLE was ever seen even in dreams."

By her knowledge of alchemical theurgy, the Lady of the Castle wrought the animated statues that protected her chosen realm:

"She sealed upon the road of the high Castle,

Through her wisdom, talismans in number,
Each talisman-statue worked of iron and stone,
Each set in its grip a falchion-blade:
Whoever trod that passageway of fear
By the sting of these blades was cleft –
Save one who was warden to that Castle,
Whoever trod the passageway was helpless.
And the warden privy to the secret
This passageway wended not, save by measured step, and wary.
Whoever's foot mis-stepped the limit –
His head, of a sudden, dropped from his trunk.
The talismanic blade struck.
Life's Moon hid in a cloud.
And the gate of the sky-high battlements
Like unto the gate of heaven remained hidden.
A geomancer might run about it for a month,
To its gate no more road would lead him than into the sky."

Her approach thus forbidden by such a rampart of steel and blood, the reclusive Princess resorted now, maliciously, to an opposite measure: she attracted lovers unto herself. She painted her own portrait upon a roll of silk nailed over the gate of her father's kremlin:

"That Faerie-Image, Castle-Dwelling,
Herself a painter from China's shops,
Set pen to painting,
Water bound in knots like spiralshells –
Her pen's inkblack, like a houri's musk-lock,
Upon her painting cast a shadow of Light."

Her self-portrait's fame spread throughout the universe; countless suitors sought her hand. But she set four conditions. Her suitor must needs be young, handsome and noble. He should thread his way to her Castle between the talismans and so court risk of decapitation beneath their falchions. If successful in reaching the Castle wall, then he should discover its hidden portal or again forfeit his head: to be cut off, this time, by an

*SAMARKAND
(UZBEKISTAN),
MAUSOLEUM
OF TÔMÂN ÂGHÂ,
1405,
AND MAUSOLEUM
OF SHÎRÎN BÎBÎ ÂGHÂ,
1385*

executioner. And should he fulfil all the preceding trials, still he must solve a set of riddles posed by the Princess, or yet again offer his neck to the sword:

> "Whosoever holds good this counsel,
> The Alchemy of Happiness be his lot!
> Whosoever measures not my words –
> However great – falls shortened."

From all lands, princely lovers thronged to sacrifice their lives. All fell beneath the talismanic blades by the second trial at the latest. Severed heads piled as high as the battlements of her father's kremlin.

Then came the turn of the Prince fated to be the chosen one. This lover understood that without magic, afsûn, he had no chance of foiling the traps of the Brazen Hold. The young man consulted sages that he might learn of the existence of a supreme spiritual guide until "he heard of one master of all the arts, one who bound demons in chains, and linked himself to angels". Towards such a master, Nezâmî tells us (in an explicit reference to a spiritual parable by his fellow-poet and contemporary, the Persian mystic 'Attâr), the Prince hastens "from mountain to mountain" like those birds symbolizing souls in quest of their king the Sîmorgh *or Griffin-Phoenix as manifestation of Divine Wisdom. Once found, this master – further assimilated by Nezamî to the prophet Khezr, another archetype of mystic initiation – reveals to the Prince all the Castle's spells, and the secret spiritual bonds that caused the talismans' movements. The Prince finds himself ready, henceforth, to challenge the Brazen Hold. He dons Red:*

> "His garment Red he made. This was matter for blood,
> And such oppression – Heaven's tyranny.
> Since in blood's river he would dip,
> His clothes like his eyes he tinged in blood,
> Self-care cast off,
> The world's blame-shout he cried
> And said, 'Not this ordeal for myself I endure,
> No. I seek blood-price for a hundred thousand heads.
> Either their heads I prise free from this web of bondage,
> Or my own head I lay down at ordeal-end.'

So for this task his garb he steeped in blood;
Drew sword, fared forth, pitched tent on such a field."

Through the craft taught by his master, the Prince smites with his sword each murderous statue with a blow which cracks their metal at the precise required spot, annuls their magic and precipitates them down the cliff-face. When he reaches the Castle walls, he strikes with a leather thong a drum suspended from the battlements. The drum's reverberations, multiplied in hollow echoes, reveal to him the secret portal to the fortress. The Princess is now constrained "from behind her curtain to turn player of wiles". She asks the Prince to answer four riddles, which she secretly hopes he might solve: for now she loves in turn.

She takes from her earrings two pearls equal in weight and lustre, and has them conveyed to the Prince. He weighs them and adds to the scales three further identical pearls. She weighs all these in turn and finds them to be equal. Then she crushes the five pearls together in a mortar and mixes them with powdered sugar. This mixture again she orders borne to the Prince. He pours milk over this pearly sugar in a cup. When she receives the cup, she drinks the milk, then kneads a paste with the residue at the bottom – which her scales reveal not to have diminished by a single ounce from the weight of the five pearls which had first been weighed together. Then she takes from her finger a ring bearing a pearl of the finest lustre, and places this precious ring on a dish to be borne to the Prince. He deposits in turn by its side another pearl, in all ways similar to the one on the dish. When the Princess sees both these pearls side by side, she detaches still another from her necklace and adds this last gem to the pearl offered by the Prince, stringing it along with the Prince's pearl upon an identical cord, which is again borne to her suitor. Nothing any longer distinguishes these last two pearls:

"A knowing glance upon them cast,
The twain so bound, one from another no longer might he know
Except that they were twain: between these pearls of such fine water
No other difference remained, for shine or lustre."

The Prince then adds to this pair of pearls a seal fashioned of a Stone of Azure, lapis lazuli (mohreh-ye azraq): *"For no third pearl might be added to these two." The Princess welcomes the lapis lazuli seal, so joined to the twin pearls: "This Seal she placed upon her lips, and smiled."*

The wedding could now be celebrated. What remained to be explained were the solutions to the puzzle, the meaning of "the Face hidden beneath the Veil". The first two pearls had meant that life "only lasts for a pair of days". By adding three pearls, the Prince had replied that even if such earthly life might be prolonged, it should only be "for three more days". The Princess had crushed these five pearls together and mixed them with powdered sugar to signify that the brief span of this earthly life remained so "polluted with lust" that none might separate them except "by magic and alchemy". Now this the Prince had been able to effect by pouring milk upon them: the sugar became mixed with the milk, while the crushed pearls remained at the bottom. To show that she was now in love, the Princess drank the milk. Then she sent the Prince another pearl set in a ring to signify that she accepted wedlock with him. He added a pearl of equal water to proclaim himself her equal. The Princess answered with a new pearl from her own necklace; she strung it with the Prince's pearl to mean that she too recognized that they were wedded peers. Then the Prince sealed their union with lapis lazuli "to keep away the evil eye". This the Princess acknowledged: "The Seal of his love lies upon my breast: it is a Treasure-Seal, fixed upon my Treasury":

"He lived with her in grace, to his desire.
Like to her Redrose cheek he dyed his robe in Red.
For the initial day in his white-marked state
The Red of his robe he took as omen.
Through Redness from Blackness escaped,
Red finery he bound to him fast
For by Red he was granted safe-passageway.
The Red-robed King they called him.
Red bedecks new customs.
Gems are prized for their Red.
Gold they call the Red Sulphur –
For from Red glows its worth.
Blood mingles with the breath of life
And Reddens with souls' virtue.
Those in whom shines forth good nature,
Their Ruddy face shows forth their noble seed.
The Red Rose might not rise Empress of her garden
Did not her Ruddiness show forth."

When this rare story reached its end,
The air filled with Red Roses, scented in its essence;
The countenance of Bahrâm, from all the Roses scattered,
Reddened like spiced wine;
He stretched his hand to the Red Rose,
Hugged her to his bosom; and slept in grace.

The greatest painter of medieval Herât evokes the bustle of activity surrounding the building of the Friday or Cathedral Mosque of Samarkand, raised in 1399 by Tîmûr, who had elephants brought up from India to speed the work. But the minaret just rising out of the ground in Behzâd's painting seems to reproduce, with striking accuracy, the corner tower on the facing page from the shrine at Mashhad — the painter must have ridden out to see it, since the city is only a short journey from Herât. Empress Gôhar Shâd's minaret, erected in 1416–18 for a shrine dedicated to one of the holiest figures in Shî'ism, displays on its honey-coloured bare brickwork a shower of ceramic medallions, each emblazoned with one of the 99 names of God, above a strip of calligraphy woven in "masonwrought" technique.

99

Between 1440 and 1443, the craftsmen commissioned to redecorate this shrine, then already two centuries old, amused themselves by inserting into their mosaics, which were otherwise of traditional pattern, a waterfowl flying in profile. This was a visual quotation from a motif found on Chinese pottery of the sort exported to the Islamic world since T'ang Dynasty times in the 8th and 9th centuries AD.

102

TORBAT-E JÂM (IRAN), SHRINE OF SHAYKH AHMAD
IBN ABI-L-HASAN, 13TH–14TH CENTURIES AND 1440–43

The Chinese
Princess
beneath
the Sandalwood-
coloured Dome

نشستن بهرام روزِ پنج شنبه در گنبدِ صندلی

The day of Thursday is a Day of Good
And its fortune linked to Jupiter.
The breeze of morning opened a muskpod:
The Sandalwood-coloured earth flamed into aloes-wood –
To display the Earth's manner, all Sandalwood-coloured,
A Sandalwood tinge took the SHÂH for his coat now and cup
To emerge from the Turquoise Dome,
Wended his way to a Dome-Palace tinted like Sandalwood
Where he fell to wine-drinking from the hand of a doll-like one – from a
    Chinese shadowplay:
Drank Water-of-Kawsar, heavenly fountlike – from the hand of a houri to
    his eye –
Until eve in his path of joy such wine he drank:
In wine-drinking, mirth.
Night encircled them, lined with kohl; and its spiral shell
Filled the Night-Dragon's maw with starpearls:
So the SHÂH with the narrow-eyed one, China-fostered.
He wished her to scatter the dust from his thoughts:
The Lady of China smoothed his brow's furrow
And a stream of honey, from her plenty, opened
And said: "Oh you through whom souls live in all the world,
High Emperor to all Emperors
More than sand in sahara,
Stone in mountain, water in sea –

Life be friend to your Fortune
And you, breadsharer of Life and Fortune.
Oh you are like the Sun! Bestower of Light:
Ruler, Bestower of Rule.
I feel like one forever vexed
Over this my tongue so broken and bound:
Before spiced wine
Needs must I pour forth such vinegar?
Yet since the SHÂH wishes joy for his soul
And for his mirth requests something of this my saffron
I shall open my bag of crooked speech.
I shall increase his mirth: by his laughter."
So, her invocation uttered, this Moon worshipped her Sun:
She kissed the SHÂH's hand.

The tale of the Chinese Princess unfolds, not in the Far East, but in the northern Mesopotamian steppe at the foot of the Kurdish highlands. One day, two young travelling-companions on their way to a certain city crossed this stretch of scrubland on foot. "The name of this one was Khayr (Good), and of the other Sharr (Evil): in each his deeds with his own name accorded." Each traveller bore his own bag of provisions and water gourd. But Khayr had not been aware of the length of the way, carried insufficient food and soon had exhausted his scanty water supply. Sharr, however, who had often crossed this stretch, husbanded his water. After seven days, Sharr still had more than enough to drink, but shared nothing, while his companion was raked with thirst.

Khayr was soon aware of this "evil gem-essence" in Sharr — in Persian the word for essence and for gem can be the same — and so at first forbore to ask him for any water. But then he was overcome with thirst and collapsed on the sand. Khayr begged Sharr for a drop of mercy, offering him, in exchange, two rubies of immense value which he carried in his scrip: "He had with him two rubies of the colour of fire, of finest water — but stone's water; lustre rippled in water from two hidden gems — but water to the eye, not his tongue."

Sharr — "God's wrath upon him!" says the poet — laughed suspiciously at Khayr's offer. What, asked Sharr, should befall if Khayr, once they reached the city, were to denounce his travelling-companion to the watch as a thief in order to recover his gems?

No, in exchange for a draught of water, Khayr must needs offer two gems far more precious still, but such ones as he should never recover: his eyes. (Sharr indulges here in cruel word-play between the Persian words chashmeh, *a source of water, and* chashm, *an eye.) "Said Khayr: 'For God, have you no shame? Would you give me cold water in exchange for searing fire?'"*

But Khayr, in thirst to the point of death, finally accepted. At once Sharr was upon him with the point of his dagger which he swiftly drew across Khayr's orbits, so changing each eye into a ruby: "The white narcissus by his blade he bloodied into a rose, so gouging two gems out of a crown." But Sharr not only took Khayr's sight, he stole his real gems and clothes to boot, leaving his victim to grovel on the bloodied sand — without offering him so much as a sip of water. Here Khayr would have died if Kurdish tribesmen had not happened to be pasturing their flocks on the desert scrub nearby.

The tribe's chief had a daughter of fetching beauty, slender as a cypress, mouth like a pistachio blossom and with curls of black hair that bewitched all with the spells of Ancient Babylon, Bâbel. *Nor did such charm lie only in the eye of the beholder, for this Kurdish girl was also versed in Ancient Babylon's magic lore of healing. That day she was returning from a spring known only to her tribe with her jug on her shoulder, when she heard Khayr's groans. So it was she who saved Khayr as a "Heavenly Angel", gave the blind man water, examined then bathed his wounds while calling on God, and bandaged them: "While each ball's white humour had been slashed, each pupil's virtue yet remained within the eyelids."*

Khayr was able to rise and walk. The Kurdish girl guided him to her camp by the hand — propriety being observed, however, since the victim was sightless. The girl's mother laid Khayr to rest and fed him. That evening, on his return from grazing his flocks, the kindly Kurdish chief also searched the wounds, and knew at once where he might secure the needed salve:

"Said he: 'From the branch of one great Tree
A bunch of leaves must be gathered,
These leaves ground, their juice expressed,
Thereby the wounds anointed, and their fever abated.
If such a salve be wrought
The eyes again shall find their light.
Harsh though the slash through the eyes has been,
They shall heal through the juice of the Tree's twin leaves.'

Then he showed where stood that Tree.
Said he: 'By the water which flows from our source
Rises an ancient growth, a Tree resplendent,
Its scent expands the mind.
Its trunk from the root splits into twin shoots,
The gap between them wide,
The leafage of one, like to the raiment of a houri,
To a spent eye brings light,
The leafage of the other like to the Water of Life
Delivers those who suffer falling sickness from their fits.'"

The young girl tended Khayr's wounds for five days, then "the sightless one opened his eyes: twin narcissi blossomed at dawn." Khayr was cured. A tremor of goodwill and love for the young man spread throughout the Kurdish chief's household. Khayr thanked his hosts and told them his story. Then he showed his gratitude by offering to graze their flocks in the desert as their servant and shepherd. But the Kurdish chief and his wife came to consider as their own son this young man to whom they had restored sight — and their daughter loved him, and he loved her:

"From the many pains which she took and felt for him,
In love fell the daughter of the Kurd."

Now that Khayr had recovered his sight, she took care to appear in his presence only veiled, yet "Khayr through her mercy fell in love with her lovingkindness."

After many months spent herding the tribe's flocks, Khayr became ashamed of his wretched dependence upon his hosts. He dared not ask the Kurdish chieftain for his daughter's hand. He even expressed the wish to take his leave. But the gruff old Kurd in tears would not suffer it. He himself offered his daughter's hand to Khayr and proclaimed him both his son-in-law and his heir, so that "the thirsty one to the point of death found Water of Life, and the Light of the Sun shone upon him and caused his flower to bloom." Nor did the Kurd's kindness stop there. He allowed Khayr also to harvest leaves from the Tree of Healing, to bring relief in turn to other sick. So "Khayr went unto the Tree of Sandalwood-scent, by which his soul sought remedy."

Together, Khayr and his father-in-law led a camel loaded with twin panniers filled with leaves culled from the Tree — one lot to heal the blind, the other to cure epileptics — and travelled to the nearest city.

Now the King of this city had just made known this edict: whosoever might heal his only daughter, of matchless beauty but sorely afflicted with the falling sickness, might win her hand and inherit the kingdom. But whosoever attempted her cure and failed, and so looked on her beauty in vain, perforce surrendered his head to the executioner's sword. When Khayr and his Kurdish father-in-law entered the city gates, a thousand would-be healers had already failed to expel "the devil's woe from the Faerie's person" and died for it. Khayr prepared his brew of leaves. This he gave to the Princess to drink. She recovered her wits. The King kept his promise, wedded his daughter to Khayr and proclaimed him heir to the throne. A second miraculous application allowed Khayr to heal the equally beautiful daughter of the Grand Vizier of blindness. He wedded her also. So, not long after, Khayr became King, renowned for justice, and found himself the spouse of three exquisite wives – "Three turns in the world's backgammon play he won." At King Khayr's side his Kurdish father-in-law was appointed Commander of the Guard.

And the Kurdish chief executed justice. For the day came when Sharr, now a rich craftsman, was seen and recognized by King Khayr as the monarch rode with his train through the city market. Sharr was at once arrested by the watch and taken before the King, whom he failed to recognize. Sharr hid his own true identity, lying when questioned by the King, saying his name was "Mobashsher the Traveller, master of all arts". But by the side of the King stood the Kurd, naked sword in hand. When Khayr revealed himself in wrath to Sharr, the guilty one threw himself on the floor and cried out that, since his real appellation was Sharr, he was limited and doomed to Evil by his very name. Therefore he begged forgiveness of Khayr as of one limited and constrained for his part to doing only Good by his very name. "Khayr, this point of argument driven into his mind, on the spot freed him from death."

Sharr took leave and ran "as if he would fly", rejoicing to be off scot-free. But the Kurdish officer, warden of his Lord's Wrath, ran faster, caught Sharr in the garden and struck off his head with his sword. "Said he: 'If Khayr is Good, and may only conceive Good, you are Sharr, Evil; naught but Evil may befall you.'" Then he searched Sharr's clothes and found in his sash the two gems that he had once stolen from Khayr in the desert. These he restored to the King:

"He came and presented them to Khayr exalted,
Said he: 'Gems to Gemsoul return!'
Khayr kissed the gems and set them back before him,

To reward the Kurd's Gemsoul now with these gemstones.
His hand to his own eyes he bore, and said:
'By you I now possess this very pair of gems.
Your two gems, by these, are rendered the meaner;
These twain, by my friend, are gems restored to their lustre.'
So all things with Khayr were bent to his wish.
What the people saw from him was Good altogether.
Good Fortune entrusted him with the throne.
His iron turned silver, his sackcloth silk,
And where the State yields to a leader of Good,
Thorn turns into date-palm, and stone, into gold.
Justice he strengthened:
His own kingdom made firm.
By the leaves which from that Tree he brought,
The easing of hard travails he wrought.
Time and again, to ward off his sorrow,
He would ride at a gallop towards the great Tree,
Came under the Tree, stood there beneath,
Unto its ground rendered salaam and praise.
For love of the Sandalwood-scented Tree
He had his raiment woven, Sandalwood-dyed;
Naught but Sandalwood strove he to acquire;
Robes but of Sandalwood-colour wore he no longer;
Sandalwood yields all its peace to the spirit;
Sandalwood's scent is a sign of the soul;
Sandalwood rubbed removes brainpan's ache,
Fever from heart, searing gall from the liver.
Why wonder when Sandalwood be Colour of Earth?
The Earth thereof moulded: hence its hue for such cause."

So the Chinese Tartar rounded out her tale,
In broken tongue delivered sound.
The SHÂH bestowed her rank within his very soul
And far from the Evil Eye preserved her forever.

*S*amarkand was not only the capital of Tîmûr's short-lived Empire, but also one of the Islamic world's most important markets for the overland China trade. The decoration of the mausoleum raised to Tîmûr's niece, Princess Shâd-e Molk Âghâ, displays medallions of stylized lotus-flowers of pure Chinese inspiration. Medieval Persian usage designated such floral motifs, and other matters of recognized Far Eastern origin, as Khatâ'î, "Chinese". This epithet, heard by Marco Polo and other Italian travellers in Mongol-ruled Asia, reappears in their writings as "Cathay" – the name by which medieval Europeans came to know the Empire of the Great Khân.

115

Who was this Ostâd 'Alî ("Master 'Alî"), or Ostâd 'Alîm ("Master Savant") — the name cannot properly be deciphered — who lies buried within this tomb sumptuously adorned with mazes of writing so complex that they may scarcely be read? Did esoteric coquettishness dictate such eye-teasing inscriptions? The calligraphic bands are moulded in turquoise paste so thick that they rise in relief, forming successive eight-pointed stars, Seals of Solomon, the Prophetic Talisman. In the centre of each Solomonic Seal lodges a turquoise knob like the Bezel of the King-Prophet's Ring: the very Eye by which God chose to look upon Himself, according to the teachings of 12th-, 13th- and 14th-century Sufi masters.

Western Persia and Azerbaijan

فارس وعراق عجمی وآذربیجان

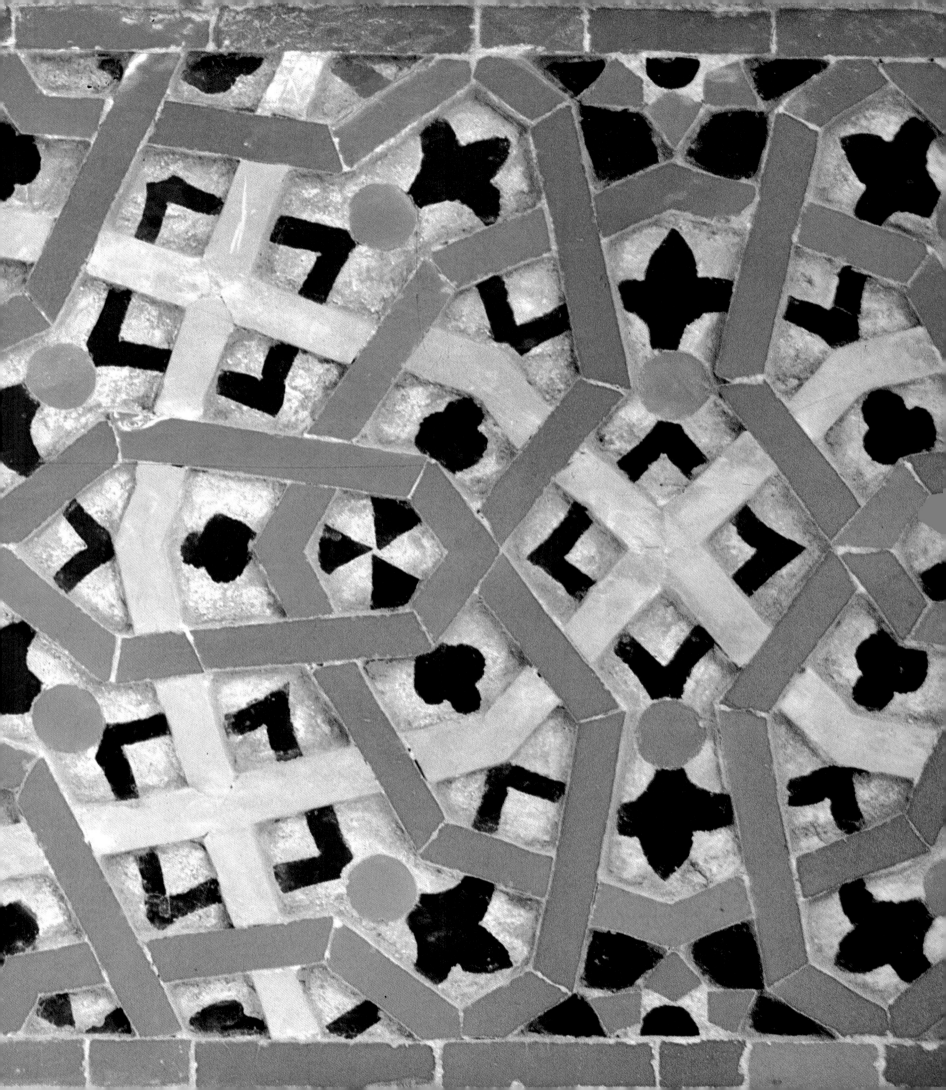

Ever denser networks of blue-tile calligraphy and starbursts begin covering walls, and so restrict the space allotted to carved stucco, in 14th-century Iranian shrines under the rule of the Islamized Mongol rulers or Îl-Khâns, the "Vassal Khâns" to the Great Khân in Peking. The blank ogee of this mihrâb, or wall-niche to show the faithful which way to direct their prayers, is an abstract gate opening only onto divine contemplation.

PAGES 122–27: NATANZ (IRAN),
THE KHÂNQÂH OR DERVISH CONVENT, 1316–17

*B*uilt in 1364, this mosque was repeatedly sheathed in tiles: first in 1375–76, when the revetment still revealed surfaces of bare brick and panels of carved stucco, then again in 1406–17, 1432–33, 1457–59, 1470–71 and many more times through the 17th century down to our own day. These details from one of the mosque's finest mosaic panels, of 15th-century workmanship, disclose the three basic motifs of Islamic ornament: tendrils and shoots of the Tree of Life; heavenly stars; and Koranic calligraphy, here made to revolve in a shamseh or sunburst.

YAZD (IRAN), THE FRIDAY MOSQUE, 14TH, 15TH, 17TH AND 20TH CENTURIES
PAGES 136–37: YAZD, VIEW AND SETTING OF THE FRIDAY MOSQUE

134

YAZD (IRAN), CHAQMAQ MOSQUE, 1437
KERMÂN (IRAN), FRIDAY MOSQUE, 1349 AND 1559

*T*o the south of the central Iranian desert, under the majestic but barren ramparts of an absolutely mineral world, a Persian oasis-city otherwise devoid of colour suddenly throws up two brilliantly enamelled towers. Although of modern workmanship, these twin minarets pursue the tradition of sacred towers everywhere — ziggurats, pagodas or steeples — as links between earth and heaven, while their vivid hues set against a desert horizon perpetuate the ancient and medieval Near East's enduring nostalgia for the Gardens of Paradise.

KERMÂN (IRAN), VIEW OF THE OASIS

The art of mosaic faïence reached its zenith on the walls of this architectural masterpiece built for Jahân Shâh, chief of the clan of the Black Sheep Turcomans who had become masters of Western Iran and much of Anatolia by the middle of the 15th century. With its perfect turquoise, ultramarine and sandalwood tones, the Tabrîz shrine, although now roofless and otherwise badly damaged, remains the Persianate world's ultimate "Blue Mosque" (Masjed-e Kabûd). The flamboyance of its decoration mirrors the violently expressionist aesthetic tastes of the Turcoman lords of Tabrîz, so different from the restrained, almost academic classicism prevalent in contemporary Herât.

In 1601, the Safavid ruler Shâh 'Abbâs had the dome of this shrine, first built in the 15th century, completely blanketed in star-patterned blue tiling in the fashion of his new capital at Esfahân. The minarets are 19th-century restorations. Within the dome's stars, the patterns created by the bricks form spider's webs in tribute to the web spun across the mouth of the Prophet's Cave which served both to hide, and to reveal, the network of emanations of the Divinity made manifest.

MÂHÂN (IRAN), SHRINE OF SHÂH NE'MATOLLÂH,
1436–1601–EARLY 19TH CENTURY

Completely sheathed in thousands of turquoise underglaze-painted tiles, the Mosque of the Mother of the Shâh was the last azure blaze of imperial Safavid art in Esfahân and summarizes the complex legacy of an entire civilization. Its thin enamelled film of colour serves to mask – and deny – the frail reality of the yellow clay brickwork beneath. Its vine tendrils of remote Hellenistic origin pass through stylized clouds ultimately derived from Chinese models. On the minarets, geometric calligraphy in mosaic entwines the names of MOHAMMAD *and* 'ALÎ *with Shî'î fervour. In these very same years in Europe, in the sunset decade of Louis XIV's rule, Antoine Galland conjured up a vision of the Islamic East garbed in similar fairytale colours with his translation from the Arabic of a medley of Egyptian, Mesopotamian, Persian and Indian stories making up the* Thousand and One Nights. *In 1722, insurgent Sunnî Afghans took Esfahân and sacked her, so putting an end forever to the Safavid dynasty's messianic dream of imperial domination throughout Islam.*

The Persian Princess
beneath
the White Dome

On the day of Friday, when the sky canopied
In an arching willow into stalactites of light
And made the house all White with Sun
The SHÂH in array White, in glory
Mounted high unto the White Dome
Where Venus passed into the fifth mansion of her clime
And struck five royal daily calls in his obeisance –
But only when the forces of Khotan – day-streaks of White –
Were put to flight by an Ethiopian vanguard of Night,
Only then did the SHÂH cut short his scope of pleasure.

Then Night dipped in her pouch for sky-collyrium, and lined
The eye of Moon, and all the stars made bright.
The SHÂH from her, she, Soul-Soothing, Heart-Yielding One
Seated in Night, and born of a White morning breeze,
Requested her to sing, to the echoing ring of her own Dome
Reverberations voiced and hummed, as of an organ Byzantine:
Blessings she, Heartbinding One
Called to the Crown and Throne exalted
And praise to raise an Empire,
Befitting Crown and Throne,
And spoke.

The tale told by the Persian Princess is the collection's merry little piece of admonitory ribaldry.

Once upon a time the all-powerful Master of a secret garden, on returning of a sudden, heard unfamiliar laughter in his home. He hid behind the lattice-work screen masking the balcony of his garden's corner tower and discovered a bevy of playful virgins sporting naked in his pool, all of perfect beauty like "fish of quicksilver". The young landowner chose to watch, unseen, peeping through the lattice-work:

"The Master eyed the lattice-hole – a spring of light this,
A narrow fount – and through it saw a waterpool spread out.
On every side they scattered roses.
Silver limbs theirs, and pomegranate nipples
And eyes bright as lamps –
More savoury each than ripe fruit.
Each bride by way of heart's-enticement
Unto his wall sent whiffs in sugar-scattered scent.
His Serpent-Dragon prone upon his treasure
Stiffened from soft fruit to hard pickle
Pomegranate nipples to watch, with apple chins
To cancel out – to write on ice – the very name of apple!

"There was in the orchard of that garden
A lawn by the side of the cypress-grove
With a pool wrought of marblestone:
The young man had written Pool-of-Kawsar – Heavenfount – thereon.
The water therein as clear as tears,
Its fish never disturbed
And all around the lustred surface of the pool
Lily, narcissus and jasmine grew.

"Lovely as Buddhist idols they moved down from the pavilion
And saw a pool shine; from Moon-zenith to Fish-nadir
The heat of the sun shone down upon them
And the water like the sun found them again: it mirrored them.
Towards the pool they wended swaying,

Opened the knots of their caftans,
Unlaced their bodices, appeared without veils,
In grace like pearls sank into the water
And struck the water with silver limbs, splashed multicolour,
Then hid their silver in the pool's shadows, darkness black,
Moongirls and pondfish together slipped through the water:
And from Moon-zenith to Fish-nadir the world burned in fever.
The Moon when it scatters mirrored dirhams of gold,
Wherever it finds a little fish, shines and puts it to flight.
These Moons, when they scattered mirrored dirhams of gold,
Aroused the Master's little fish!
For a spell they linked hands
In a chain – laughing – so they did:
For a spell cast waterpearls upon their breasts:
Pomegranate-nipples and orange-chins into a Web they spun
Each teasing her playmate with fear of a serpent:
'A serpent!' she said, and waved a braid."

The Master makes himself known to these maidens who so trespassed into his garden to make mirth in his pool. They submit to his will. She whom the Master chooses is brought to him, consenting, by her companions fully as complaisant, that he should take his pleasure with her. But each time the Master finds occasion for sport, an unforeseen incident interrupts the consummation of his desires: "The make-up stick had not yet gone into the collyrium pouch, when the curving dome of the sky again played havoc with him."

The first time, when the maidens bring up their chosen companion to the Master in the corner tower and leave them together to their pleasure, the structure, weakened because it is ancient, collapses in a pile of stones, throwing both lovers into the street (fortunately deserted at that late hour). Each lover shamefacedly shuffles off in an opposite direction, she wrapped in her veil, he in his caftan. On the second occasion, the lovers hidden in a grove are surprised by the sharp report of a falling gourd knocked off its branch by a mouse: and this sudden noise makes them fear the abrupt arrival of the "Mohtaseb" – the inspector of good morals and public behaviour – and his armed watch. *Believing themselves on the verge of capture, they panic and bolt. The third time, sheltering in the very depth of a cave, the lovers' toying is interrupted – and their carpets and cushions turned topsy-turvy – by the terrified leaps and bounds over their bedding of two foxes pursued by a wolf.*

The Master understands the lesson, and repents. He consents to enjoy his loved one only in wedlock, sanctioned according to Holy Law.

"See his kingly fortune! Once he found his water pure,
Therein he drank, as Lawful now.
He found a spring bright as a sun,
Like jasmine pure, like silver White.
White the lustre of the day.
White the Moon which lights the world.
All colours are smeared with flattering fuss:
All save White, unsullied thereby.
All those reduced to despair when besmirched,
When cleansed are given for name the 'White'.
In worship at the time of pilgrim-striving,
It has become *Sonnat,* Holy Use, to wear White."

When the Jasmine-White One spoke this speech from her breast,
The SHÂH pressed her tightly to his own,
And so from one night to another in mirth and in joy
Towards every Dome he spread his carpet-bed.
So unto him the Sky, fashioned-like-to-a-Dome,
Opened the Gates unto the Seven Domes.

Initially built in austere patterned brickwork by the Seljuk sultans between 1072 and 1075, through the centuries Esfahân's Friday Mosque was redecorated with tiling. Its mosaic panels of calligraphic compositions, dated 1475 from the period of the Turcoman sultans and reproduced on these pages, fully meet the aesthetic challenge set by the wonderful Tîmûrid revetments created

elsewhere in Iran in this same century – such as those commissioned in 1437 for his mosque in Yazd by the emir Jalâloddîn Chaqmaq, vassal to Herât's Emperor, Shâh Rokh. The calligraphic mazes resolve themselves into phrases which include the names of GOD, MOHAMMAD and 'ALÎ. Mondrian or Vasarély might not have disowned these vibrant geometric meditations.

Latter-day restorations have failed to impair the majesty of this corbelled gateway or îwân, dotted with the framed names of MOHAMMAD *and* 'ALÎ *in turquoise mosaic on honey-coloured brickwork. In Persianate eastern Islamic architecture, here ultimately drawing on a Sasanian prototype, such an ogee gateway, when yielding access to a palace, symbolized royal power and hence became known (in various linguistic hybrids of Arabic, Persian and Turkish) as a "Sublime Porte"* ('Âlî Qâpı *or* Boland Darwâzeh). *But this portal, as in all major mosques, affords entrance to the most glorious of all palaces: God's Temple.*

ESFAHÂN (IRAN), FRIDAY MOSQUE,
11TH, 15TH, 18TH AND 20TH CENTURIES
PAGES 170–71: DARB-E IMÂM MOSQUE, 1453

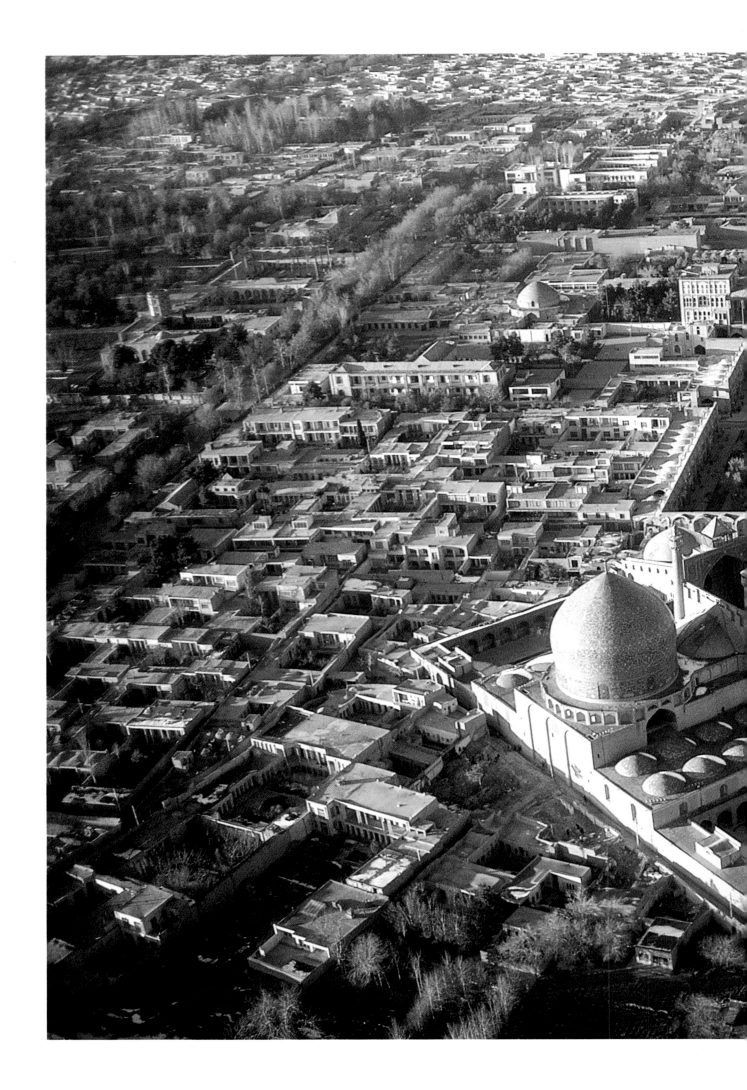

ESFAHĀN (IRAN),
ROYAL SQUARE AND MOSQUE

Shâh Bahrâm's Winter

This day for the Dawn's victory of Light,
The sky displayed a brow
Happy, bright, day-kindling:
But a day so quickfrozen – there should abide the memory of such a day!
The SHÂH
      In goodliness
           In heartbinding countenance
      Held assembly of his wise men:
This a day for the hearth, not a day in the orchard, this
First day of Winter:
The orchard's taperlike-flowers, candlelike-flowers, all spent,
Garden-tools and gear borne off,
Nightingale-lilt by raven snatched,
Its stolen caw in garden thrust,
No raven's tint save Hindu-black –
No marvel, such a theft, from the raven-Hindu thug!
Dawnwind, night-thief, turned a painter
Painting chain-rings on the water.
Winter's burn stole fire's warmth,
Froze the water to ice-sabres,
Sun's ray-sabres melted to water,
Sleetwind wielding sabre-points
Pricked eyes, fountains' eyes stitched closed with icepricks.
Ice-boiled milk curdled to cheese
And body-blood to icy wind.
The mountains ermine-clad, soil in purpure,
Skies mantled in vair:

Upon the wild game, prey-cats lay in wait
To rend their pelts for pelisses.
Grass pulled all its heads below:
Hermitgrass withdrew underground.
Now the piebald day-night world wrought Alchemy,
Concealed the fire-ruby in the flintstone's heart,
The Rose in her wisdom hid in an old alembic pot
And lidded her head in her wisdom under a sealed clay top
And ice-glass waters' quicksilver
Plaque upon plaque turned into silver pure.

In such a season the SHÂH's palace
Held in ward all four seasons' temper:
Dizzy incense-fumes in plenty
Tempered the snow-charged wind,
And candied fruits and wines like honey
Numbed the brain and stirred the heart.

AS FOR THE PALACE'S FIRE:

FIRE kindled of sandalwood and aloes-wood
In a ring of smoke like dark Hindus prostrate –
A FIRE to bolster good cheer –
Zoroaster's mine of red sulphur,
Blood seething and curdled,
Shot-silk blooded,
Henna-dyed jujube,
Quicksilver reddened to ground cinnabar-sulphide,
Core-hollowed red apple
Core-crammed with pomegranate seeds,
Straw-magnet amber tinged with pitch,
Sun muffled-veiled in musk,
Morsel of Light resolved in Darkness,
Red poppy twined in a houri's hair,

A pallid Turk, sprung from the race of livid Greeks
To a merry twinkle in a Hindu's blackest eye.

A Firebrand for the Prophet Jonah,
Torch of Moses,
Jesus's Feast of Tongues of Flame,
Abraham's Garden of Flames-Turned-Roses.
Ingots of embers coloured like musk
Circled the fire like rust on a mirror.
There her colour like jetbead, here her virtues carnelian.

Her Gem-Essence feeding the eye
As she sparkled from gold to gules to azure like a gem
And flashed like a new bride's jewelry
With a glowing necklace of ambergris-embers on her nipples
Beneath her bridal curtain and canopy, gold-embroidered;
But her curtain, aloes-wood, and her canopy, strewn with
    pomegranate-flowers.
The yellow flame flickered in a brazier of thorns
Like a treasure of gold beneath a black Dragonsnake.

As for the Palace's Fire:

For her Hell and her Heaven famous both:
Hell from her Heat, Heaven from her Light;
Hell to those treading heathen caravan-tracks;
Paradise on the path of wayfarers Heaven-bound.
Zoroaster's Zend-Book of Hours sang to her,
And the Magi danced around her,
Moths spreading patched caftans before her like wings
While she opened the frozen water's pores.
The pity of it! Why should her name (like Hell's) be Fire?
Around the Fire from a crest of grace descended
Doves, the Shâh's women, beat their wings to the dance

Around the FIRE-curtain stitched of Flaming Silk:
A bevy of partridges and quails! They linked hands,
The household waxed more thriving-green than a cypress-shade
And the wine more rose-red than a pheasant's blood.
The dove-coloured sky scattered
Snowflake-doves from a dove's slit throat: the air's dusk-blood.
Wine stood before the eye in cups of glassy Gem-Crystal,
Liquid congealed, liquefied fire!

And the Onager-eyed ones drank wine
And ate kebabs of the haunches of Onagers,
And SHÂH BAHRÂM, slayer of Onagers, with his boon-companions
Drank wine as do the world's rulers!

Anatolia

رُوم

*W*hile Central Asia and Persia cringed under the Mongol onslaught – whose first murderous cavalry raid had thundered into Eastern Islamic territory by 1220 – 13th-century Seljuk Turkey was mostly spared. Its tileworkers pursued those artistic developments initiated under the Ghôrids in the far-off lands of Herât in relative safety. Although Anatolia's good building stone hardly needed protective revetment, nonetheless many walls in Turkish Asia Minor became ever more thickly enmeshed in blue ceramic geometric and calligraphic patterns. Knotted kufic script, here adorning the entrance to the tomb of Sultan Keykavus I, proclaims: "Truly we belong to God and truly to Him shall we return" (Koran 2:156).

SIVAS (TURKEY), HOSPITAL (ŞIFA'IYE),
AND MAUSOLEUM (TÜRBE), OF KEYKAVUS I, 1217
PAGES 184–85: ESKI MALATYA (TURKEY),
GREAT MOSQUE (ULU CAMII), 1225–70

ESKI MALATYA (TURKEY),
GREAT MOSQUE (ULU CAMII),
1225–70

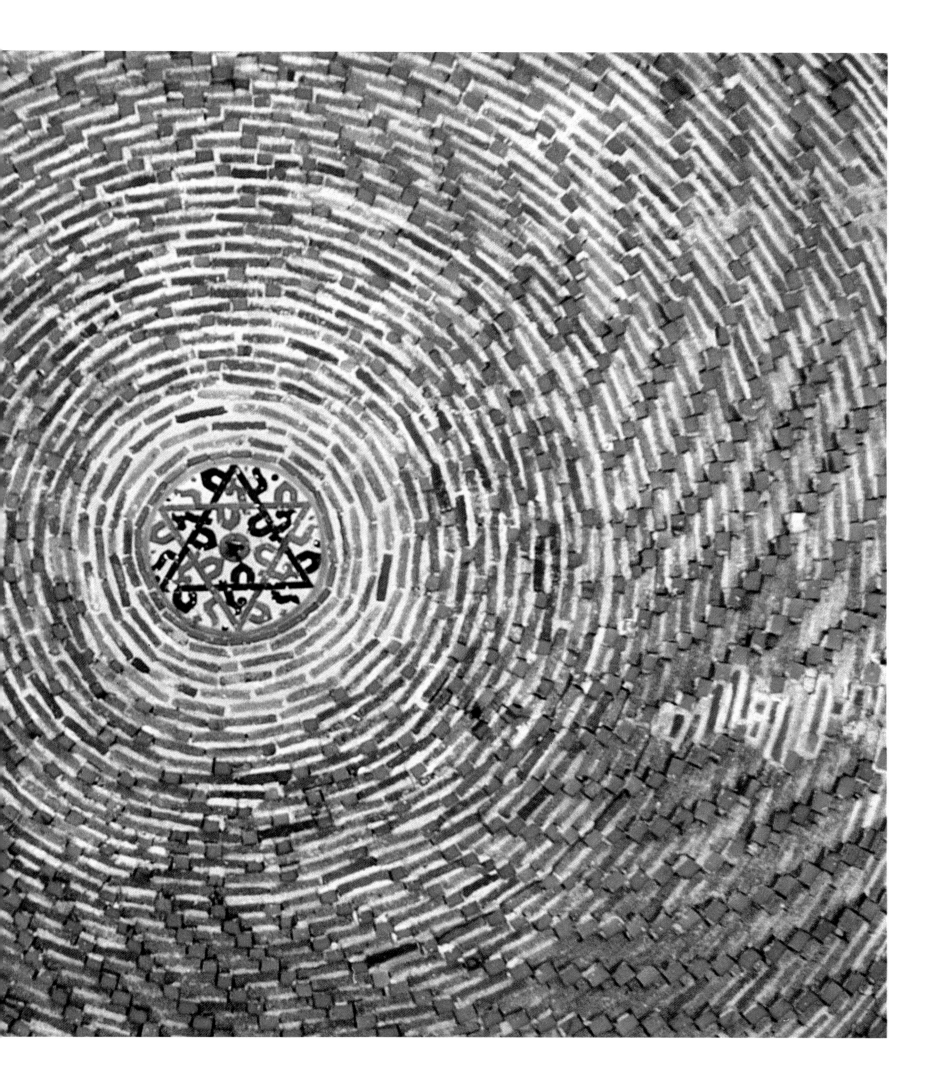

ANKARA (TURKEY), ARSLANHANE MOSQUE, MIHRĀB, 1289
SIVAS (TURKEY), BLUE (GÖK) MEDRESE, 1271–72

KONYA (TURKEY),
"TILED" (SIRÇALI) MEDRESE, 1242

By the middle of the 13th century, the Islamic world reeled under almost simultaneous assault from Castilian knights in the West, French Crusaders in the Levant and Mongol horsemen in the East. Seljuk Asia Minor offered a haven and became Islamic civilization's most creative centre in this age. The Spanish Muslim mystic, Ibn 'Arabî, both visited and taught here. The Persian poet Rûmî, from a family of refugees originally from the northern Afghan town of Balkh, saw this medrese *or theological college as it rose in his new home in Anatolian Konya, where expanses of tiling began engulfing traditional patterned brick surfaces to give colour to the poet's vision of a "green sky".*

With a range of colours limited to blue-green and ultramarine, Konya's tileworkers caused thorny sunbursts to rise over horizon-bands of exuberantly floriated kufic calligraphy, pursued in almost baroque fugues. The spikes of the sunbursts intersect to create new fields of stars in a "green sky".

The Byzantine
Princess
beneath
the Yellow Dome

B AHRÂM SITS ON SUNDAY
BENEATH THE YELLOW DOME
AND THE DAUGHTER OF THE CAESAR OF ROME,
RULER OF THE SECOND CLIME,
TELLS HIM HER STORY

نشستن بهرام روز یکشنبه در گنبد زرد

Gorges of the cliffs, and the hem of the desert:
The morning's scales tipped and filled them with Gold.
On that day of Sunday rose the world's brand
Wrapped in Gold like the Sun hidden in its own flare
To take the Gold Cup, Jamshêd's Grail,
And crown himself in Gold like to the Sun,
Upon his finger bound as by a marigold in splendour
A seal of amberstone upon a saffron-shining ring –
Scattering Gold flashes he went up to the Yellow Dome
Where his heartjoy increased a hundredfold
Piling up mirth
Through rejoicing in wine and tune of song.
When night fell – night? Bridal-curtain to his loveplay!
A night-screen for lovers' private fondling! –
The SHÂH spoke to her, candle-stature, sweetmeat-scattering,
That from her rubymouth should flow preserve of rosewords:
He wished her to raise through her song
Under such a Dome, such harmony.
No flight from the SHÂH's command –
No excuse to be brooked in his heart by His Splendour!
Said the Byzantine bride in all her Chinese splendour:
"You are Overlord to Rome and to China, both –
As far as Tarâz in Turkestan between!
You are life-bestower to the souls of kings!

Ever victorious the Overlord of Kings!
Whoever, save to serve you, should venture a thought
Lays his head to be trod down upon your footpath!"
When she had uttered the faultless invocation
Her breath exhaled whiffs as sweet as incense-burner's wisps,
And so she spoke.

According to the tale of the daughter of the Emperor of East Rome, once upon a time there was a King whose palace was filled with numerous concubines. Not one of them satisfied him, however, because none of them showed proper love and obedience. Each noisily demanded costly gifts and arrogantly claimed first rank — that is, wished to relinquish servile status to become a legally wedded wife with queenly title. Gifts of gold and jewels to rival the mythic wealth told in Holy Writ of Qârûn — biblical Korah — might not satisfy them.

"Each time a goodly concubine he bought
Not one seemed to observe her proper duty.
Each one within a week, perhaps more, or one less,
Stepped beyond the limits permitted,
Raised her head to be Lady, *Khâtûn*,
Wished for treasure, like Qârûn.
Now there was in the household a hunchbacked old Crone,
A woman among these fools and a baiter of fools.
Every slave-girl whom the King bought, soon
The Crone in the new girl's vanity saw profit,
Flattered the newly bought one with titles of splendour:
'Empress of Rome! Ravishing one of Tarâz!'
When the concubine's eyes were filled with pride,
She lapsed from the rule of service."

The King, annoyed by all his insolent concubines, resorts to the shrewdest slave-dealer in his realm. The merchant provides a young woman of perfect beauty, modesty and obedience, but afflicted with a single fault: incapacity to love in return. She had reduced all potential buyers to despair.

The young woman, however, shows such irreproachable docility that she charms the King. She also proves the only inmate of the harem to resist the Crone's insinuations. She even denounces the hunchback's intrigues to the King, who casts the old woman out of his seraglio. Soon the King falls in love with his own slave. Yet she refuses herself to him, gently, but firmly. In a reversal of rôles, the King becomes a slave to his slave, and dares not press his attentions upon her.

"At last love turned his head
And cast its dust in his eyes of Lordship.
Silver he threw at the feet of the silver-limbed one!
With silver he bought this silver shrine!
Only the door to one lust he bolted on himself:
He curbed his snake. Freed himself of his dragon.
And the faerie-faced one, beneath the King's purdah
Watched over the service of all the Purdah-Folk.
She was a rosebud, mercy hidden in her tight sepal-ring,
Strict without, friendly within.
Save the door she barred to the room of 'rest-and-raise!' –
No handservice neglected;
Housewardenship and trust of the inner palace –
One by one with care, all she put in their place.
While the King exalted her rank like unto a high cypress,
Like his shadow she was content to fall beneath his feet."

To woo her, and by way of offering to take her as lawful wedded wife, the King tells her a story – a tale-within-a-tale – of probable rabbinical origin, and certainly one of the strangest fables concerning married behaviour, and the mutual trust owed by spouses to one another, known to us in the entire corpus of medieval Islamic narrative literature – another one of Nezâmî's strange feminist touches which so illuminate the normal gloom of his civilization's erotic hierarchy.

To Solomon and his spouse, the Queen of Sheba, a son is born paralyzed in all his limbs. Before the supplications of the afflicted royal parents, an angel from heaven reveals that if each of the two spouses will at last honestly answer a single question raised by his or her partner, then the child might be healed. Solomon asks his spouse if, after

*marrying him, she still ever looks with desire on any other man. Yes, she confesses —
and at once the child stretches forth his hands. The Queen in turn questions Solomon:
despite all his God-given wealth, has he ever lusted for more? Solomon confesses he has
— and at once the child moves his legs as well.*

*Although moved by the tale, the King's slave still denies her person to him. At a loss
the ruler calls the Crone back to the seraglio to ply her wiles. The ancient Go-between
thus finds her accustomed indispensable place in the household again. She advises the
King to make love to another concubine under the eyes of his favourite and thereby
overcome her resistance by exciting both her senses and her jealousy.*

*Vanquished at last, the modest slave confesses that she has fallen in love with her
master also, but that a curse hangs over her race (Nezâmî's tale here shows reminiscence
of the Amazons of Greek lore). Any woman of her Amazon-people who knows a man,
and then bears a child, dies at once afterwards. But the King's slave is ready to die for
love. She yields to him. He weds her and makes her his Queen. She gives him a son —
and does not die. The curse has been lifted through the very gift of love.*

"The King drew the silk curtain from his Chinese idol-image,
Opened the Golden lock to her sweetmeat-casket
And saw a treasure there worthy of all his Gold,
Arrayed her in Gold, made her more Golden still.
Gold is that which yields full joy:
The taste of Saffron-coloured *halwâh* lies in its dye.
Why look to see whether Saffron is Gold?
See the Golden laughter of who has eaten Saffron!
The light of the candle shines through a veil of Gold.
The Golden Calf of Moses drew her value from her hue.
Gold, which is Yellow, is a fount of joy:
Precious the Yellow dust thereby."

The SHÂH heard the tale to its end,
Took her to his bosom and slept in joy.

IZNIK TILES (TURKEY), 15TH–16TH CENTURIES

Shâh Bahrâm's Spring

Under good trine Jupiter trigoned with Saturn,
The Stars' Sun-King proceeded from Fish to Ram –
Then Grass and Khezr Evergreen found youth
In the Life-Fountain of Youth:
The navel of every spring bubbled into a River Nile
And every stream into a Heavenriver.
Aloes-ashwhite soil blackened to musk:
The merchantbreeze picked up her scent of musk
And scatter-sold her musk.

Naw-Rôz is New Year's Day: warming air
Straightway kindled the universe:
The *Naw-Rôz* breeze sealed a fresh pact
With the field-wild herbs, and pawned her soul.

Heads of grass sprang up from the earth's core.
The Sun wiped his mirror's rust.
Dew spurted from under the upper air's hem.
Warmth cracked open winter's shell.
Camphor-white snows on the clifftops
Wept tears into rivers of splendour.
So Verdure lustred her Gem before all eyes,
And greened Creation.
Then the damp narcissus peered through eyes bleary with sleep
On those with eyes to see: and snatched their slumber!
The dawn breeze in a whiff opened a muskpod

And rubbed civet on violets' purpure-sable.
The cypress cast her shadow across windruffled grass
And mingled with shrubtrees like a comb striking curls.
The water-lily's pistil-eye smarted with sleep,
So she hurled her soul into the safety of her water-fort.

Branches bloomed into fresh blossoms
Pearl-like: so the petals of the opening tulip.
The lily, besotted on a tipsy narcissus-crown,
Placed her stamen's gold ingots on his leaf's open palm.
Thus scentladen spring breezes
Scattered blossomstars – though it was not Judgment Day!

The fenugreek shed his dewtears;
Ate his saffron; then laughed.
The Scribe of the Book of Flowers inspired
In Water of Life wrote this judgment:
To bloody the windflower!
To pearl the wildrose's petals!
To smear with collyrium the lily's stem!
The purslain shook his long mane of curls upon curls
Back over his shoulders, like Daylam-folk.
Grassblades and treeleaves in mirth
Split into shears and curved into crescent arrowheads;
The hyacinth goaded with musk
Coughed over the open clove;
The hollyhock on clause coeval
Inscribed the jasmine heir-apparent;
The wild mint's scent in ardour
Dissolved the Zodiac Scorpion's sting;
Then a roseblossom winked at a camomile's eye

And a bird sang secrets to an elephant's ear: iris;
Camphor-tinted, musk-whiff scented, the white rose curved
Like the earlobe of a beloved hung with gold and silver;
And the Egyptian willow, like the aloes-shedding tree
Shed camphor here, there musk.

WAR AND SOVEREIGNTY IN THE ORCHARD

Judas-Tree and Jasmine faced off Willow,
Unfurled their standards of gules and silver;
Stung with fernwind's willow-whittled arrows,
Willow in a branchful of leaves bit painwrithing hands;
So Rose girded her waist with sovereignty's swordbelt.
Soil and breeze together wished her good cheer.
The nightingale warbled a wartrill of cymbals
Through the night till the cock-crow's watch,
And Rose's gules charged on field of vert
Five times rang out Rose-Sultanate's salute!
So on cypress-tops the turtledoves called
In the merry songs of heartsoothers –
But the turtledoves' flutes in morning plaint
Sheared the mountain-partridge's yearning to laugh –
And the francolins sang on the hemlands
So piercingly high that they sheared through Heaven's pavilions.

Then the nightingale turned Magus,
Cantor of the Zend-Avesta,
By night from Heaven brought down Zend Scripture,
Sang its words:
So the nightingale moved by his own yearning's dirge
Grew as thin as a harp's silk strings.

ISTANBUL (TURKEY),
RÜSTEM PAŞA MOSQUE, 1557

And so the Garden became painter's Tablet: Image-Bonder's:
Bird and fish to sport therein.

And so SHÂH BAHRÂM on such a day
Held royal court, luminous
Through Seven Domes
Raised higher than Heaven's Dome itself!

Barbary

المغرب

The Moorish Princess
beneath
the Turquoise Dome

AHRÂM SITS ON WEDNESDAY
BENEATH THE TURQUOISE DOME
AND THE DAUGHTER OF THE KING OF THE FIFTH CLIME
TELLS HIM HER STORY

نشستن بهرام روز چهارشنبه در گنبد فیروزه رنگ

Wednesday the Sun blossomed and turned
The Sphere's pitch Turquoise
And the SHÂH world-kindled, robed him
In Turquoise-tint from victory
Unto the Turquoise Dome wending from splendour's crest.
This day would be short; long its tale.
The night enfolded in musk-hair purdah
The SHÂH who rose from within the purdah of his chamberlains
To wish the Lady Storyteller of his Castle
As Lady-Storytellers' wont
To tell him through her loveplay
A tale for his heart's joy:
Roseblossom-mouth opened she, cypress-tall she
Placed upon her rosepetal-lips, pastilles of candywords
And said: "The Sphere be slave to your commands
And its propitious Star sing praise to you,
I and better than me a thousand slave-girls
By kissing the ground you walk on become noble;
Foul should she be before your fount of honeyspeech
To tap a vinegar-seller's bitterwordshop;
But since from the SHÂH's command there be no flight
I shall speak: To the SHÂH's head, pangs! Be it accepted!"

According to the Princess of the Western Desert of the Moors, there once lived by the banks of the Nile a young, rich, idle merchant named Mâhân (Moonlike), as handsome

221

as a Joseph in Egypt. With his friends Mâhân indulged in endless merrymaking, with no care for higher things: "How many days, beneath the Azure Sphere, merry they waxed with jest and song." One evening Mâhân was guest at a feast in a garden in the suburbs of the Egyptian capital. Tipsy with wine under the bright light of the moon, he thought he recognized through the palms one of his caravan-merchant associates who had arrived suddenly. The latter beckoned to him:

"And said: 'Tonight I have come from a far-off road.
In my heart to see you there remained no patience.
I have brought profit beyond compute.
From such profit there will be much to praise.
When I arrived before the city it was late,
The city gate was closed, and no way home;
Hence to the caravanserai outside
I bore the merchandise and placed a seal upon it.
When I heard that the Master was a guest
I came – to return is easy.
If you should come before the city it were best.
Their Master's presence is his people's safeguard.
Also it should prove possible in this dark night
To hide half our profit from the excise-tithe.'"

Mâhân, goaded by greed, followed his fellow merchant out of the garden. His guide preceded him at a brisk pace through the darkness, treading ever faster to reach the caravanserai before dawn. It seemed to Mâhân that the path was becoming too long, that they were straying too far from the Nile – but he attributed such confusion in his senses to tipsiness. A rooster crowed, and Mâhân, his brain drowsy with drink, collapsed on the path and slept. When the sun, already high in the sky, burned his forehead and awakened him, his guide had disappeared, and Mâhân found himself under the cliffs of the Western Desert:

"He opened his eyes to look upon his path,
All around him cast his glance,
The rosebower sought, not a rose in bower saw,
Nothing but a thousand searings from his own heart perceived:

Cave upon cave he saw this caravan-halt,
And the snake in each cave dragonlike and worse."

Mâhân wandered at a loss until dusk, then:

"Collapsed in a swoon at the mouth of a cave,
Every prong on a bush appeared to him a snake,
In that demon-den lost consciousness;
Then a human voice struck his ear."

An old peasant and his wife appeared, bent under bundles of thornbushes for kindling. The man drew nigh:

"And uttered a cry: '*Hân!* Who are you?
With whom have you ado, with only the wind for road-companion?'
And he: 'A wretched man, my matter raw!
My name is Mâhân, son of Hôshyâr!'
The other: 'In what manner did you fall into such a place?
This is the desert. There is no dwelling here.
This land of desolation is home to the demon-folk: the jinn-devils.
The very lion roars in dread of them.'
And he: 'For God in God! Good man!
Perform out of humanity what befits a man!
Of my own will I fell not here!
Leave talk of demon-folk: I am a son of Adam!
Yesterday I lay in softness and ease
A host upon the carpet of Eram, the Garden of Delights.
A man came and said: "I am your companion,
One of the partakers in your wealth and trade."
From that paradise he drew me and threw me in this waste.
He was lost to my sight just as the day rose.
With me that friend so unlike a friend
Either lost our way or misled me quite!
Show humanity to me for the sake of God!
My lost way unto me now show!'
And the man: 'Oh handsome-faced youth,

By a hair you escaped, by a single hair.
He was a demon, whom you call a man.
His name *Hâyel* – Dread – of the Desert.
He showed himself to you as your partner in gain.
His purpose was to destroy your soul.
Like you a hundred folk has he borne astray,
Each to perish under these cliffs!
I and my wife shall be your companions and friends.
Both of us, this night, shall be your guards.'"

The two peasants led him through the desert without another word. Dawn rose; they disappeared "like a prison's keys", stranding Mâhân even deeper in the rock-strewn waste. "When the day mirrored the rising light, the reddening sand bore witness to the dying night's blood." Mâhân sucked on the prong of a thornbush to allay his thirst and hunger, crawled under the shadow of an overhanging cliff-ledge and slept. At dusk, hoofs rang out on the stones, an armed rider appeared, leading a second horse by the bridle. When he saw Mâhân he drew his sword, charged – then pulled his horse up short:

"'You there! Sitting upon the road bleary-eyed!
Who are you? What is your place here?
If you give report to me of your secret doings – well!
If not, I strike off your head!'"

Mâhân, trembling, told his story. The horseman gnawed his knuckles in apparent dismay:

"'Male and female, those were two crafty ghouls
Who lead humans astray from the right path
To throw them in a cave and spill their blood.
But when the cock crows they flee.
The female was *Hîlâ* – Deceit – and the male *Ghîlâ* – Disaster.
Their work is making evil and woe.
Render thanks that you have escaped their doom.
Hân! Show some spirit if you are a man of parts!
Mount this spare horse, hold the reins in hand,
Whatsoever you see, good or evil, hold your tongue!'"

PAGE 219: FEZ (MOROCCO), MEDERSA BÛ 'INÂNIYA, 1351–58
PAGES 226–27: RUINED FORTIFICATIONS
IN THE SEISTAN DESERT, AFGHANISTAN

Mâhân and his new guide cantered like a desert wind out of the gorges, into an undulating plain of sand, a "sahara" (sahrâ) flickering with a thousand sparkles of light: torches. Mâhân discovered a host of demons dancing amidst cries and roars. The demon-folk (Persian dêw) on all sides screamed out songs, plucked on lutes and clinked wine-cups. Each devil betrayed a shape more grotesque than the last:

"Each sported a trunk, and on the head horns to maul,
Bullock and elephant blended in one,
Each gripped a torch,
All loathsome and foul like a drunkard's speech.
Flames darted from their gullets.
They screamed verses and shook rattles and clappers of bones.
With the jingling of the bells tied to their tails
They set the whole world to dancing."

Mâhân's horse, too, began to dance. Its rider felt bulges swell between his legs – and become a pair of wings. He looked down and saw his horse turning "into a Dragon with four legs and two wings, and stranger still, Seven Heads". Mâhân's mount looped into twists, tossed its helpless rider in its coils – then shook him off at dawn:

"He saw around him a desert stretching without end.
Coloured sands folded in carpet upon carpet
Red as blood, and searing as hell."

Mâhân staggered forth until dusk. He found a small pool of water lying stagnant next to a dry well, and drank. For fear of more night-visions, he sought refuge down inside the well-shaft, which was deep by "a thousand steps", to hide therein "like Joseph in his own well" protected by darkness as if by "a veil", and sleep. A sparkle of light awakened him. A small round breach appeared to open in the wall in the very bottom of the well, no larger than "a dirham" or silver coin, whence a moonbeam shone through. Mâhân scratched at the hole with his nails and fingers until he could pass his head, then his whole body, through the opening. Like the character trapped in a well in the Thousand and One Nights *story of the Serpent Queen, Mâhân passed through and "saw a garden, nay, a Paradise, finer than the Garden of Eram wrought and fashioned". Its orchards were heavy with jujube, dates, figs, apples, pistachio-nuts, peaches, quinces, pomegranates, oranges, almonds, pears and grapes. The sweetness of their taste was unrivalled. Mâhân ate until he was glutted.*

"Suddenly from a corner rang out a cry:
'Seize the thief: you there to the left, you to the right!'
An Old One appeared, aboil with wrath and rage,
Brandishing a cudgel over one shoulder.
He said: 'Devil! Thief of my fruit! Who are you –
By night stolen into my garden – for what?
For so many years have I dwelt in this garden,
From night-attacks of thieves have remained without care!
You, of what people are you? Of your line who knows aught?
How came you here? Who are you? How called?'"

Mâhân begged pity and told his story. The Master of the Garden relented: "You have freed yourself from the bonds of woe, a safeguarded stronghold you have reached." The Old One told Mâhân that all these demonic assaults had been mere illusions, for "if your heart had been rightly placed, your mind would not have shown you such fancies." Then, with a sudden display of love, he offered Mâhân not only the hospitality of his garden, but also all its wealth both apparent and hidden, including vast stores of gold, and held out his hand – which the young man took. Whereupon the Old One, musing aloud that he had no son, offered to adopt Mâhân as his heir: "If you be pleased with this, oh you whose serf I am, I shall do all this in your own very name."

Mâhân kissed the Old One's hand and swore to be his serf in turn; their pact was sealed. The Master of the Garden designated for him, while waiting to prepare a more proper chamber in the Castle for him, a temporary couch settled on a platform nestled in one of the bower's trees – provisioned with white wheat-cakes and jugs of water, and accessible by a ladder of leather thongs which the occupant of the perch must then, however, pull up after him. "Until I should return, be patient in this place, by no means from this sleeping-perch descend."

The Old One departed. Mâhân began to eat his white cakes when the night filled with spots of candle-lights. A troop of exquisite girls adorned like princesses disposed carpets under the tree to welcome their Queen, whose beauty was witchery. Their lutes and songs caused Mâhân's wits to spin: "A hundred times he thought how he might cast himself down from his tree."

His senses came under new trial with the scent of an enormous gemmed food tray loaded with meats seasoned with cumin and which was placed before the Queen. The

Queen's words caused him to waver further – she raised her eyes to him, and said to one of her women: "I sense the scent of a friend wafted down from this tree. He boils in his lust. Call him down nigh to me that he might toy with me as I shall fancy." Mâhân forgot all the Old One's advice and climbed down to sit by the Queen. He ate and drank, tipsy with the wine she poured for him. She offered her mouth. "He laid his lip upon that fount of spicy wine." But then, aghast:

"Saw an *'Efrît* from head to paw
Wrought from all the Wraths of God:
A buffalow-cow with tusks of boar,
A she-dragon such as none has ever seen –
Leave talk of dragons: she was an Ahriman, the Fiend of Darkness!
From earth to sky she opened wide her maw,
Humped her back – we seek shelter in God! – with a curve
Like those bows which they string hard in Tûz:
And her back like a bow and her face like a crab
And her stench extended a thousand leagues
And her snout like a brickmaker's kiln
And her maw like a tanner's vat
And she opened her chops like a crocodile's jaws
And squeezed her guest tight to her udders."

Mâhân screamed like a child in the she-ghoul's clasp. She dropped him on the sand at dawn, when "the Curtain-Web of Darkness rose from the world and all these fancies were lifted with it."

Mâhân crawled over the sand to find "a tortuous hell in place of the paradise" of the preceding night. Its garden was only thorns; its fruits were revealed to be ants swarming among snakes; and its meats old carrion. The flutes, harps and rebecks were abandoned animal bones. The jewel-embroidered hangings were strips of leather smelling of the tannery. Pus dripped from the earthenware pots whence Mâhân had caroused that night, thinking them cups of wine. In the pool whence he had first drunk, the water that stagnated in it was that of a privy. Mâhân pondered all these horrors hidden under fair semblance, and in repentance cried out: "I seek refuge in God!" Then he set out through the desert weeping bloodflecked tears. Finally he discovered, in the sands, a spring of purest water. This he drank, performed his ritual ablutions and prayed prostrate, weeping out to God as he rubbed his face in the sand. But:

"When he raised his head from his breast
He saw one of same form and appearance as himself,
Greenwearing like the season of spring,
A ruddy countenance like the Dawn of Light.
He said: 'My lord, who are you in truth?
Precious are you, a Gem your Gem-Essence!'
He said: 'I am Khezr the Evergreen One, oh worshipper of God;
I have come to take you by the hand;
It is your own pure intent which has now come forth.
This is what conveys you to your own home.
Give me your own hand, with all your being.
Close your eyes. Then open them.'"

Mâhân opened them: he had returned at once to his "abode of peace", salâmat-gâh, the very garden "whence the demon had first led him astray." From there Mâhân returned to the city, where his friends, in despair over his sudden disappearance, had put on mourning clothes dyed blue (azraq). Mâhân told his story to his friends. Then he decided to adopt forever the same coloured clothing as they:

"The colour Blue became one fixed unto his person.
Like the sky, he took upon him the colour of Time.
Blue is a colour, Heaven on high
For its silken raiment a better never found.
Whoever becomes of like colour as the sky:
The sun unto him becomes his food of life,
Like the wafer-disc upon a Christian's dish!
The Turnsol, Blue, thus judges wise,
Which feeds on its own pistil: the very disc of the sun!
Whichever direction the sun may turn,
Thither the Turnsol, Blue, shall bend its gaze.
Perforce every flower that is a Turnsol-Blue,
The Hindu shall call it: Worshipper of the Sun."

Such a tale so uttered this moon of lovely countenance;
The Shâh folded her to his breast with love.

Hindustan

هندوستان

The Indian Princess
beneath
the Black Dome

نشستن بهرام روز شنبه در گنبد مشکین

Since Bahrâm in pleasure-worship
Planted eyes on the Seven Effigies in paint,
This day of Saturday, from the Fire-Temple of Shammâs the High Priest he wended
And planted his tent in Blackness, in 'Abbâsid sable;
Towards her Palace-Dome tinged in musk,
Towards the Lady of India he wended, gave her salaam;
Until evening indulged there in mirth and sport;
Aloes-wood burnt; incense sprayed.
Then the Night, SHÂH-like,
Drew muskblack across a white day's silk.
Then the SHÂH asked her – and she like a fresh spring in Kashmir –
To scatter fragrance like a Dawn's Nightscattering breeze
To scatter sweetmeats from her casket of pearls:
To say to him, Ladylike, a few words
Of such a tale to lustre a love-lip
And make the drunk desire repose.
Fawnlike, Turk-eyed but born of India,
She let slip the knot to her muskpod:
"First," she said, "let the royal musicians
Five times resound higher than the Four Elements –
Cushion-Thrones to the Moon!
As long as the world may endure may his soul endure!
May all heads lie down upon his threshold!
Whatsoever he wishes, may he seize in his grip!

May his royal fortune in no sadness delay!"
So she sealed her invocation, bowed
And from her sweetmeat produced a lulling scent of aloes-wood.

According to the tale of the Indian Princess, once upon a time there lived a King always dressed in Black. He revealed to none the reason for his perpetual mourning until a favourite concubine cajoled the secret out of him. Nezâmî here skilfully draws on the typically Hindu narrative technique of the tale-within-a-tale to pursue his story in the first person as the doleful King himself becomes the narrator. Then the poet concludes in the words of the royal concubine who herself reportedly told the story to the Princess of India, now recounting the matter as Shâh Bahrâm's bride. Here it is the Black-robed Indian King who narrates what befell him.

"One day a stranger came to my court from the high road.
His sandals, his turban, his garment, all were Black.
I ordered food for him as fit.
I called him into my presence, showed him honour,
And said: 'Oh you whose story I have not read!
On what account is all your garment Black?'
He said: 'Leave off this matter! Leave off!
Of the Bird Rokh none may ever give report.'
I said to him: 'Say yet again! Seek no pretext!
Give me news of your pitch and your City of Pitch – *Qayrawân!*'
He said: 'You must hold me excused
For to this your wish may I not yield by far.
Of the matter of such Black shall none enjoy report
Save he who such Black wears – and enough!'"

Pressed by the all too curious King, the mysterious traveller finally consented to reveal at least this much:

"'There is a city in Chinese Turkestan
Adorned like Highest Paradise:
But its name is the City of the Bewildered.
It is the abode of mourning, of those garbed in Black.

*PAGES 232–33: UCHH-E SHARÎF (PAKISTAN),
SHRINE OF BÎBÎ JÂWANDÎ, 1498
PAGES 234–35: MULTAN (PAKISTAN),
SHRINE OF ROKNODDÎN, 1320*

The countenances of all there are like unto the Moon,
But like the Moon veiled in Black silk.
Whoever quaffs of the wine which they serve in that city,
Its Black dregs will cause him to wear Black.
Whatever the fateful reason for that garb of woe –
Leave it unread! It is the strangest tale.
Should to the very blood my throat you wish to slit,
More than these words I shall not tell.'
These words he said, bound his things on his mount,
And locked the door upon my wish."

Irked by curiosity, the Indian King quit his palace in secret, took to the road disguised, located the City of the Bewildered and indeed found all its inhabitants clad in Black. But none would disclose their common secret to him until a humble tradesman, abundantly paid to speak by the royal traveller, at long last lifted a corner of the veil:

"He said: 'You have asked that which is not proper.
I shall give you what may serve you for answer.'
When Night spread her musk over camphor's Day,
The two men stole far off from all other men.
He said: 'For what you asked the time is come,
See, learn,
Rise! I now solve the riddle for you!
The picture left unseen, I now show to you.'
These words he said, left the house,
Guided my path,
And so fared, with me, lost stranger, behind –
And of living creatures none other with us.
Faerie-like he cut me off from all mankind,
Into a ruin dragged me.
Once within the ruined house,
Faerie-like veiled, we two, from all eyes,
We saw a basket there hanging, tied to a rope.

He went and set it gently down before me,
Its rope wrapped about it, compass-round,
Like a Dragon around a snake-basket coiled.
He said: 'For a moment sit you down in this basket,
Manifest your splendour both to heaven and earth,
Until you shall know all that lurks concealed,
The meaning of the Black garb,
And all that lay hidden to you of good and evil:
This shall you not see, except by this basket.'"

When the Indian King sat down in the basket, it was suddenly hoisted by magic and spun in mid-air, then overturned, spilling its terrified occupant upon the platform of a tower rising as high as the sky. Upon this platform the marooned King found the empty nest of the giant Bird Rokh. This proved his only means of escape. For like the lost seafarer of the Thousand and One Nights *and other Arabic tales of odd travel lore, the King waited for the huge Bird and was able to cling unseen to its talons when it alighted and then flew off again, this time to deposit the wanderer in a Paradise-like garden.*

Here, for thirty nights, the Indian King was entertained by a wonderful Faerie Queen, surrounded by faerie ladies-in-waiting hardly less comely. Each evening the Queen sat the traveller by her side, plied him with the finest food and wine, teased him and so caused his senses to swim with desire for her – but still she denied her person. If only he might prove patient until the right time, she repeated, then "a thousand nights of pleasure" she would offer him. And to cool his ardour while he waited, each night she gave him to choose for his bed one of her own ladies-in-waiting: like the Divinity denying her Pearl and granting only reflections until the time of full union. But finally the King grew too insistent, even though the Faerie Queen assured him that only a single last night of trial remained before she satisfied his wish:

"When she saw me so unyielding,
So impatient, so unbridled,
She said: 'For an instant only close your eyes,
Until I open the door to my sweetmeat's Treasury.
When I have unlaced that for which you lust,
Press me to your bosom – and open your eyes!'

And I, lulled by the sweetness of her sham,
Shut my eyes to her Treasure.
When for one instant only I had obeyed her delay,
She said, 'Open your eyes.' I opened them.
I sprang yearningly forward in hope of my prey,
To hug my bride to my side.
But when I directed my gaze to my bride
I saw myself – in the basket.
No one was around me, neither woman nor man.
I sat alone with my cold sigh for company.
I remained like a shadow from that shaft of light:
A predator Turk – from my Turk-lovely bride fallen far.
Such things I muttered when beneath the tower
My still basket was stirred.
My friend came, and from the high tower
Unloosed the basket's rope from its knot.
Fortune, quenched with teasing me,
Let slide my basket down from the tower.
And he who first led me, then fled,
Now took me in his arms, begged forgiveness,
And said: 'If I had told you of this for a hundred years
You would not have believed the truth of it.
You went and saw what was hidden.
Such a tale to whom might be told?
I too in this seething have seethed,
From this tyranny have robed myself in Black.'
I told him, 'Like me you have seen such oppression.
To all you said I assent.
I bear witness to the pain. In silence
No other resort remains to me but wearing Black!
Go, bring me Black silk!'
He went, and laid before me a night-dark cloth.
Over my head I cast the Black silk,

That very night set out on my road,
To my city returned, heart knotted,
Over myself donned the tinge of Black.
I am the King of the Wearers of Black:
Like a Black Cloud weeping.
I seethed with yearning for my pleasure –
And my yearning stays raw!"

His favourite slave-concubine then told the following to the Lady of the Black Dome,
who recounted it to Bahrâm in the very words used by the concubine:

"When my lord of the hidden riddle
Told me his tale,
I, whom he bought with a silver coin,
Chose what he chose:
With this Alexander for the sake of the Water of Life
I went into the Blackness of Eternal Darkness.
In Blackness Her Majesty the Moon
Like an Empress beneath her black canopy
Favours no Colour fitter than Black:
Her silver crescent narrows before her hidden Black phase!
To youth befits Black hair.
Black sets off a young face.
Through Black the eye's pupil looks upon the world.
Pure Black suffers no dust.
If the Night's pure silk were not Black,
When might she prove worthy to be the Moon's cradle?
Seven Colours lie beneath Seven Heavenly Thrones:
Not one is higher than Saturn's Black."

When the Lady of India unto Bahrâm
Altogether finished her tale,
The Sнâн praised what she said,
Clasped her; and slept in joy.

The Seven Walls of Ecbatana

Tile Decoration in Middle Eastern Architecture

THE BABYLONIAN AND ACHAEMENID BACKGROUND

Ancient Egyptian craftsmen were familiar with a form of cobalt-based faïence and used it not only for occasional coloured wall-plaques – like the depictions of Syrian and Nubian captives fired on tiles inside Ramses III's temple at Madîna Hâbû (now in Boston) – but even as raw material for small animal statuettes without so much as a clay core. Egyptian monumental architecture, however, for the most part remained a matter for carved stone, from ancient times to the mosques of medieval Fâtimid and Mamlûk Cairo.

Enamelled brick facings were, nonetheless, a main feature of ancient Mesopotamian clay architecture. The earliest known examples of protective coloured revetment, from around 2000 BC, are baked-clay wedges with black, red and white glazed heads, thickly embedded in triangular patterns into the sun-dried walls and pillars of the remains of the Sumerian temple of Uruk (now partly preserved in Baghdad and Berlin Museums). Tiled art appears in full maturity on Babylon's famous turquoise-dominant Gate of Ishtar (also now in Berlin), dating from the turn of the 7th and 6th centuries BC. The glazed bricks here were moulded in high relief with the different colours on a single piece already separated in *cuerda seca* manner with black iron oxide lines (as opposed to the manganese-based lines of medieval potters). In addition to turquoise and night-blue, Babylonian tile colours included green, yellow, tan, white and black. The Gate of Ishtar's glazed brickwork not only soothed the eye and shielded its architecture from the elements, like later Islamic revetments, but furthermore afforded magic protection. Between friezes of stylized palm leaves, Babylonian tilework normally depicted fierce symbolic guardian figures – snarling lions with maws striped in yellow and green, bulls with swelling leg-muscles highlighted in blue – alongside unreal creatures such as dragons and griffins who united the properties of earth – with their reptilian or feline bodies – and those of heaven – with their enamelled wings.

Once they had become the declared imperial masters of Babylon in 538 BC, the Achaemenid Persians in turn adopted glazed brickwork. The frieze from the palace of Darius I (521–485 BC) at Susa, now in the Louvre in Paris, adds blue-bearded archers with turbaned helmets to the guardian beasts of Mesopotamian lore.

The 5th-century BC Greek historian Herodotus, in his description of the seven-walled city of Ecbatana in Media (on the site of modern Hamadân in Iran), already hints at the symbolism of the Seven Colours linked to the Seven Heavens in a deliberate architectural ascent. What we cannot ascertain from Herodotus's text, of course, is whether Ecbatana's architects glazed or only painted their walls. What oxide did they use to secure their red? Arsenic or vermilion? And how much gold and silver leaf did they need to coat their citadel's keep and crenellations?

"[Deioces] built walls great and mighty, now known as Ecbatana, each one encircled within the other. They were so wrought that each wall rose in height above the next by its battlements alone. Not

ARCHERS OF SUSA
ACHAEMENID ENAMELLED BRICKWORK
5TH CENTURY BC
MUSÉE DU LOUVRE, PARIS

only does the hill upon which it was built help the place to appear this way: all this was further contrived on purpose. There are seven circles in all, and within the innermost are the Royal Seat and the Treasures. The largest wall is equal in circumference to the encircling ramparts of Athens. The battlements of the first circle are white, those of the second black, those of the third circle purple, of the fourth night-blue, of the fifth vermilion. Thus are the battlements of all these circles coloured with tints. The last two, now, have had their battlements, in the one case, silvered: and in the other, sheathed in gold." (*Histories,* I, 98)

Alexander's conquest of Persia in 330 BC extinguished Western Asia's art of glazed brickwork façades for the next 1500 years, although Near Eastern craftsmen never forgot the technique of glazing itself. In its place, Hellenistic and then Roman rule in the Levant ushered in the fashion for mosaic floors in coloured marble pebbles and bits of glass. The re-emergence of glazed brickwork architecture in later medieval Islam, from the first hints in 11th-century Iran to its full flowering under the 15th-century Tîmûrids of Central Asia, appears all the more surprising, as if an ancient Near Eastern art had been resuscitated. But the legacy of Hellenistic mosaic work also contributed greatly to the art of medieval Islamic tile design.

HELLENISTIC MOSAICS ISLAMIZED
(4TH CENTURY BC–10TH CENTURY AD)

The earliest known Macedonian examples of mosaic work, dating from the 4th century BC, are arrestingly realistic depictions of human and animal figures executed in white, black and brown pebbles embedded in cement, found on the site of the royal palace of Philip and Alexander at Pella. Further refinements under the Hellenistic kingdoms in Western Asia and under the Roman Empire caused mosaic artists to reach new heights of illusionistic verisimilitude – which is what they aspired to – with ever finer tesserae assembled in many colours. In the Levant, the artisans of the Greek-founded city of

Antioch, which became the metropolis of Roman Syria, influenced mosaic work throughout the Near East. Before the conversion of the Roman Empire to Christianity in the early 4th century AD, however, mosaics remained mostly restricted to floors or to the ornamentation of fountains.

The aesthetic lessons drawn by Islamic civilization from this earlier Graeco-Roman mosaic tradition in the Near East cannot be overstressed. Hellenistic tessellated floors offered later Muslim craftsmen not only models of figurative design but also manifold abstract decorative patterns, both vegetal and geometric, to imitate. Vine tendrils, wreaths, mazes, linked Greek keys and cords twined or knotted were further stylized for Islam's own symbolic purposes.

The religious revolution of the 4th century AD affected all of the Empire's arts, and none more so than mosaics. While the centre of power was transferred to the new city of Constantinople on the site of former Byzantium, mosaic craftsmen of the new Christian Roman or "Byzantine" Empire learned to cover minute earthenware cubes with a thin sheet of gold laid under glass, and then to fuse all three elements into a single golden tessera through vitrification in the kiln. Mosaics now shone with new light as the gold cubes were deliberately set to catch the sun's rays at different angles or, indoors, the reflections from candles. Moreover, these gold-dominant mosaics now moved up from the floors to sheathe the inner walls and cupolas of the new shrines in order to manifest the symbols and saints of the triumphant faith. Still, for all its glowing haloes and gilt skies, early Byzantine mosaic work – with Antioch still a centre of Near Eastern artistic production, second only to Constantinople itself – very much perpetuated the illusionistic techniques and motifs of earlier Hellenistic art down to the period of the Arab conquests in the Levant in the 7th century AD.

Nor did Hellenistic influences spare Iran. To be sure, the Persian Empire – as resurrected under its native Parthian dynasty by 250 BC and carried to a new surge of power by the House of Sâsân, fired by Zoroastrian religious zeal after AD 226 – stubbornly

ROMAN MOSAIC AT ANTIOCH
ANTAKYA MUSEUM, TURKEY

fought with, progressively pushed back and finally restricted Greek and then Roman rule in Asia to the Anatolian peninsula and the Syrian coastal strip. Finally, the Persians also tried to prise this strip from Christian Roman control in the ruinous wars of the 6th and 7th centuries AD, which fatally weakened both powers on the eve of the onslaught of Islam.

Still, Graeco-Roman aesthetics left a deep mark to the east of the Euphrates military frontier. Medieval Persian scribes, long after their conversion to Islam, perpetuated (at first in Arabic-language chronicles) the record and memory of the constant border warfare between Sasanians and Romans. These Muslim scribes were also somewhat aware of the many cultural borrowings of their forebears from the people of "Rûm". From such Islamized Iranian sources the early Arab chronicler Mas'ûdî, writing in Egypt in the 10th century AD, narrated one particularly revealing episode – as remembered in the Near East of his own day – from a major Persian military foray into Byzantine Syria more than 400 years before. In AD 529 Antioch herself had been briefly captured, and sacked, by the Sasanian Emperor known to the East Romans as "Chosroes", and by his own people as *Khosrô Anôshagh-Rovân,* "Chosroes of the Immortal Soul", before appearing as *Kisrâ Nûshirwân* in Mas'ûdî's Arabic transcription. King Chosroes, Mas'ûdî tells us, was astonished by the mosaics at Antioch – and the medieval chronicler takes this opportunity to dwell on the particular art form of the Greeks and Romans which he calls, in Arabic, *fusayfisa:* "One designates as *fusayfisa* a composition of painted and shiny glass and stones, used in the shape of cubes to adorn floors and buildings; some have the appearance and sparkle of crystal goblets. After returning to Iraq with his costly spoils, he [Chosroes] ordered built, near to Madâ'in [Mas'ûdî's Arabic name for the Sasanian capital of Ctesiphon], a city which he called *Rûmiyya,* the 'Roman'; this he adorned with mosaics upon its monuments and inner walls, according to what he had seen in Antioch and in the other cities of Syria. The walls of Rûmiyya still exist, although they are half in ruins, and bear witness that what we have described is true." In the tradition of all medieval chroniclers, Muslim or Christian, Mas'ûdî was also a moralist who liked to intersperse his prose with pointed fables, later taken up by other Islamic writers; it is he who tells the first known Islamic version of the famous story, from a lost Persian source, of the King moved to piety by the speech of his counsellor at the sight of owls nesting in a ruined building.

The Arab caliphs, after their decisive victory over Sasanian Persia at the battle of Qâdesiyeh in Iraq in AD 637, laid claim to the Sasanian imperial inheritance for themselves. They took up the Sasanian struggle against East Rome. As early as AD 636, the Arabs had shattered the backbone of Roman rule in Syria by conquering Damascus; they took Jerusalem the following year. In 661, Damascus in turn became the imperial capital of Islam under the caliphs of the Umayyad dynasty.

The Umayyads repeatedly attacked Constantinople itself from 673 to 718 in a vain attempt to substitute a new world rule, installing the temporal successors of the Prophet wherever the Christian Roman Emperors had once held sway. Regarding themselves as rivals to Caesar (*Qaysar*) and as heirs both to Chosroes (*Kisrâ*) and Solomon (*Sulaymân*), the caliphs 'Abd al-Malik ibn Marwân (685–705) and Al-Walîd (705–15) raised two buildings in the heart of their newly won domains as twin visual symbols of the new religious and imperial order: the Dome of the Rock in Jerusalem, on the deliberately chosen site of Solomon's Temple; and the Great Mosque of Damascus, upon the almost equally significant foundations of the city's former Byzantine Basilica of Saint John the Baptist. Local craftsmen employed by the caliphs were fresh converts to Islam, but were steeped in a thousand years of Hellenistic training. They adorned the inner walls of these two shrines at Jerusalem and Damascus with mosaic work in the East Roman manner, in a naturalistic and even illusionistic style. By depicting vine tendrils, Corinthian acanthus scrolls, gemmed vases and even fantastic Pompeian-like Roman palaces, they ensured the survival of

MOSAIC OF THE TREE OF LIFE
UMAYYAD MOSQUE, DAMASCUS, SYRIA
8TH CENTURY AD

such motifs in Islam's nascent art. Still, Islam's first aesthetic victory was secured by the new faith's iconoclastic assault upon these very motifs. The mosaic craftsmen of the Damascus Mosque were forced to banish all human and animal figures from their Graeco-Roman imaginary cityscapes. As a result they turned their theatrical palaces into a strangely empty, abstract and cerebral dreamworld, well on its way to full aesthetic transformation into an Islamic style. Springing up among the fairy-tale Graeco-Roman castles of the Damascus shrine, a vigorous plant motif makes its first Islamic appearance – one already fraught with ancient Near Eastern religious symbolism, and destined to figure on mosque walls for centuries to come: the Tree of Life.

In the distant Islamic West, further transmutation of the Byzantine manner was to occur in the 9th- and 10th-century Great Mosque of Cordova, for which the Spanish Umayyad caliph Al-Hakam II (961–76) even requested the despatch of a master mosaic artist from the reigning emperor of Constantinople himself, Nicephorus Phocas. According to the Moroccan chronicler Ibn 'Idhârî, the solicited Greek artist arrived in Cordova with 320 quintals of glass cubes as a gift from the Christian Emperor of the East to the Muslim ruler of Spain (then on friendly terms because both were opposed to a common enemy, the 'Abbâsid Caliph in Baghdad). Only after he had satisfactorily trained local Spanish Muslim disciples in his art was the Greek master allowed to return to his home, laden with gifts from the Caliph of the West.

As in Damascus, the banishing of human and animal figures from the mosaics of the dome and mihrâb of the Cordova Mosque resulted in suspended abstract gardens with Trees of Life, acanthus wreaths and vine tendrils – and despite some stylization, still handled, even as late as the 10th century AD, in something of the old illusionistic Graeco-Roman manner. However, the Greek master, or his Andalusian pupils, did introduce among the mosque's rhythmic plant-forms a new, purely Islamic decorative pattern: kufic calligraphy in gold tesserae, set in a deep blue ground.

The issue of Islamic iconoclasm – such a determining factor for the course of its sacred art – should however be seen in some historical perspective and be very carefully qualified. Of course, figurative art was from the first banished from Islamic shrines for fear of idolatry. Islam, which here consciously and explicitly resuscitated Judaic strains, arose in the tormented religious atmosphere of a Near East that was soon to be divided between Byzantine Christian worshippers and destroyers of sacred imagery. Muslim theologians in the first two centuries of the Islamic era, out of iconoclastic exasperation with a Levantine civilization hitherto saturated in image-worship, proceeded to attribute to the Prophet himself a number of *hadîth* (sayings), whose authenticity it is now utterly impossible to prove or disprove, in order to condemn the making of icons. A harsh conversation, recorded and sanctioned among those *hadîth* regarded as sound by the rigorous 10th-century canonist Al-Bukhârî, might indeed have taken place, as recounted, only a few generations before – for example, in the workyard of the mosaicists of the Damascus Mosque:

"It is related that Sa'îd ibn Abi-l-Hasan said: I was in the home of Ibn 'Abbâs, when there came unto him a man who said: 'Oh Ibn 'Abbâs, I am a man whose livelihood depends upon the work of his hands; and I make such images.' Ibn 'Abbâs told him: 'I shall only relate unto you what I have heard said by the Prophet, upon whom blessing and peace: Whoso shall make an image, God shall chastise him until so far as he shall be able to blow therein the spirit of life: the which he shall forever be incapable of doing.' The man choked violently and his face turned sallow. Ibn 'Abbâs said: 'Woe unto you! If you cannot eschew such work, then there remain trees and all such other things without souls to depict!'"

While such an attitude did banish figurative art from mosques and Koranic illumination, the historical fact is that on the contrary Islam's princely dynasties, beginning with the Umayyads themselves, deliberately patronized imagery elsewhere: at first on their palace walls, then increasingly as illustrations in their books (other than the Koran). The "Desert Castles" or hunting pavilions of the 8th-century Syrian caliphs are adorned with some of the very last reflections of Graeco-Roman illusionistic figurative art in the Near East, both in fresco and mosaic: depictions of the chase on horseback, of animal combat, of tributary princes, even of plump nude concubines on the wall of the caliph's private bath. Notwithstanding stylistic changes, this initial divide between abstract *cult* art and figurative *court* art was destined to endure throughout the entire lifespan of traditional Islamic civilization. The different fates that befell figurative art in Islam and in those countries belonging to, say, the Buddhist or Christian cultures lay in this: in Islamic lands, figurative artists could not rely on the patronage of a durable sacerdotal class, but depended on the protection of princes alone – whose patronage inevitably vanished in the event of political disaster.

Hence, in a given Islamic region, the disappearance of an attested school of figurative art will invariably be found to have followed hard upon the overthrow of its local dynasty (if such a dynasty had been imperially pretentious enough to patronize figurative painting to begin with). The fall of a princely line, and the transfer by victorious rivals of the imperial capital to a new site, normally reduced conquered regions to provincial status, where only the clerics remained to dominate, by default, an ever narrower cultural life. The schools of Islamic figurative painting that did flourish in Damascus, Baghdad and Cairo were also successively snuffed out when their court artists flocked to the new centre of power and patronage of the day – ultimately, to the Ottoman palace workshop in Istanbul. Even the medieval Islamic West enjoyed its own spurts of figurative creativity, from the carved ivories of the caliphs of Cordova down to the palace frescoes of the last emirs of Granada. The sterilization of this figurative tradition in the Maghrib after the 15th century reflects not so much harsher local clerical strictures as the area's general political, and hence cultural, decline, with the

general transfer of Islamic civilization's creative energies to Eastern centres of power – Turkey, Persia and India. As for Islam's two most brilliant schools of figurative art – the court libraries of Herât and Tabrîz at the turn of the 15th and 16th centuries – these witnessed a full convergence between the skills of the abstract decorator and that of the painter of "souls". The illuminator who represented palaces and mosques on paper adorned them with designs identical to those of the tilemaster working on his walls. Tîmûrid archives thus record that the court artist Khwâjeh 'Abd-or-Rahîm was "busy making designs for book-binders, illuminators, tentmakers, and tile-cutters" alike (M. Rogers tr.). But the 15th-century Herâtî and Tabrîzî book-painters who reproduced tiled buildings in shadowless and perspectiveless miniature also filled them with tiny dancing figures and so brought them back to dream-life – at least on paper – in contrast to the empty dream-castles on the mosque walls inaugurated in 8th-century Damascus.

THE NEO-SASANIAN REVIVAL OF STUCCO (9TH–11TH CENTURIES)

The Umayyads of Damascus were overthrown in AD 750 by their Arab rivals of the House of 'Abbâs. In 762, the 'Abbâsids set up the new seat of their caliphate in Baghdad – not far, significantly, from ancient Ctesiphon. The feud between Arab aristocratic clans was fed by a major Near Eastern revolution. Of course, the many social and messianic expectations aroused among the Near Eastern masses by the spokesmen for the House of 'Abbâs were ultimately – as usual – betrayed. But the 'Abbâsids did manage to hunt down the Umayyad princes and slaughter them to a man (barring one survivor who reportedly escaped as far as Spain to found an independent emirate – if he was not a local Spanish or Moroccan impostor). The Umayyads had represented the interests of the narrow caste of Arab warlords, descendants of the conquerors from the desert. The ruling Damascus Arabs had rejected the demands for social parity raised by the mass of new converts, mainly Persian, but had also proved incapable of containing them. The 'Abbâsids, although themselves Arab nobles, were supported by the Persians – ranging from the former Sasanian scribes and landowners, now formally Muslim, to the desperate Iranian peasantry who hoped (in vain) to improve their earthly lot. With their victory in AD 750, the new caliphs cut loose the Islamic régime's military dependence on Bedouin tribal warriors and took the old Sasanian scribal and landowning class into full ruling partnership, transferring their capital from Syria to Iraq, closer to the Persian heartlands.

Thus Islam's pole of cultural gravity shifted to the east. The 'Abbâsid caliphate was a resuscitated, albeit deeply Islamized and superficially Arabized, Sasanian Empire. Its viziers and scribes were Persians, who managed the new realm and court according to the laws, manners and harsh social code of the old Sasanian order – although carefully harmonized with the letter of the Koran. The Empire preserved its Arab mask for a while, however, because the caliph's legitimacy was closely tied to his noble Arab status as descendant of Al-'Abbâs, uncle of the Prophet. The Muslim Persian scribes, as haughty a caste of literati mandarins as any recorded, chose to express themselves in chastest classical Arabic, which their own grammarians and writers – all of them Iranians like Sîbûyeh and Miskûyeh or master prose-writer Rôzbeh, otherwise known as Ibn al-Moqaffaʾ ("The Son of the Maimed One") – codified into one of history's more exuberantly complicated élite languages, as incomprehensible to the Iranian masses as Achaemenid cuneiform or Aramaicized Sasanian Pahlavî had ever been. The Empire's Iranian administrators translated into this scribal idiom those ancient Sasanian works that dealt with court étiquette and the moral instruction of princes. Covering former Roman and Sasanian territory and reaching eastwards as far as the old Sasanian Empire's Indus frontier, 'Abbâsid civilization thus fused Graeco-Roman, Persian and even (a little later) Indian elements in the crucible of the Arabic language. The resulting culture was highly

distinctive, and marked, as is well known, by various negative traits such as political despotism, a harsh legal code and an obsessively misogynistic patriarchal family structure, but also by far-reaching creativity in mathematics, Neo-Platonizing mystical speculation and abstract art. With the transfer of power from Damascus to Baghdad, mosaics in the Byzantine manner tended to yield their place on walls to stucco revetment in the former Sasanian fashion. All the non-figurative Hellenistic motifs persisted, however: the vine tendrils, acanthus wreaths, palmetto friezes, knotted cords and the rest. These were easy to carve in deep relief in plaster, then touch up with paint or gilding. Since the 'Abbâsids in Baghdad, like the Sasanians in Ctesiphon before them, built mainly in brick, both in the capital itself and then, after 834, in their caliphal residence of Sâmarrâ ("he rejoices who sees her", according to popular etymology), stucco revetment covered vast surfaces. Repeated decorative motifs might be reproduced from wooden moulds.

Ninth-century 'Abbâsid Mesopotamia also, however, made a decisive contribution to the future evolution of ceramic revetment. In their efforts to imitate Chinese porcelains, which reached Baghdad by overland caravan or from the Gulf trade, Iraqi potters learned to mask their own ceramics, moulded from an argillaceous paste, with a lead-based glaze whitened and opacified with tin oxide, resulting in history's first faïence, in the strictest sense of the term.

'Abbâsid power disintegrated in the 10th century, even though in the East, Persian, then in increasing numbers Turkish princes continued formally to acknowledge as overlord a caliph reduced to ruling no more than his own crown lands in Lower Iraq. The artistic development of 'Abbâsid-style revetment in carved stucco and light-and-shadow play in brickwork was further refined in the new Eastern princely capitals of Nîshâpûr, Bokhârâ, then Ghaznî – in what are now Iran, Uzbekistan and Afghanistan – which closely imitated the ideal model of caliphal Sâmarrâ just as later European courts copied Versailles. Arthur Upham Pope has arrestingly compared the effect of the chequered light-and-shadow brick patterns in high relief on the mausoleum raised in 907 by the Sâmânid Persian emir Esmâ'îl in Bokhârâ to "basketwork" capped by a round baked-clay dome.

Despite the invention of true faïence in 9th-century Baghdad, brickwork with stucco revetment continued to hold sway in Eastern Islamic architecture down to the 12th century. Aesthetic change followed, though was not necessarily caused by, a fresh political upheaval: the advent of Turkish and Mongol power.

THE TURCO-MONGOL AGE
AND THE RENAISSANCE OF TILED BRICKWORK
(11TH–14TH CENTURIES)

The full Persianization of Eastern Islam – and the virtual renaissance of the Achaemenid architectural aesthetics of enamelled walls – was paradoxically achieved not so much under native Iranian as under new Turkish and Mongol rulers. The Turkish bodyguards in Sâmarrâ who cut down their incompetent caliph Al-Mutawakkil in 861 to replace him on the throne with his own son thereby betrayed the 'Abbâsid "secret of Empire", the caliphate's own *arcanum imperii,* to borrow the famous phrase from Tacitus. Just as the Western Caesars had done when faced with barbarian German pressure on the Rhine, so the 9th-century 'Abbâsid caliphs and their main Persian vassals – the Sâmânids of Bokhârâ – tried to contain mounting Turkish nomadic thrusts along the banks of the Oxus and Jaxartes, or Amû-Daryâ and Syr-Daryâ, the classic dividing lines between the sedentary Persianate world and the steppes beyond. The Turkish horse-nomads of the early 9th century had still been "pagan". In High Imperial manner, the 'Abbâsid and Sâmânid rulers dealt with these Turks by resorting to a Roman-style frontier tribal policy: bribing certain clans of tribesmen to defend the Empire against incursions by other tribesmen along the frontiers, and buying and training the children of loyal tribesmen to serve as élite praetorian bodyguards to the person of the sovereign in his own capital. Both in late Imperial 4th- and 5th-century Rome and in late Imperial 9th- and 10th-century Baghdad, barbarian mercenary troops eventually realized that they themselves amounted to the main military force of the Empire, held its balance of power and so "pierced its secret". Once the Empire's basic weakness had been disclosed, its partition between barbarian military commanders was only a matter of decades.

But the Turks no more sought to destroy the 'Abbâsid Empire than the Germans had Rome. Like the German kinglets who parcelled out the West Roman lands, the Turkish emirs of mounted warbands throughout the former 'Abbâsid domains reverently sought to perpetuate the forms of the civilization that they inherited – and in particular adopted its prevailing religion to secure the backing of local clergy. Precisely as the Merovingian and Carolingian Franks had done, Turkish warlords posed as inflexible defenders of their own area's religious orthodoxy, and in similar manner mercilessly repressed all sects regarded as heterodox – in their case, the various forms of Shî'ism. Nor does the parallel end there. While a Frankish ruler like Charlemagne carried his adopted Roman Christianity deep into German lands where the Roman legions had never penetrated, so the Turks took Islam to heart – and geographically far beyond the reaches of the old Arab Empire.

In Ghaznî, between 997 and 1030, the Turkish warlord Mahmûd united under his standards – and so converted – those Afghan highlanders tempted by promises of booty by raiding India, and planted Islam's colours as far as Lahore. The Ghaznavid Indo-Afghan frontier state thus became the first Islamic Turkish principality. The Caliph acknowledged Mahmûd as the "Right Arm" of his Empire. Farther west, Tügrül Beg, leader of the Saljûq or Seljuk Turkish warbands, entered Baghdad itself in 1055, ostensibly to expel the mayor of the palace, an Iranian Shî'a and hence abhorred heretic, and in reality to impose himself in turn as lord protector to the impotent Caliph in the name of proper Sunnî orthodoxy. The Caliph therefore granted Tügrül Beg the title of *sultân,* an Arabic word meaning simply "power": the starkest possible admission of who, in the Near East, now truly wielded it. In 1071, Tügrül Beg's successor, Alp Arslan, overwhelmed Byzantine defences at the battle of Manzikert and led his Seljuk forces into the heartland of Anatolia: a peninsula now destined to become the core of future "Turkey" but which the Seljuk Turks themselves were still content to designate simply as *Rûm,* the land they had torn away from "Rome".

For all their orthodoxy, the Turkish "powers" had little use for classical Arabic, now increasingly restricted to the liturgy, Holy Law and scholastic theses in those areas where Arabic's spoken forms had not become firmly entrenched. In place of Arabic, the Turkish chanceries favoured Persian, or rather an Islamized neo-Persian, a language still Indo-Iranian in basic structure but now written in Arabic script and filled with Arabic loanwords. Throughout non-Arab Islamic Asia, that is, from Anatolia through Iran and Central Asia to northern India, this form of Persian became the new "court idiom", or *darî.* Thus Persian's literary renaissance flowered not so much under the native Persian-speaking Sâmânid rulers of 9th- and 10th-century Bokhârâ as under the 11th- and 12th-century Seljuk and Ghaznavid Turkish sultans in the Near East, Central Asia and the Punjab.

Why this Turkish partiality for Persian? The usual explanation offered, valid as far as it goes, is that the Turks first penetrated the Islamic world through its eastern, Persian-speaking land frontier. A more cogent reason might be that the Persian scribes, who continued to staff chanceries throughout the Islamic East after the decline of the 'Abbâsids, were now free to develop their native idiom under their new Turkish royal masters. The issue became clear to all with the enthronement of the third Seljuk ruler in 1072, Sultân Malik Shâh – whose name, as it happened, simply combined the three royal titles of the Turks, Arabs and Persians. The new Sultan appointed as his chief minister in Baghdad a learned

Sunnî Iranian civil servant who might almost be regarded as the archetype of the great Persian scribes of medieval Islam – a man likewise remembered less by his now largely forgotten given name than by his official (Persianized) Arabic title: *Nezâm-ol-Molk,* "Administrator to the Realm". Nezâm-ol-Molk's reputation in history rests not so much on his administrative abilities – brilliant as these were – as on his treatise on government (at any rate attributed to him), written, no longer in Arabic, but in neo-Persian prose of unsurpassed lucidity. By the middle of the 11th century, it becomes inadmissible to speak of a solely "Arab" civilization in the Near East; there now emerges rather a rich, complex "Islamic" or "Islamicate" culture (the latter was Marshall Hodgson's preferred adjective), trilingual and nicely balanced between the military power of the Turks, the literate administration of the Persians and the liturgical writ inherited from the Arabs.

The cultural parallel between Turks and Germans does not even end with the founding of the Seljuk and Carolingian Empires. While Turkish chanceries encouraged Persian, so a strikingly similar linguistic development occurred in the medieval West under the last wave of Germanic invaders, the Scandinavian "Normans". Once settled around the mouth of the Seine and duly Christianized, Norman barons – not the kings in Paris – first extended the use of the budding French language, as distinct from liturgical and scholastic Latin, so that it became the international idiom of knighthood and courts as far as England, Sicily and the Holy Land. The oldest known manuscript of the French *Chanson de Roland* has thus been traced to England, much as the great epic of the neo-Persian language, the *Book of Kings* by the poet Ferdawsî, was first recited at the court of the Turkish sultan Mahmûd of Ghaznî on the eastern Afghan marches of Islam. And where Norman barons soon became fond of naming their sons after characters from French-language Arthurian romances, so, in these same years and as if in a mirror image, Seljuk Turkish princes in Rûm likewise adopted the appellations of the legendary Persian heroes from Ferdawsî's epic to become known as sultans "Kay Qobâd", "Kay Farîdûn" and "Kay Khosrô". When Norman and Seljuk knights first clashed in the late 11th- and early 12th-century Levant, this proved to be the opening battle of the Crusades.

The only significant exception to the general pattern of Turkish rule throughout 12th-century Eastern Islam was offered by a single native Persian-speaking dynasty from the central Afghan highlands, the Ghôrids, who managed to extend a short-lived sway from Herât to Delhi from 1150 until their own political collapse in 1206. Elsewhere Turkish power was undisputed, even though the Empire of the "Great Seljuks" fragmented into smaller Turkish principalities after the death of its last great sultan, Sanjar, at Merv in Central Asia in 1156. Well into the 13th century, however, Seljuk princes continued to rule firmly in what had been the most glorious conquest of their forebears: Anatolia, or Rûm.

After 1220, however, the highly acculturated, Islamized and Persianate Turkish rulers of the Levant succumbed in turn to mounted "pagan" invaders from their own ancestral steppeland: the Mongols.

For the first time since the Arab tribes had overrun Iraq and Iran more than 600 years before, 13th-century Western Asia under Mongol rule was forced to acknowledge non-Islamic sovereignty. The Mongol princes or "vassal Khâns" (*Îl-Khân*-s) who governed much of the Levant from the Western Iranian city of Tabrîz recognized the Great Khân in distant Peking as their overlord and sent him tribute in return for titles of investiture. The first Îl-Khâns continued to rely on Persian-language adminis-trators. But they were most emphatically not Muslims: the Îl-Khâns sacked Baghdad in 1258 and executed its last puppet caliph, toyed with conversion to Buddhism or Nestorian Christianity, and meditated an alliance with the Crusaders along the Syrian coastal strip to trap in military pincers the last powerful Islamic ruler in the region, the Mamlûk sultan of Egypt. Meanwhile the *Pax Mongolica* opened trade routes across Asia from Acre to Karakorum, not only to the mounted couriers of the Great Khân and his vassals, but also to merchants and missionaries of all faiths, even to men from the West like Marco Polo or Friar William of Rubruck.

But when Ghazan, Îl-Khân of Tabrîz, embraced Islam in 1295, and so cast off fealty to Peking, the underlying kinship between Turks and Mongols throughout the Near East and Central Asia became very apparent again. Once converted to ensure their political legitimacy among their Muslim subjects, the Western Mongols, always a numerically tiny military caste, intermarried and became assimilated with the Turkish aristocracy, to the point of adopting the Turkish language for daily use themselves while preserving Persian for written administration. With the death in 1335 of the last powerful Îl-Khân (now bearing the typically Muslim name of Abû-Sa'îd), the various Turkicized West Mongol princes and their Turkish princely in-laws fought to secure fiefs from what was left of the Empire from Baghdad to Bokhârâ.

The contender who emerged from the post-Mongol political chaos in 1370, and attained world fame, was the Turkish emir of Samarkand, Tîmûr, *Tîmûr-e Lang*, the "Lame" (the English "Tamerlane"), or, as he always preferred to entitle himself, the *Kürägän* or "son-in-law" to a puppet Mongol prince descended from the great Chenkkîz Khân himself, and whose daughter he had married to endow himself with proper Mongol legitimacy as heir to the mythic founder. Tîmûr rampaged with his East Turkish warbands down to the Indian plains and as far west as Anatolia. He gave these looting sprees the pious pretext of resuscitating the legitimate Mongol Empire, while paradoxically invoking orthodox Islamic rule. In point of fact, Tîmûr slaughtered his fellow Muslims throughout the Middle East – though sparing artists and craftsmen for deportation to Samarkand – while drinking himself to a stupor after battle with Shîrâz wine or fermented mare's milk. To complete and cap the full "legitimacy" of his neo-Mongol realm, Tîmûr lacked only Ming China, which he set out to conquer in the frozen winter of 1404–5 with characteristic megalomania, disregarding his advancing age. He died of pulmonary congestion in early 1405 at Otrar on the frontier of Chinese Turkestan, still raving in his cups – Marlowe's bombastic portrayal is not so very far off the mark – and so spared the Far East his visitations. To his sons he left a splendid new imperial tiled architecture in Samarkand.

Medieval Islam's two centuries of Mongol and Tîmûrid bloodletting from 1220 and 1405 proved, in the strange ways of Providence, culturally luminous – at least regarding poetry, mysticism, painting and the rebirth of tiled architectural revetments. Indeed, philosophical and artistic creativity not only marked the tormented East in this age, but even the Moorish West then reeling under the impact of an inexorable Christian *Reconquista*.

Islam's almost Toynbee-like creative response to the combined Mongolian and Castilian military challenge in the 13th and 14th centuries may be illustrated by the extraordinary receptivity, coupled with supple but unbreakable resilience, shown by its arts throughout this age. The Spanish Alhambra is a well-known example, with Gothic elements so skilfully absorbed into its traditional Moorish patterns that they pass unnoticed by most Western visitors. The case of Islamic manuscript figurative illumination as practised in the Near East is even more instructive. The Baghdad School of book-painting down to the opening of the 13th century – like its parent civilization – was mostly a blend of Byzantine and Sasanian influences. This largely derivative synthesis was revitalized in the boldly original treatment of an Iraqi painter of genius, Al-Wâsitî, in the decades immediately preceding the Mongol sack of Baghdad in 1258 – which ended manuscript production in the ravaged caliphal capital for more than a century. But manuscript illumination continued elsewhere in the region under the Mongol princes, and for the first time violently registered the impact of Chinese art. Chinese artifacts in the shape of figurative embroideries, painted vases and illustrated Taoist and Buddhist scrolls poured into the Near Eastern stronghold of the Îl-Khâns at Tabrîz as gifts from their overlords in Peking. Throughout the 14th century, a new artistic synthesis between the old Baghdad manner and the new Chinese models was wrought not only in the royal library of Tabrîz, but even in Baghdad itself, now raised up again from the dead by the Islamized and thoroughly Persianate Mongol princes of the House of Jalâ'ir – whose last sultan, Ahmad, wrote Persian poetry himself. The exquisite result was the creation of what has conventionally come to be called the "Persian miniature", which crystallized in form in illustrations to Persian poems at the very end of the 1390s in Baghdad at the court of Sultan Ahmad Jalâ'ir by the master painters Jonayd and 'Abd-ol-Hayy. This was the school of figurative art which the Tîmûrid masters inherited and pursued.

A masterpiece of cultural complexity, the late medieval "Persian miniature" partly draws on Islam's older traditions of Arabic calligraphic line and taste for geometric compositions to illustrate romantic subjects ultimately derived from Sasanian lore – known through such poets as Ferdawsî and his successors – but always seen in the idealizing light of Neo-Platonic mysticism, this being the crucial Byzantine legacy. No less important, however, was the influence of the Chinese scrolls and vases accumulated in the treasure-houses of the Îl-Khâns, which Muslim painters in the Western Mongol courts took infinite trouble to imitate. They painstakingly reproduced Chinese-type cloud-scrolls, phoenixes, dragons and twisted trees in the margins of Persian books. But the Muslim artists were uncomfortable with the monochrome washes and wet mountain vistas of Sung and Yüan landscape paintings. Instead, they desiccated, as it were, the landscapes of their Chinese models by bringing harsh desert sunlight and brilliant colour to bear; the sharp outlines of their Arab calligraphic split-reed pens replaced subtle contours only suggested by the Chinese inkbrush, which they filled with jewel-like hues actually ground from such semi-precious stones as malachite and lapis lazuli.

The rise of the Persian miniature may ultimately be traced to a complete artistic misunderstanding, though a very fruitful one. The literati of the Chinese court – even under the Mongol Yüan dynasty – despised the taste of the barbaric princes of the West, Mongol or Muslim, to whom they were content to send gifts of what they themselves regarded as mediocre or inferior art – especially works garishly coloured, which higher Chinese pictorial tradition abhors. (Similar scorn, entertained in a later age by the literati of the Ch'ing Dynasty regarding other "Western barbarians", underlay their export to 18th-century Europe of those shoddy trinkets and ghastly curios that made up "chinoiserie".) For their part, while Muslim painters admired the technical virtuosity of the Chinese works they saw, they utterly ignored their original Taoist inspiration (or whatever lingered of it in the second-rate stuff they received), and considered artifacts from the land of *Chîn* to be the work of craftsmen supremely skilled in things material, but devoid of the least spiritual insight.

However, Byzantine civilization, whose Neo-Platonic thought medieval Muslims scholars had appreciated, translated, understood and fully absorbed into their own mysticism, remained an object of admiration as late as the 14th century. Anecdotes told in verse by such major medieval Persian poets as Sanâ'î, Nezâmî and Rûmî stress the mystical superiority of the painters from *Rûm,* Byzantium, over the mere shallow gaudiness of the painters of *Chîn.* The point is that if Muslim manuscript illuminators of the Mongol period were able to absorb and transmute brilliantly the lessons of basically mediocre Chinese works, and marry this chinoiserie style to the calligraphic and geometrizing legacy which they shared with the tilemasters of their own culture, this is because they could wed the Far Eastern motifs to their own Neo-Platonic world-view and system of aesthetics, thereby confirming the fundamentally Mediterranean orientation of medieval Islamic civilization.

But both before and after the climax in such exchanges reached under the Yüan and their Îl-Khân

FIGURED TILES
IN CROSS- AND STAR-PATTERNS
FROM THE KÂSHÂN WORKSHOPS, IRAN, 1267
MUSÉE DU LOUVRE, PARIS

kinsmen in the West, mutual intellectual misunderstanding did not prevent constant mutual artistic influence between the Persianate and Chinese worlds in strictly technical matters, notably in the case of ceramics. For lack of kaolin, as we have seen, 'Abbâsid potters tried to reproduce the visual effect of T'ang porcelain by means of a glaze opacified with tin. Literary sources supplement our lack of material remains to document the taste for Chinese luxuries in the Persianate world even before Mongol rule. For the late 12th century, the Ghôrid scribe Nezâmî 'Arûzî ("The Prose-Writer", so called to distinguish him from his contemporary namesake the poet) already testifies to indoor revetments on the lower parts of palace walls in what he specifically calls "Chinese porcelain", or *îzâr-e Chînî* (the writer refers here to the interior decoration of a legendary 'Abbâsid castle), "and its effect was more felicitous than the Eastern dawn!" (*khorramtar az Mashreq*). In the Mongol period, Yüan China received from Muslim potters both its knowledge of cobalt and the technique of underglaze painting, whence the blue-and-white porcelains of the Ming Dynasty (in power as of 1368), which Muslim rulers in turn collected.

According to Donald Wilber, domes, as symbols of the sky, were perhaps the first Islamic architectural elements to receive outer revetment in blue-green tiling: a spirited illumination of the Baghdad School, painted by the great Iraqi master Al-Wâsitî in 1237, depicts two camel-riders in animated conversation passing before a mosque of monochrome yellow brick capped with a uniformly sky-blue cupola. The early 13th-century Arab geographer Yâqût noted of the now ruined tomb of the Seljuk sultan Sanjar (d. 1156) at Merv (in modern Turkmenistan) that its "dome is blue and could be seen from a day's journey" (Wilber tr.). At Rayy near modern Tehran, Wilber further points out, Yâqût saw "carefully made fired bricks with a bluish glaze painted on them in the same manner as on pottery bowls in other parts of the world", and that when referring to the Iranian oasis of Kâshân the geographer recorded that "from it are brought

the *kâshânî* bowls, which the common people call *kâshî.*"

Surviving fragments of 13th-century tiled wall-panels from these Kâshân workshops afford us, better than any literary guess, a direct glimpse of what internal revetments on Iranian soil, fashioned according to the emerging taste of the age, might have looked like. The Louvre in Paris preserves a set of 15 Kâshân tiles carefully fitted together, some cut in the shape of a Saint Andrew's cross, others into eight-pointed Solomonic stars, destined to line the mausoleum of a saint at Dâmghân in Khorâsân. Their inscribed date – corresponding to AD 1267 – belongs to the age of Mongol invasion. But their figurative designs are still handled in the pre-Mongol, Sasanian-derived manner which lingered for centuries beside Byzantine influences throughout the Persianate world, before the full impact of Chinese pictorial models had made itself felt.

Although created to decorate a Sufi shrine, these Kâshân tiles cast off iconoclastic fetters to come alive with human and especially animal figures: 2 bears, 4 gazelles, 6 jackals, 2 fish, 3 hares, 21 birds – the whole bestiary from the *Kalîleh and Demneh* book of fables by Rôzbeh ibn al-Moqaffa' – in addition to an astrological lion passant. The three haloed humans, seated cross-legged with round moon-like faces, are drawn frontally in the Sasanian manner. They represent a princess in a palace garden on one side, and on the other, seated in conversation beneath a cypress, the twin Prophets Elijah, young, and Khezr, bearded, by the Fountain of Life in which swim their two resuscitated fish, emblems of their souls immortalized.

The dominant tone of these tiles is darker than will be the case in succeeding centuries: in addition to two tones of blue, black and white, their colours include a rich brown and also an "aubergine" or eggplant shade. The tiles are brightened, however, with metallic reflections, for they are lustred. Based on siliceous paste under glaze opacified with added tin oxide, enamelled in fire and then highlighted with lustre, these pieces glow with all the art of 13th-century Kâshân pottery then at its creative zenith – despite the contemporary thunder of Mongol *chapâo*-s or cavalry-raids outside the workshop walls. In 1301, tilemaster Abo-l-Qâsem 'Abdollâh, heir to five generations of Kâshân potters, noted his observations and technical tricks in a unique Persian treatise entitled *The Book of Those Brides That Are Gems and Scents.*

Glaze is the thin vitreous layer, smooth and glossy, transparent and colourless if nothing is added to it, which protects a clay piece by rendering it waterproof. Glaze is always made with siliceous matter: sand, or, as recommended by Abo-l-Qâsem, powdered quartz. In order to lower a glaze's melting temperature to the capacities of a medieval kiln, craftsmen added a "flux" or melting agent to their siliceous powder. This flux might be lead oxide, or an alkali such as soda or potash – which in either case still left the glaze transparent. "Alkaline" flux, apparently adopted in the course of the 12th century, allowed underglaze painting; motifs painted on the underlying paste and left to dry were then fired under the alkaline glaze, which kept the protected designs neat and sharp. To opacify his glaze – for example, in order to paint not under, but upon it, as was the case here – the medieval artist added tin oxide. The bold designs on the Louvre pieces were thus painted upon opaque tin oxide glaze, fired at high temperature, then fired again at lower temperature for the lustring process described below. Other oxides – for example, cobalt for blue, manganese peroxide for brown or for the "aubergine" tint encountered here, and copper mixed either with lead for green or with an alkali for turquoise – served to colour the basic quartz-derived glaze-paste, as they continue to do in Herât to this day.

By way of modifying the earlier 'Abbâsid recipe for vessels wrought of thick clay fired under opaque tinned glazes, 13th-century Persian potters mixed powdered quartz, or basic "sand", with the alkaline soda or potash derived from the ashes of saline plants, then added the bright white clay for which Kâshân was famous to the proportion of some ten per cent in order to render the paste more plastic. Thus Master Abo-l-Qâsem in 1301:

a. First comes powdered quartz (as in the practice of Herât's modern masters): "The first stone is *mahâ,* which in Arabic they call *hasât,* and in the expression of the craftsmen, 'sugar of stone'. This stone is white, pure and sparkling, of lesser purity than crystal, but whiter and purer than marble, hard to such an extreme that many sparks fly forth when struck with the flintstone."

b. This pulverized quartz becomes vitrified paste – or frit – when mixed with soda or potash and melted: "And it shall be such that of the sugar of stone, pounded, powdered, crushed and strained through silk, they shall take one hundred and five parts, and of potash [*shakhâr*], pounded to grains the size of nuts and almonds, one hundred parts, and such a mixture, altogether mixed, they shall cast into that kiln which in their expression they call the *barêz.* … It shall heat over a low fire, and with a ladle of iron which they shall have forged to the measure of the kiln, they shall stir it all together from dawn even unto the time of sunset until it be well mingled and mixed into a single essence like unto molten glass [*âbgîneh-ye godâkhteh*], and this is the matter for glass vessels [*zojâj*]. After eight hours of equal heating, portion by portion shall they take it out upon the ladle: and below, before the kiln, they shall have dug a trough filled with water. The molten essence into this water shall they pour. And when water and fire meet with one another, then from amongst them shall rise forth a hiss and roar like unto you would say thunder and lightning from within their midst."

And further: "This is the composition which the craftsmen call the essence [*jawhar*]: and pounded, powdered, crushed, strained, they preserve it until such time [as it shall enter further] composition."

c. At this juncture the artist resorted to Kâshân's fine white clay: "The Kâshânî is white and is so to full extent," Master Abo-l-Qâsem explains; and his 16th-century copyist adds here: "In the art, the condition is that [the clay] be white; now, the clay of Kâshân is white in the extreme." Abo-l-Qâsem himself notes: "Of it there is a sort like unto white snow; its mine lies in the hills of Nâ'în in the surroundings of Esfahân; this they mix with plaster and withal whitewash houses."

As for the tinctures to their glazes, 13th-century Kâshânî craftsmen, like their 20th-century Herâtî successors, drew them from what Master Abo-l-Qâsem in 1301 designates as the "Seven Metals": "I mean tin, and lead, and copper, and iron, and lazuli [*lâjward,* meaning here cobalt], and coat-of-mail [*mozarrad* = apparently graphite], and other sorts of essences [Abo-l-Qâsem here forgets to add a seventh element to close his conventional list, such as either the manganese peroxide or the 'golden and silver marcassite' or *marqashîthâ* which he mentions elsewhere] – which they pound further upon the oblong mortarstone which they use."

If Master Abo-l-Qâsem, to enrich his palette further, resorts to magnesium oxide, yellow vitriol, sulphite of arsenic, antimony and zinc before returning to copper ("which yields green"), he owns himself partial to lead: "And the best of the sorts of lead is that whose essence is white to an extreme, and the worst is all that which is *Rûmî* ['Byzantine' here, or 'Anatolian'?]. And from thence the painters derive their use of litharge, red and yellow vermilion, and white lead." Adds the copyist: "And the advantage of both tin and lead is in its sealing [*mosmat*] of the colour turquoise [*fêrôzeh*], and the advantage of lead is in the varied manner of its enamellings [*mînâhâ*]."

Abo-l-Qâsem's text yields all the ingredients to the pieces in the Louvre: "If to every forty portions of molten essence they should cast in a portion of lazuli [= cobalt], then there shall come forth a translucent blue [*kabûdî-e shaffâf*] like unto a sapphire [*yâqût-e ak'hab*]. And if, to every ten portions [of the molten glaze], they should cast in a portion of magnesite, then there shall come forth a black like unto jet. And if they cast in less, then there shall come forth a colour red like unto the hue of the aubergine [*rangê sorkh-e bâdanjân-gûn*]."

We might note, to stress the pungency both of Abo-l-Qâsem's text and of the Louvre pieces' dominant colour, that English "aubergine" derives,

through French, from the Arabic of medieval Spain – and thence from this same Persian *bâdanjân.* More important, however, is Abo-l-Qâsem's comparison of the blue he derived from cobalt – which here as elsewhere he persists in calling lazuli – to the effect of a sapphire. In medieval France also, such was the awe aroused by the intense blue light – caused likewise by cobalt – shed by the stained glass windows of the basilica of Saint Denis that Abbot Suger's chronicler believed that it was due to "the sapphires in great abundance that were pulverized and melted up in the glass to give it the blue colour which he delighted to admire: *materia saphirorum*" (Henry Adams tr.).

But the master touch of the Louvre pieces lies in the metal sheen of their lustre, a technique of pure medieval Islamic invention going back to 9th-century 'Abbâsid Iraq, and which Andalusian Muslim craftsmen transmitted in turn to their Christian Spanish fellow potters. Spanish practice has perpetuated to this day the medieval Islamic lustre process, which the Kâshân master calls the "Twin-Fired" (*dô âteshî*). Upon his piece already decorated and fired at high temperature (between 750°C and 950°C), the late 13th-century Persian artist applied, with the tip of his brush, metal oxides including copper and gold, powdered with pestle and mortar and diluted in vinegar. A second firing at lower temperature (around 650°C) – using fuel this time specifically selected to emit a lot of smoke – rarefied the oxygen in the kiln precisely by the large amount of smoke generated. Such a "reducing" atmosphere, as technically termed, precipitated the oxide particles so as to form a pellucid, and translucent, metallic epidermis, which indelibly penetrated the slightly yielding glaze. Depending on one's angle of vision, or on how one turned the piece in one's hands, the surface of the vessel mirrored the sun with multiple metallic flashes. According to Abo-l-Qâsem:

"They shall further take one weight and a half of red and yellow arsenic, one weight of silver or gold marcassite, one half weight of yellow vitriol from Tabas or Cyprus, a quarter portion of burnt copper, kneaded, pounded, powdered, crushed. Thereof, with six dirams of pure silver, burnt, powdered, they shall pound upon the mortarstone for two days and two nights, until it shall be soft to an extreme. Thereupon, when dissolved with a measure of grape-syrup or vinegar, they shall paint with this upon the vessels as they desire. Then they shall place these in the second kiln or *shâkhûrâ* wrought by them just for this purpose, and for three days and three nights they shall cause soft smoke to be emitted forth until these should take on the Colour of Twin Fires, *rang-e dô âteshî*. Once they have cooled they are taken out, and with damp earth they shall rub them until there should come forth a hue like unto that of Gold."

Master Abo-l-Qâsem did not hesitate for his lustreware to resort to real gold – like the artists of Empress Gôhar Shâd's dome in Herât a little more than a century later: "If they wish to gild vessels both translucent [*shaffâf*] and opaque [*mosmat*], they pound 24 sheets of a *mithqâl* of red gold; these gold sheets they interleave with paper rubbed with gypsum; then they cut this into piece after piece with scissors, and with diluted gum-ammoniac upon the tip of a pen cause it to adhere upon the vessels, and with cotton equalize it."

It is no cause for surprise, then, that Master Abo-l-Qâsem should have looked upon his craft as "in truth, a branch of Alchemy" and upon himself as a member of the select brotherhood of its practitioners, since he could secure that "that which is brought forth from middling fire like unto Red Gold shall sparkle, and similar to the Refulgence of the Sun shall glow!" Having attained full mastery in their art, the ceramists of the 13th century were ready at last to apply it again, on a large scale, upon the walls of palaces and shrines. So stricken by Mongol warfare in this age were the territories corresponding to modern Uzbekistan, Afghanistan and Iran, that almost no tiled walls have survived from this period (save for a few remnants at Mashhad). Such monuments do exist, witnesses to the rapid evolution in 13th-century Eastern Islamic architectural adornment – but they are in Turkey.

The Mongols spared the Anatolian territories of the Seljuk sultans of "Rûm" for a longer period. His defeat in the battle of Kösé-Dâgh in 1243 forced Sultan Kay-Khosrô to acknowledge the Îl-Khâns as his overlords, but the victors allowed him to retain his throne as tributary prince under a Mongol protectorate. The chamberlains to this vassal Seljuk court – now rendered all-powerful within their own sphere of authority, and adorned with the curiously poetic title of *Parwâneh* or "Butterfly" (meaning one turning about the royal flame) – managed and milked of tribute the Anatolian sultanate in the interests of the Mongol overlords in Tabrîz. But until the utter breakdown of the Seljuk sultanate at the turn of the 14th century into a sandheap of contending West Turkish warlordships – from which the Ottomans ultimately emerged the winners – Anatolia suffered only the odd punitive Mongol expedition, but nothing on the scale of the bloodshed endured by Khorâsân, Central Iran or Iraq. Thus Konya, capital of the Seljuk sultans of Rûm, became a haven for Persian scribes and poets fleeing their devastated homeland to pursue their creative activities in security under the patronage of the vassalized but still wealthy Anatolian rulers and their "Butterfly" prime ministers. The representative figure usually cited for this age is the 13th century's leading mystic poet in Persian, Mawlânâ ("Our lord") Jalâloddîn, who was born in 1207 in the northern Afghan town of Balkh, was taken to Asia Minor by his refugee family as a child and founded the most famous of all dervish orders in Konya – where he died in 1273, to become known throughout Eastern Islam by his sobriquet of Rûmî, "He of Rûm". In this westward wave of fugitive Persians emigrating from the Persianate world to safe Anatolian soil were included craftsmen and architects as well. The flow, however, had already begun in the preceding century. We know, for example, that the mosque of the Seljuk stronghold at Divriği was built in 1180 by an architect from Marâgheh in Iranian Azerbaijan. In 13th-century Rûm, to be sure, Islamic conversion and linguistic Turkification among the native population proceeded apace. At the same time, however, a Persia-in-exile, as it were, was given the opportunity to perpetuate its culture in the midst of a nascent Turkey.

The tile decoration of several significant 13th-century Anatolian monuments is itself a telling indication of the Persianate acculturation of the Seljuks of Rûm – precisely because tile revetment corresponds to no structural necessity in Asia Minor. Anatolia possesses superb building material and a tradition of stone sculpture going back beyond Hellenistic to Hittite times. The Seljuks themselves also raised buildings in Rûm whose adornment, while Islamic, was carved in hard stone alone, as at Sivas, Nigde, Kayseri, Erzurum and Divriği.

Still, to follow the new aesthetic dictates of their Persian neighbours, Seljuk architects sheathed some of their most important shrines in the finest surviving 13th-century ceramic revetments – because solidly sealed on stone – on their original walls. Thus the tiled *Shifà'iyeh* or "House of Healing" in Sivas, built in 1217, looks like an early Anatolian response to the decorative innovations of Ghôrid Herât on the other side of the Iranian plateau. Persian tilemakers may have been responsible for its turquoise and night-blue bands, now densely threaded among the façade's bare bricks to form fields of stars and carpet-like weavings of plaited and knotted calligraphy. At Eski Malatya (Old Melitene), the Great Mosque, dated 1247, alternates strips of bare and enamelled brick, whose virtuoso design culminates under the dome in a spiral that whirls around a central medallion – itself a six-pointed Prophetic Star marked with repeated calligrams composing the name of Mohammad and figuring the Seal of Creation as made manifest in ceaseless circling emanations. At last, in Konya, capital of the sultanate, the Büyük Karatay *medrese* or theological college, built in 1241, displays total tile revetment on its inner walls. With a palette restricted to black, white, blue-green and ultramarine, the tiling expresses the Cosmic order with plaited Koranic calligrams and star-bursts. The poet Rûmî, who is known to have taught in this very

building, evokes in his verse the aesthetic equivalence which his civilization perceived between the sky and a "green dome" (*gombad-e khazrâ* – R.A. Nicholson tr.):

> Hark with the soul's ear to the sounds innumerable
> In the hollow of the green dome, rising from lovers'
> passionate cry.

The classical phase of the art of tile revetment was in sight. With the conversion of the Mongol Îl-Khâns to Islam in 1295, it resumed its full development on Persian soil.

Despite its now deteriorated state, the mausoleum raised to himself between 1307 and 1313 by the Îl-Khân Oljâytû, near the northwestern Iranian town of Soltâniyeh, constitutes the first surviving Persianate funerary monument in high classical style: a brickwork octagonal building two storeys high, still partly covered by its original tiles, with ogee niches and a blue-tiled, sky-like dome visible from a distance.

Pursuing the decorative trends of the preceding century in Anatolia, the craftsmen of Oljâytû's mausoleum interlaced bands of turquoise and ultramarine tiling into ever tighter networks, leaving far less bare surface of brick between the strips of colour. Such narrow reticulation, or "strapwork", of blue tiling likewise appears upon the walls of a shrine again raised by Oljâytû the Îl-Khân over the grave of the 9th-century Sufi saint Bâyezîd in Bastâm in Khorâsân in 1313. In the interstices left by the ceramics at Bastâm, the now extremely reduced bare monochrome surfaces of brick are themselves carved with tiny abstract motifs to play with light and shadow among the tile strips: no expanse is left plain.

With the stage set for full inner and outer revetment, blanket outward architectural tiling makes its full appearance at the end of the 14th century in Tîmûr's royal capital of Samarkand with the complex of tombs on the outskirts of the city known as Shâh-e Zendeh, the "Living King". These were raised by Tîmûr to honour the reputed resting place of Quthâm ibn 'Abbâs, cousin to the Prophet.

CHINESE DISH WITH PATTERN OF FLYING WATERFOWL
AND EIGHT-LOTUS CROWN
LEADED GLAZE, SPOTTED
T'ANG DYNASTY, 8TH OR 9TH CENTURY AD
RIETBERG MUSEUM, ZURICH

of medallions in high relief along its side-panels. These many-lobed medallions correspond to fantastic flowers ultimately derived from the lotus, or to chains of "eight-lotus crowns" with petals and pistils highly stylized into rounded octagonal stars – a recurrent motif of Chinese decorative art already seen on the T'ang pottery exported to the Islamic West. The general effect of this Tîmûrid gateway in turn suggests the blue-tiled panels soon to rise in Ming China, such as the Wall of the Nine Dragons at Ta T'ong, itself undoubtedly a response to western Central Asian Islamic influences. The late medieval Persian and Turkish languages designated motifs of deliberate Chinese inspiration as *Khatâ'î,* "Chinese-like": one might almost translate it as "Islamic chinoiserie". From *Khatâ'î,* one of the possible adjectives for things Chinese in Persian, was derived the name "Cathay" used by Marco Polo and other medieval European travellers to the Far East.

The inner revetment of Princess Shâd-e Molk Âghâ's dome, however, reflects not Chinese but complex Near Eastern astronomical symbolism: a central starlike eight-pointed Seal of Solomon, in its midst a sunlike planet surrounded by six other stars, all encircled in turn by medallions enclosing still more planets with their attendant minor stars to form successive little constellations of the Seven Heavenly Bodies.

While Tîmûr rode forth to massacre his fellow-creatures elsewhere, his niece's tomb bore the following admonition in Persian verse, as recorded and translated by Lisa Golombek and Donald Wilber:

This is a garden in which lies buried a Treasury of good fortune,
And this a tomb in which a precious pearl has been lost,
In it the one of cypress stature finds Grace;
One may take solace in that we both may be under the ground;
Just consider that Solomon was carried away by a gust,
Despite the fact that the seal of Protection was in his ring.

Tîmûr's own mausoleum, the Gûr-e Mîr or "Tomb of the Emir", with its highly visible ribbed and blue-tiled dome raised over the conqueror's remains after his death in 1405, proclaimed far and wide that a

One of the gems of the complex is the mausoleum to Tîmûr's niece, the princess Shâd-e Molk Âghâ , or "Lady Joy of the Kingdom", who died in 1371 in her girlhood to the royal clan's grief. Pressed by other duties, the artists were not allowed leisure to complete the revetment of the outer walls and domes, but they did manage entirely to sheathe the portal in blue-green tiling which they in turn moulded and carved in very deep relief, as if they were dealing with stucco – thereby playing both with colour and light-and-shadow.

Samarkand was always a main market for the China trade. When the Arabs conquered the oasis in 712, they discovered here, for example, the Chinese-invented craft of paper-making out of rags, which ultimately, through Arab transmission farther West, replaced papyrus and parchment everywhere. Reflecting the nearness of Chinese Central Asia, the ogee arch to Princess Shâd-e Molk Âghâ's mausoleum in turn displays, not only underglaze-painted tendrils in expected Persianate style on its spandrels, but also markedly Chinese-inspired rows successor to the Mongol Îl-Khâns in Soltâniyeh now lay in imperial state in Samarkand.

AZURE CLASSICISM AND ITS HEIRS (15TH–18TH CENTURIES)

As political heir to Samarkand, Herât, capital of the Tîmûrid domains from 1405 to 1507, was the academy of Eastern Islam, as we have seen, where the civilization's classical achievement – in literature, philosophy, painting and architecture – was summed up and "brought to perfection", in Prince Bâber's words. With the model of the Gûr-e Mîr before it, the dominant colour of 15th-century Persianate architecture was night-blue, tinted with cobalt posing as *lâjward,* or lapis lazuli.

Concerning lapis lazuli, the 16th chapter of the Persian-language *Lapidary* of one Mohammad ibn Mansûr, written about 1450, deals with just this Stone of Azure which so impressed the imagination of his age: the mines of the stone, its properties, supposed alchemical origins (the scribe believed lapis lazuli ultimately to have emerged from copper), its medicinal and even magic virtues and the techniques used by the manuscript illuminators to crush, cleanse and transmute the lazuli stone into pigment for their paintings.

According to Mohammad ibn Mansûr, two sorts of lapis lazuli exist, "one sort dotted with spots of gold, and the other without". The finest stones are mined in Badakhshân, in the present Afghan northeast, for "the *lâjward* of Badakhshân is of a good pure colour, with upon it spots of gold, and better than other sorts of *lâjward.* One examines the excellence of a *lâjward* by casting a piece thereof upon a fire that throws off neither sparks nor smoke. If an azure-coloured tongue of flame shoots forth, then it is sound [*nêkû*]; if one does not shoot forth, then it is not sound." Its uses are numerous: "Out of the *lâjward* are wrought cups and bowls and seal-stones and belt-ornaments and rings and the like. If powdered *lâjward* is scattered upon a fire, multicoloured smoke should appear. And [the planet] Venus is the guardian of *lâjward.*"

Hence its virtues: "The *lâjward,* despite the fact that it is cold and dry, for the purging of bile is more powerful than other remedies. Cleansed *lâjward* is more profitable than the non-cleansed for melancholy, sleeplessness and liver pain. If *lâjward* mixed with oil is rubbed upon the hair, the beauty and lustre of the hair will be increased, and the hair curled thereby. If hung around the necks of infants, it reduces their fear. Illuminators and painters use *lâjward* for most of their pictures."

Mohammad ibn Mansûr further dwells upon the crushing of the stone and the cleansing of its powder with pitch and olive or linseed oil to obtain the finest azure pigment.

In Iran, the shrine known pre-eminently as the civilization's "Blue Mosque" – *Masjed-e Kabûd* – still stands in Tabrîz. Dating from 1465, it is more than half ruined and has lost its dome and vaultings. But those mosaic tiles that do still cling to its remaining brickwork arches under the open sky are, arguably, the most beautiful architectural revetments left in the Islamic world. Patterned with flaming white calligraphy, turquoise Seals of David and Solomon, burning amber-toned wreaths of the Tree of Life and leaping constellations of diamond-shaped jet-black medallions, their ultramarine ground has never been equalled before or since for intensity and depth.

The west Iranian city of Tabrîz came to constitute the other major pole for the arts in the 15th-century Persianate world with Herât to the east. Tilemasters from Tabrîz worked on monuments throughout the Levant ranging from Ottoman Brusa to Mamlûk Damascus (where one Ghaybî at-Tawrîzî, "He of Tabrîz", signed his name on a panel in 1420). Where Tîmûrid Herât's taste in art, in architectural revetment and manuscript illumination alike inspired a cool, jewel-like classicism, the workshops of Tabrîz, the former Mongol capital of the Levant, harked back to aesthetic traditions inherited from the Îl-Khâns with their collections of flamboyant Chinese Taoist and Lamaist Buddhist scrolls. Much like the surviving tilework of the Tabrîz Blue Mosque, the book-paintings produced by the 15th-century Tabrîz royal libraries show equal vibrancy, boldness of drawing and colour, even romanticism: as distinct from Herât's search for balanced, luminous perfection with taut academic restraint. Where, in terms of contemporary Early Renaissance Italian art, Herât might have stood for the Florence of the Persianate world, Tabrîz was its Venice.

The cultural distinctiveness of Tabrîz reflected its political resilience as a major centre of trade. When Shâh Rokh of Herât died in 1447, his vassal in Tabrîz, Jahân Shâh ("World-Ruler"), emir of the Turcoman clan known as the *Qarâqoyunlu* or "They of the Black Sheep", at once severed all political ties to the House of Tîmûr to show that his fealty to the ruler of Herât had been personal, not dynastic.

While Jahân Shâh admired Herât as the focus of the civilized world he knew – he himself took but failed to hold the city in 1458, during the bout of anarchy that followed Shâh Rokh's demise – he and his Black Sheep Turcomans had shaken off Tîmûrid rule over central and western Iran within a decade. The Turcomans re-established Tabrîz both as a leading capital of the Persianate world and as Herât's great western rival, both politically and artistically. The Tabrîz sultans raised their own "Blue Mosque" in 1465 and sponsored a school of manuscript illuminators with a penchant for the visionary and the fantastic. When a rival Turcoman clan, the *Aqqoyunlu,* "They of the White Sheep", overthrew "They of the Black Sheep" and in turn ruled Tabrîz from 1467 to 1501, the new sultans continued to patronize this same mood in art.

In terms of tile revetment, as in all other artistic fields, the 15th century for Eastern Islam is the high water mark of aesthetic achievement in Samarkand, Herât and Tabrîz alike. The artistic and general cultural heritage of this golden 15th century was shared between the four late Islamic dynasties that ruled over the Turkish, Persianate and Indian domains from the 16th to the 18th century:

The Uzbeks in Samarkand: After hounding the last Tîmûrid princes out of all their Central Asian territories by 1501 and occupying Herât itself between 1507 and 1510, the Özbeg or Uzbek ("Self-lord") Turks (properly speaking, this was a dynastic, not an ethnic name) were content to perpetuate Tîmûrid forms of civilization in their own twin capitals of Bokhârâ and Samarkand – whether in manuscript illumination or architectural tiling. The Sunnî Uzbek emirs welcomed painters and tilemasters from Herât – who fled the imposition of Shî'a rule in their own city after 1510 – but by the middle of the 16th century this generation had died out and Uzbek Central Asia's post-Tîmûrid creativity fossilized into imitative, cold academicism.

The Safavids in Iran: Fervently Shî'a, the Safavid shâhs laid claim to the political and artistic – but not religious – legacy of both Turcoman Tabrîz and Tîmûrid Herât. As a young Turcoman chieftain in western Iran fired with messianic passion for Shî'ism, the head of the Safavid clan, Esmâ'îl, denounced his Sunnî rivals, overthrew the rule of the orthodox Turcomans of the White Sheep in Tabrîz in 1501, pushed the equally orthodox Uzbeks out of Herât in 1510 and thus united under his sway the western and eastern rims of the Iranian plateau. But the slaughter of his mounted archers under matchlock fire by the most powerful of all his Sunnî opponents, the Ottomans, in the battle of Châlderân (near Tabrîz) in 1514, shook his confidence and blocked his designs to spread Shî'ism throughout Anatolia and the rest of the Islamic world.

Esmâ'îl's purpose had not been to revive an Iranian-centred, Persian-speaking empire. He himself, as a Turcoman, wrote his poetry as well as his letters of abuse to the Ottoman sultan Selîm in Turkish (Selîm retorted, as a cultured gentleman, with worse insults – in Persian). But the wall of Sunnî military hostility, Ottoman in the west, Uzbek to the east, which shut Esmâ'îl the Safavid within the confines of his Persian kingdom, virtually restricted Shî'ism to the Iranian plateau. Here, of course, Esmâ'îl and his successors were able to impose Shî'ism as state creed by persecution of all other schools of thought, so that Shî'ism did eventually become – fortuitously – identified with the modern Iranian nation-state. Lying, however, under constant Ottoman threat, the Safavid shâhs were even forced to renounce their residence in Tabrîz, their first capital now too exposed to attack from the Western Turks, and retreat towards the central Iranian plateau. In 1598, Shâh 'Abbâs fixed the site of the new capital at Esfahân: *Esfahân, nesf-e jahân* ("Esfahân is half the world!"). This Persian rhyming pun reflected the prestige the new Safavid metropolis rapidly came to enjoy not only in the eyes of its own population, but even in the perception of increasingly numerous European visitors in the course of the 17th century – Portuguese, then Dutch, English and French merchants connected to the India trade and usually come up by sea through the Gulf, then on by caravan through Shîrâz. Under its 17th-century shâhs, Esfahân became the ultimate expression of Persianate architectural classicism in Eastern Islam.

The revetments of those shrines in Esfahân raised under Shâh Esmâ'îl in the earliest years of the 16th century while the capital was yet at Tabrîz – such as Esfahân's mausoleum of Hârûn Welâyat, built in 1513 – still show the taste of the former Turcoman rulers with their romantic, visionary flamboyance.

But the tilework of 17th-century imperial Esfahân betrays a slackening in design. No doubt in general urban layout, Esfahân has as fully majestic a Royal Square as Samarkand's older *Rêgestân.* In this open space, Safavid horsemen played the Iranian nobility's favourite game, polo, under the eyes of courtiers favoured to sit on the terrace of the Royal Pavilion overlooking the square known as the 'Alî Qâpı or "Sublime Porte" – like the entrance to the rival Ottoman Hall of Government. To respect the perfect symmetry of the square, the early 17th-century Safavid architects of Shâh 'Abbâs boldly masked the orientation of his Royal Mosque – which faces Mecca at a sharply differentiated angle – with a second façade aligned with all the other portals of the esplanade. But it is the details that disclose Manneristic repetition. The blue or yellow-brown ceramics that cover the huge surfaces of the

Royal Mosque and Shaykh Lotfollâh Mosque with vast expanses of tiles, all executed in *Haft Rang* or "Seven Colours", reveal an increasingly flaccid facility of design which also affected Esfahân's school of miniature painting in this age. But the general coloured effect is splendid. Seventeenth-century Safavid taste also covered with tiles the city's older and more austere brickwork shrines inherited from Great Seljuk times, just as Esfahân's own Shî'a divines brought new and subtle glosses to bear on older philosophic works. The turquoise Mosque of the Shâh's Mother, *Masjed-e Mâdar-e Shâh,* dating from 1706–14, was the final flowering of certain exotic plants. In 1722, insurgent Sunnî Afghans took Esfahân and sacked her, and so ended Iranian neo-classicism.

The Osmanli or Ottoman Turks: As paramount Sunnî power after their conquest of Constantinople in 1453 and annexation of the sultanate of Egypt in 1517, the Ottomans inherited from their Seljuk predecessors a deep respect for Persianate cultural models – while ever more bitter hostility pitted them against the Shî'a Safavids in Tabrîz and Esfahân. The Ottoman sultans relied on their Uzbek allies to keep military pressure on the Safavids in the east, and likewise granted warm asylum to those Iranian artists who rejected the "heterodoxy" now prevalent in their homeland to seek safety in exile at the Western Sunnî court. Sultan Selîm took tilemasters with him from Tabrîz after his brief occupation of the city following his victory at Châlderân in 1514. For the year 1526 alone, the records of Istanbul's imperial library workshop, known as the *Naqqâsh-Khâneh* (*Nakkaş Hane*) or "House of Painters", list ten masters from Tabrîz among the 41 designers for books, textiles and tiles appointed to the Ottoman court.

Osmanli architecture, however, soon turned away from Iranian models. Ottoman artists beheld before them the Seljuk tradition of stone building in Anatolia and also, in the capital, such Byzantine models as the great basilica of Hagia Sophia, the archetype for all heaven-domes. The peerless 16th-century Ottoman master-architect Sinân creatively adapted the Byzantine dome to Islamic use in his mosques of Süleymâniye in Istanbul and Selîmiye in Edirne, with powerfully balanced masses of hard bare grey masonry surrounded by, and contrasted to, slender, taper-like minarets. Under the leaden winter skies of Turkish Thrace, Ottoman tilework abandoned outer walls and instead sheltered under the domes to adorn inner walls.

Based on patterns designed by the masters of Istanbul's Naqqâsh-Khâneh, and fired in kilns in the nearby specialized potters' town of Iznik, Ottoman tiles also quickly parted company with contemporary Iranian styles. While still drawing on Eastern Islam's common basic visual vocabulary of floral and calligraphic motifs, as well as *Khatâ'î-* or "Chinese"-derived designs and the knotted arabesques of Greek keys, which were a legacy of the Seljuks (and ultimately of the Byzantines) and hence known as *Rûmî,* the illuminators and textile designers of the 16th-century Ottoman palace workshop and the ceramic artists of 16th-century Iznik developed a powerfully original manner.

Iznik tiles usually lined Ottoman mosque and palace walls with underglaze-painted gardens depicted in perpetual spring, marked by sinuous but always vigorously intertwined and very boldly stylized stems pertaining to the "Four Flowers" – actually seven plants in all: roses, peonies, carnations, tulips, eglantines, lilies and cypresses. These floral patterns were often enhanced, in large bursts of colour, with huge, stylized pine-cones. To these designs ultimately drawn from nature, Iznik potters also often added an imaginary, fantastically elongated, jagged leaf-form. To designate such garden-compositions, Ottoman Turkish, borrowing from the Persian, used the word *sâz,* literally "a fashioning". The ubiquity of the tulip capped with its long bell-like petals not only underscored the Ottoman court's infatuation with this flower – the early 18th century, which heralded the Empire's decline, has been aptly termed the "Age of Tulips" – but carries a nice etymological twist. Ottoman Turkish often called this favourite plant the "turban"

flower or *tülbend*: the same word thus yielded "tulip" and "turban" in European languages when the flower was imported from Turkey and cultivated, especially in Holland, in the early 17th century.

The most striking innovation of the Iznik potters was their discovery of a brilliant red, one which could finally hold its own in the kiln, derived from "Armenian bole", an Anatolian clay rich in iron

273

oxide. As soon as they became aware of the virtues of "Armenian bole", Ottoman masters spread it in such thick layers on plates and tiles alike that it often stood out in relief. "Iznik red" appears for the first known time, and already juts out from the surface of its tiles, on the inner panels of Sinân's Süleymâniye Mosque, finished in 1557. In 1561, it may be observed thickly splashed across the opulently tiled interior of the Mosque of Rüstem Paşa, probably the richest storehouse of Iznik wall-ceramics from the golden age to be found in the Ottoman capital.

Long before they saw other Islamic wares, 16th- and early 17th-century Europeans first developed a taste for Iznik ceramics in the portable form of decorated jugs and plates. Iznik's serpentine plant motifs do show common traits with the ornamental style of Italian Mannerism and the late Renaissance. As the 17th century wore on, resemblance between the Ottoman Empire's decorative arts and the European Baroque became more marked, until the overwhelming influence of the latter almost suffocated the creativity of the former in rapidly weakening 18th-century Turkey. The last flowering of traditional Ottoman art coincided with the so-called "Age of Tulips" under the reign of Sultan Ahmed III, between 1703 and 1730 – just as Turkish power began permanently to yield in the Balkans to Austria, and the Empire to totter.

The Moghols: The architectural adornment of Islamic India ought perhaps not even to figure in a list of ceramic arts for buildings derived from the Persianate school of wall-tiling. Not that the Moghol emperors were unaware of their cultural roots in Central Asia. These most powerful of all the Muslim rulers to dominate the northern half of the subcontinent were authentic scions of the Tîmûrid clan, descendants of Prince Bâber of Kabul, who founded their dynasty's fortunes on Indian soil by his seizure of Delhi in 1526. The very sobriquet by which their line became known in later days to their Indian subjects, *Moghol,* is merely the Persian form of "Mongol". Persian was always their court

language. Classical Persian poetry enjoyed a final season of creativity on Indian soil through their munificent patronage. But far more even than Turkey, Islamic India (on a par with Egypt) remains a land marked by carved stone architecture of the very highest quality, with no need for revetments – or masks – of tiles.

The Ghôrid sultans, the first Muslim conquerors of Delhi in 1192, had themselves immediately resorted, not to the traditional brickwork of their Central Asian homeland, but to hard local sandstone carved by converted Hindu craftsmen in order to raise the first monument to their rule on Indian soil, the towering victory minaret known as the Qotb Minâr. The Indo-Islamic kingdoms of the 13th, 14th, 15th and early 16th centuries likewise reproduced the forms and symbolic motifs of Persianate architecture and ornament – ogival gateways, domes, Seals of Solomon, calligraphic bands and the rest – transmuted into stone. The finest Indo-Islamic depiction of the Tree of Life is thus to be found in the Mosque of Sîdî Sayyed in Ahmadâbâd, dated 1571, in what was then the sultanate of Gujarat, carved in stone lattice-work within an ogee window.

The Moghols in turn, once their power had been fully consolidated under Emperor Akbar between 1556 and 1605, pursued this architectural blend of Persianate form with traditional Indian stone carving down to the decline of their own dynasty in the course of the 18th century. Their builders used such hard materials as red sandstone and white marble, with insertions of semi-precious stones imitated from late Renaissance Italian *pietra dura* work introduced by the many European craftsmen who sought employment at the Moghol court – hence there was no need for brittle tiles. Nevertheless, such was the prestige of Persianate culture in the subcontinent that Indo-Muslim patrons and craftsmen occasionally indulged in what amounted to visual quotations from the artistic repertoire of the neighbouring civilization by having occasional coloured tiles inlaid upon stone surfaces – structurally useless, but superficially in Persian taste.

Early 14th-century examples – since much restored – include the ceramic bands which adorn the stone mausoleums of Muslim saints at Uchh and Multan. Among Hindus, the rajahs, as princes and members of the *kshatrya* warrior class, tended to show the greatest receptivity at least to the outward, more material aspects of the imperial Islamic culture in northern India. Thus Rajah Man Singh, ruler of the mighty red sandstone fortress of Gwâlior from 1486 to 1516, had a ceramic frieze of yellow mosaic on turquoise grounds inserted beneath the purely Hindu projecting *jharoka* balconies of his ramparts. This frieze almost suggests a deliberate Indian parody of Persianate architectural ornament with its playful animal designs of dancing elephants and even ducks. So exquisitely are the animals drawn, however, that they only mitigate, with a touch of humour, the overbearing majesty of the Rajah's fort.

Occasional Imperial Moghol resort to tile revetment, however, was not parody, but cultural tribute, whether on the northern wall of Lahore Fort, founded by Akbar in the later 16th century but redecorated in 1631, or on the walls of the Mosque of Wazîr Khân in the same city, dedicated in 1634. The decoration of both structures was patronized by the emperor Shâh Jahân, the greatest builder of the dynasty, who elsewhere multiplied architectural experiments in sandstone and marble, such as the Tâj Mahal in Agra.

In Lahore, however, on which Shâh Jahân also lavished much architectural attention, the Emperor apparently also wished to recall the aesthetic tastes of his Tîmûrid ancestors in Persia and Central Asia. The Lahore mosque raised in honour of his court official 'Elmoddîn Ansârî Wazîr Khân ("Minister lord") is a Persianate brickwork structure sheathed in predominantly yellow tiles; the vegetation they portray is also Persianate and Central Asian, especially the cypresses. But the minarets roofed with *chhatrî* or "parasol" pavilions and the projecting *jharoka* balconies on either side of the ogee gateway cry out how Indian this pseudo-Persian building truly is.

The northern wall of Lahore Fort, for its part, displays an aesthetic manifesto unique in Islamic art. On the brickwork ramparts bedecked with *jharoka* balconies, mosaic panels designed in night-blue on yellow grounds, and others – in reverse – in yellow on blue, framed with borders of bare brick, together compose what might be termed a 17th-century Moghol equivalent of "Pictures at an Exhibition": moustachioed and whiskered horsemen of the Imperial guard, elephants with howdahs, camels and their drivers. These mosaic figurative plaques ordered by Shâh Jahân are an anthology of visual quotations. Elsewhere on the wall, the usual abstract tendril- and star-patterns repeat common Islamic themes. Even some of the rampart's figurative decorative elements draw on traditional Persianate tile-designs: for example, the motif of eastward-flying geese, which Iranian craftsmen themselves once borrowed from a painted subject often found on Chinese vessels going back to the T'ang period. Most of the figurative compositions, however, mirror the style of book-paintings popular with the Moghol court.

In the Persianate world, manuscript illuminators had often reproduced the patterns of tiled walls on paper. But here the opposite occurred: Shâh Jahân ordered a series of favourite "miniatures" – really much too large to be referred to as such – to be executed on this castle wall. Among the celebrated paintings thus quoted on his "Wall of Pictures" is an animal design whose archetype goes back to Master Behzâd of Tîmûrid Herât – two dromedaries locked in combat, with necks entwined.

With Lahore's "Wall of Pictures", the artistic evolution of Islamic architectural ceramics comes full circle. The tiles of Iran and Central Asia had served to protect, mask and ultimately transfigure frail and homely walls. India enjoyed walls both handsome and solid with no need to hide them under tiles, and so its architects, despite Persian influences, finally renounced them. But its greatest imperial builder did choose to raise this final, magnificent and structurally gratuitous wall-revetment of tiles in nostalgic praise of Persianate tradition – almost by way of farewell.

Mîr ʾAlî Shêr Nawâʾî (1440–1501),
Nezâmî's chief adaptor into Turkish,
kneels in the magic garden of the Other World before the
shades of the great Persian poets of the past.
Seated in lordship over them all,
Nezâmî welcomes him to their group.
Nawâʾî, hiding his hands in the lengthy sleeves of his caftan
in the traditional gesture of humility,
is introduced by his living guide and mentor,
the Persian poet Jâmî (1414–92).
So Dante describes himself
guided by Virgil into the presence of Homer
in Canto IV of the *Inferno*.

NEZÂMÎ IN THE MAGIC GARDEN
OF THE POETS
FRONTISPIECE
TO THE *WALL OF ALEXANDER*,
A TURKISH ADAPTATION
OF NEZÂMÎ'S EPIC
BY NAWÂʾÎ OF HERÂT
ILLUMINATION BY QÂSEM ʾALÎ,
HERÂT, 1485

Nezâmî's *The Brides of the Seven Climes:* The Poet and his Symbols

Nezâmî (1141–1209) was recognized throughout Eastern Persian-, Turkish- and Hindustani-speaking Islam, within his lifetime, as the greatest narrative poet of his civilization (although he remains paradoxically unknown, to this day, in Western, Arabic-speaking Islam). For all his worldly fame, he chose to live the life of a country gentleman – of semi-Kurdish, Sunnî stock – in his quiet native Caucasian valley of Ganjeh, on the marches of the medieval Christian kingdom of Armenia. Modern Turkish-speaking Azerbaijan regards him as its national hero. Yet he expressed himself in Persian, in a richly imagistic, highly hermetic and exceedingly difficult style. The various Seljuk vassal princes who ruled Azerbaijan and Eastern Anatolia in his day vied to attract him to their castles and showered him with gifts – but he never once bestirred himself to call on their courts in person. No poet has been paraphrased and imitated throughout Eastern Islam as much as Nezâmî: manuscripts of his works, in the finest calligraphy, abound from Anatolia through the Caucasus as far as India. Classical Turkish adaptations of his poems are legion. Moreover, his romances provide the subject-matter for the very large majority of the so-called "Persian miniatures" produced for the Tîmûrid, Turcoman, Safavid, Ottoman, Uzbek and Moghol royal libraries – paintings that are indecipherable without reference to his works. Like Dante in medieval Europe, Nezâmî in medieval Islam was the literary giant in whom a civilization's imaginative expression converged.

In his collection of biographies of famous mystics, the poet and learned divine Jâmî of Herât (1414–92) summarized the regard in which Nezâmî was held by traditional Eastern Islamic literati:

"The shaykh Nezâmî possessed full knowledge of the outward sciences and manners of this world. But he chose retreat from the affairs of this lower world to turn his countenance towards God Most High, praised be He! From beginning to end, he spent his long life in contentment, devotion, retreat and solitude.

"His five romances in rhyming couplets have found fame under the name of the 'Five Treasures'. Most of these were commissioned by the sultans of his age, who hoped thereby to inscribe their names durably upon the pages of time.

"Although the majority of his works appear to be, on the surface of it, mere fairy-tales [*afsâneh*], from the point of view of Truth this was only a pretext – at once to unveil the Higher Truths, and to display the means of Knowledge thereof. The meaning of this is revealed by what the Sufis or mystics have said: for those who seek Union, and are lovers of the Beauty of Truth, the syllogism [*dalîl*] of His Existence is tantamount to His Existence itself, and to offer proof that one bears witness of Him is tantamount to bearing witness of Him."

Nezâmî's masterpiece, *The Brides of the Seven Climes* (in Persian, *Haft Paykar,* "The Seven Effigies"), masks its spiritual purpose at first under a cascade of fairy-tale imagery.

The outward aspect of the work is that of an epic lay to the glory of the Sasanian shâh (king) Bahrâm V, who ruled Persia between AD 420 and 439. Within the loom-frame of this heroic poem, Nezâmî weaves seven tales of initiation told by the Seven

Brides of Shâh Bahrâm. Each Bride comes from one of the Seven Climes of the world, and is housed under a differently coloured Dome according to the prevailing hue of her homeland and its ascendant star. By means of their Seven Tales, the ruler is educated into acquiring universal wisdom.

The earlier, 11th-century epic poet in Persian, Ferdawsî, had already sung the glory of Shâh Bahrâm in ruggedly powerful, linear verse. Even under Islam, the proud Persian aristocracy had continued stubbornly to treasure the memory of this ancient hero-king who had reigned over their own homeland before the days of the caliphs. Bahrâm had ruled as overlord over the pagan Arab princelings of Hîra in Mesopotamia. He had waged successful warfare against the Eastern Romans (Byzantine historians call him *Vararanes*); and he had saved Persia from invasion by the 'White' Huns – an Eastern branch of the same horse-nomads then ravaging Europe – in a major victory that shattered their horde in Khorâsân in the year AD 427. Gold-chased Sasanian silver cups depicted him in his own lifetime as an idealized, heroic mounted hunter, charging after game which he slaughters with arrows, his chief prey being onagers or wild asses, the swiftest animals of the desert – whence his sobriquet, Bahrâm-Gûr, "Bahrâm of the Onagers".

After his death there crystallized around his name all the emblematic legends of his civilization pertaining to the ideal rôle of prince and warrior, thus turning him into a culture-hero. According to the epic tradition, Bahrâm was sent by his royal father to be raised the hard way, in the vassal kingdom of Hîra, among Persia's tributary Arabs of the desert. Bahrâm succeeded to Persia's imperial throne by ordeal – he was the sole contending prince to dare snatch up the crown from between two lions in an arena. At first given to wine and the chase, he shook off his listlessness to annihilate a nomad invasion. He also destroyed a dragon whom he first blinded with his arrows, then rent asunder with his lance, winning the treasure hoarded in the monster's den. This dragonfight episode in Bahrâm's legend betrays the hero's link to a more ancient godly

prototype: even in Islamicized neo-Persian, *Bahrâm* still designates the planet Mars; its etymology goes back, beyond Middle Persian *Vahrâm* or *Varahrân,* to Avestic *Varathragna,* which yields the meaning of the appellation of the ancient Iranian war-god, "The Slayer of the Dragon Varathra".

In a hymn sung upon the occasion of each New Year, that is, on the day of the spring equinox that marked emergence from winter, pre-Islamic Persia, following Babylonian precedent, celebrated the creation of the world through ritual slaying of the Dragon. The solar war-god, whose visible emblem was the reigning king officiating as high priest, had shot forth his arrows – his rays – to pierce the Dragon, the emblem of night and chaos, and from its lacerated remains had wrought with his lance – another ray – the visible world, this treasure. In Mesopotamian mythology, from the punctured eyes of the monster had poured forth the Tigris and the Euphrates, symbols of life. On the high Iranian plateau, the New Year ritual signified spring thaw: the Dragon of winter darkness, overcome by the solar shafts of light, released its icy grip on the vivifying waters.

Such a mythological undercurrent seeps through the apparently Islamicized aspect of the medieval versions of the epic. Under the Baghdad caliphate, the converted Persian scribes tendered their ancestral culture-hero Bahrâm as rôle-model to the members of the new Arab and Arabized ruling class. As chosen hero for Nezâmî's crowning rendition, Bahrâm is portrayed as uniting in his person all the converging virtues of the civilized world. He rides to the chase, conquers in war, deals justly with his subjects, loves beautiful wives and delves deeply in learning. He masters the three cultured languages: Persian, Arabic and Greek. He manifests Bedouin valour and Sasanian royal dignity. He reads the constellations in Ptolemy's *Almagest.* In a patent medieval Islamic transmutation of the ancient Mesopotamian myth of Gilgamesh, he overcomes the twin lions – rage and lust – to master his own passions even as he rules the universe. If Nezâmî's hero still slays a Dragon on earth, such a feat also occurs, in the eyes of the poet, on an analogical, mystic plane. For before Bahrâm penetrates the garden of his Seven Brides, the King is shown celebrating the winter solstice. But when he emerges from under the Seven Domes, the world rejoices at the miracle of the equinox of spring. His week of initiation has been a ritual slaying of the Dragon of dark ignorance. Now initiated, Shâh Bahrâm holds assembly of his people, hears the seven plaintiffs against the cruel vizier who oppressed the realm during his absence, hangs this vizier, again curbs the boldness of invading nomads and reveals himself as ideal monarch. Nezâmî's poem thus discloses itself, among other things, as a moral fable destined for the education of princes through the offered rôle-model of Shâh Bahrâm – and was read as such. The epic was copied and illuminated for royal libraries by leading calligraphers and artists in Eastern Persianate Islam. The storybook's legendary Sasanian King was usually depicted with the (somewhat idealized) features of whatever ruling prince happened to patronize the manuscript: thus one may recognize, say, the Tîmûrid prince Bâysonghor of Herât or the Turcoman sultan Ya'qûb of Tabrîz, in this or that miniature of the Black Dome, or the Green Dome. Perhaps no monarch in Eastern Islamic history, however, took Nezâmî's message so much to heart as the second Moghol Emperor of India, Homâyûn son of Bâber, in the earlier half of the 16th century. According to the Indo-Persian chronicler Abo-l-Fazl 'Allâmî, Emperor Homâyûn patterned the ceremonial of his own court on the model of Shâh Bahrâm in *The Brides of the Seven Climes.*

In order to symbolize his lordship over the world of the Seven Climes, the Emperor took his seat upon a round carpet, "The Carpet of Felicity", whose concentric rings of different colours marked the spheres of Saturn, Jupiter, Mars, Venus and so on. Homâyûn himself sat in state upon the golden ring of the Sun, while the officers of his court were settled upon the rings corresponding to their ethnic group: thus the Hindu officers sat on the ring of Saturn, while descendants of the Prophet were placed upon the ring of Jupiter. The ruler "on each day clad himself in a garment agreeing with the Colour that was linked to the ascendant Star of that same day. Thus on Sunday did he clothe himself in a caftan [*khal'at*] of Gold, appropriate to the ruling Sun, and on Monday in a Green garment pertaining to the Moon."

Missing from this Moghol court charade, however, on account of traditional Islam's rigid exclusion of women from all public life, were the true key characters in Nezâmî's poem: the Seven Brides themselves. Nezâmî, whose proclaimed affection for women in his verse stands in such marked contrast to the usually misogynistic tone of his civilization, always grants them the central rôle in his narratives, for they are men's Initiators. Thus, where Nezâmî found in the traditional form of the epic, for example, that Shâh Bahrâm had trampled to death, beneath his mount, a favourite singing-girl who had dared scorn his prowess – and cruelty – in the hunt, the 12th-century poet deliberately modifies the tale: in Nezâmî's poem, the Shâh ends by begging his singing-girl for forgiveness. On the terrestrial plane, the womenfolk in Nezâmî's tales take the initiative in action, manage their way around multiple social barriers and from the depths of their purdah influence and guide the hesitant, confused behaviour of their menfolk. On Nezâmî's more mystical plane, male lovers perceive Divine Beauty through Its reflection in female countenances. And finally, on the level of the poet's heavenly or demonic image-archetypes, it is again faerie-women who toy with the male protagonists and lead them to salvation or perdition, like their sisters on earth. Shâh Bahrâm's Seven Brides are his moral teachers.

In this they play a rôle analogous to so many Sheherazades – indeed, Nezâmî obliquely refers to the "Thousand Tales" or *Hazâr Afsâneh,* the earlier Persian title of the later Arabized *Thousand and One Nights,* in his romance of *Chosroes and Shîrîn.* The poet draws on an identical, originally Hindu narrative device – first adopted by Sasanian Persia from India in the 6th century AD – of cunningly setting tales within an encompassing frame-story.

Brahmins destined such story-collections to the education of young rajahs as "mirrors for princes": a literary technique which ultimately reached Europe through translations from Arabic to Latin made by Spanish Jews.

In Nezâmî's rendition, Prince Bahrâm, while still a ward of the Arab vassal kinglets of Hîra, encounters his fate under the guise of Seven Effigies in a secret hall of Castle Khawarnaq. This wonder-castle was wrought, on the orders of the Arab king No'mân of Hîra, by a Byzantine master builder, Semnâr, "one who sealed Tables of Stars, and Talismans resolved", and whose completed Dome "lustred with gypsum and milk" mirrored the Three Moods of the firmament: by turning turquoise at dawn, yellow with the sun and white in mist, before sinking again, at dusk, into black. But when the artist had boasted that he might have raised a castle more marvellous still – one crowned by Seven Domes – the ungrateful King No'mân had had him blinded and cast down from the battlements before being stricken himself with remorse and madness and running into the desert where he disappeared forever, leaving his throne and the wardship of Prince Bahrâm to his wiser son and successor, King Monzer.

Upon returning one day from the chase, Prince Bahrâm discovers, within Castle Khawarnaq, an out-of-the-way door. Behind it, the luckless architect had hidden the secret of Bahrâm's fate. Once he has found the right key on a guard's key-ring, Bahrâm opens it and sees a hall adorned with inscribed frescoes depicting Seven Princesses so lovely that the Prince falls in love with their effigies at once. Each wore her own colour. Their number matched both the days of the week set under the signs of the Seven Heavenly Bodies and the Seven Climes of the world. The Seven Effigies were those of:

1. Fûrak ("Daughter of Porus"), Princess of India, daughter to the Râjâ, clad in Black, under the sign of Saturn, Lord of Lead, for Saturday.
2. Homây ("Phoenix"), Princess of Byzantium, daughter to Qaysar or Caesar, clad in Yellow, under the sign of the Sun, Lord of Gold, for Sunday.
3. Nâz-Parî ("Enchanting Faerie"), Princess of Khwârazm or Chorasmia (Turkic or Turkish Central Asia), clad in Green, under the sign of the Moon, Lady of Silver, for Monday.
4. Nasrîn-Nôsh ("On-Wild-Roses-Fed"), Princess of the Slavs, clad in Red, under the sign of Mars, Lord of Iron, for Tuesday.
5. Âzar-Gûn ("Angel-of-Fire-Like"), Princess of the Moors, clad in Blue, under the sign of Mercury, Lord of Quicksilver, for Wednesday.
6. Yaghmâ-Nâz ("Prey-Enchanting"), Princess of China, daughter to the Khâqân or Great Khân, clad in "Colour-of-Sandalwood", under the sign of Jupiter, Lord of Tin, for Thursday.
7. Dorsatî ("Perfect One"), Princess of Persia, of the blood royal, clad in White, under the sign of Venus, Lady of Copper, for Friday.

All these figures turned their painted gaze towards a portrait of Bahrâm himself, over whose image the Master of the work had engraved the Prince's own name, with this warning:

> Thus the Seven Stars decree:
> When the World-Seizer shows his face,
> Seven Kings' daughters from Seven Climes
> To his breast as orphan pearls shall he press!

Once Bahrâm has been enthroned as master of the Empire and victor over the twin lions, the Dragon and the nomad Huns, then the six kings of the earth tender their submission and send him these their six daughters – all of whom he weds, adding the seventh, the Persian princess of the blood royal, to their number. Now the hour is set for the Shâh's seven-fold initiation.

A new Byzantine architect presents himself before Bahrâm: one Shêdeh, disciple to Semnâr and heir to his art. What Semnâr promised to raise, Shêdeh achieves. And far from imitating the now proverbial ingratitude of the Arabian King No'mân, the Persian ruler bestows gifts on the Greek artist. For the mere earthly marvel of Castle Khawarnaq has now been far surpassed by the heavenly marvel of Shâh Bahrâm's new castle. The Seven Brides are lodged therein, each under her own Dome, tiled according to the colour of her homeland as determined by the hue of her ascendant star. Again, because Shâh Bahrâm, unlike proud King No'mân, is seized with a moment of pious doubt – "all these are the dwellings of greed and of lust: but the dwelling of the Creator of all dwellings, where is that?" – he is suffered by God to enter the Seven Domes and there receive, while changing the colour of his own raiment each day, the initiation bestowed by his Seven Brides.

As Shâh Bahrâm moves from one Dome to the next in his week of initiation, in spiritual terms he rises through the Seven Heavenly Spheres, of which the Seven Brides are the wardens. The Seven Spheres, according to the ancient Mesopotamian, Persian, then Greek cosmological system inherited by medieval Islam (as by medieval Christendom), were believed to surround the earthly globe in the manner of Seven Walls or Ramparts wrought of transparent and subtle matter.

The Seven Domes reflect the celestial order, as the Byzantine architect-magician Shêdeh himself forcefully puts it to King Bahrâm in a single verse by pairing two strange images: "I shall raise the Seven Domes [*Haft Gombad*] like unto the Seven Ramparts [*Haft Hesâr*]." For the Seven Ramparts are those of the Seven Heavens: one of many clues whereby Persia's greatest narrative poet discloses, after 1500 years of tenacious astral symbolism, the key to the enigma of the Seven Walls of Ecbatana. But to these celestial images of Domes and Battlements, Nezâmî adds a third, and one that is deliberately threatening, for he also compares his Seven Skies to the Seven Folds of a Cosmic Dragon twisted around the world. The reference here is to a seven-necked monster who torments the unhappy protagonist of the tale of the Moorish Princess: "This sky that encircles us around like a sash – do you wonder that it be a Seven-Headed Dragon?" By cutting through the Seven Spheres in his symbolic journey, it is again, as it were, through a symbolic Dragon that Bahrâm victoriously hews his way. This triple stellar imagery so oddly associated in Nezâmî's poem – Seven Domes, Seven Walls and a Seven-Headed Cosmic Dragon – stems from mythological symbolism associated with one of the major schools of thought to arise in Late Antiquity in the Roman Levant: Gnosticism – which itself drew heavily on older, Near Eastern cosmological lore.

The Mesopotamian astronomers who first singled out the Seven Heavenly Bodies attributed divine status to them. Seen in ascending order from earth – as then perceived – these bodies received the names of those gods corresponding to the Moon, Mercury, Venus, the Sun, Mars, Jupiter and Saturn. The Sumerians were thus responsible for rendering the number Seven sacred and for organizing Time on the basis of the week, which became – through Jewish transmission – Church Latin's explicitly named *septimana.* Judaism's twin daughter religions perpetuated the Mesopotamian weekly calendar, only changing its titulary deities of the Seven Spheres into so many titular Archangels. Beyond the Seventh Sphere of Saturn, ancient cosmology further taught, lay the Eighth Sphere of the Fixed Stars, and beyond that still, the Ninth Sphere or Empyrean, distinguished from the first Seven because they were unmoving.

According to Late Classical Antiquity, the revolving of the Seven Spheres created both Time and Fate: "The Seven Rulers with their rings surround the sensible world: and their Rule is known as Fate." So goes the teaching of an influential Graeco-Egyptian treatise written in Alexandria around the beginning of our era: the *Divine Poimandres,* attributed by its writer to the god Hermes Trismegistus, then believed to correspond to Egyptian Thoth. The Seven Spheres were held to influence all the activities of the sublunary world, the only one thought to be subject to the cycle of birth, growth, corruption, death, dissolution and perhaps rebirth. But this seven-tiered astral hierarchy then came to be invested with more threatening symbolism by the thinkers of the Gnostic school.

Gnosticism (from Greek *gnôsis,* "knowledge") was a religious trend spawned by the deep-lying intellectual pessimism affecting philosophical schools in the great urban centres of the dying Roman Empire. Gnosticism developed at the same time as orthodox Christianity, and in bitter opposition to it. In Sasanian Mesopotamia, where numerous religious influences converged – Zoroastrian, Judaic, Christian and even Buddhist from Iran's easternmost provinces – an analogous school of thought sprang up around the teachings of the prophet Mânî, "Manes" to the Greeks and Latins, in about AD 242. Manichaean Gnosticism spread in turn through the Roman Empire. Young Saint Augustine was briefly converted to it. In the Near East, Gnosis – or 'irfân in Arabic – lingered well into Islamic times, and its various teachings deeply influenced all medieval Islamic thought, although sometimes in subtle ways undetected by ordinary Muslims. Early official Islam reacted harshly to avowed Gnosticism. The 'Abbâsid caliphs, in bouts, persecuted Iraq's Manichaeans – called zindîq-s – as cruelly as the Church later set out to exterminate those Western Manichaeans, the "Cathars", who survived in southern France down to the 13th century. But Gnostic notions secured a permanent place in higher Islamic philosophy through the teachings of Sufism.

Both Manichaeism and the Greek-speaking Gnostic schools had preached an absolute dualism: they believed the God portrayed in the Old Testament to have been an evil Demiurge, creator and master of this lower world that was wrought of sheer corruption at its worst and wrapped in mere illusory beauty at its best. The Good but Unknown God, He who was spoken of in the New Testament, ruled beyond the Seven Spheres, in a world of pure Light where corruption touched Him not. As the realm of evil, this lower world suffocated under the Seven-Sphered Sky as beneath the prison-lid of a seven-tiered Leaden Dome; one, however, pricked through and through with needle-points of Light – the higher stars – as by so many stellar holes allowing us to glimpse the Luminous World of Good beyond. As instruments of the God of Evil, the spirit-wardens of the Seven Spheres – Greek-language Gnosis also considered them evil and called them the Archons – locked fast these Spheres, like Seven Gates to Seven Ramparts, over the prison-house of this lower world. The human soul, as a fragment of the Divine Light fallen into the darkness of Matter, wished to escape the grip of the God of Evil and return to its Luminous Principle through the release of death or, in this very life, by visionary ecstasy. Thereby the soul might ascend from Sphere to Sphere and finally break beyond their bonds to reach in freedom the Luminous Skies of the Fixed Stars and of the Empyrean.

The central myth of Late Antique Gnosis found expression in the Hymn of the Pearl, which survives in Greek and Syriac versions. The Hymn describes the fall of the soul, followed by its skyward return whereby the human spirit breaks through the chains of Fate. Gnostic rituals spelt out the prayers and magic formulae by which the soul, in the course of its ascent, and fortified by "knowledge", might catch the Archons off guard and overcome the seven-tiered astral obstacle barring the visionary's way. The Hymn of the Pearl further gathers in Gnosticism's entire Near Eastern religious and mythological heritage by portraying the fall and rise of the soul as a struggle waged between the forces of Light and Darkness, and as the luminous soul's own combat against the Cosmic Dragon. As Henry Corbin has stressed, the Hymn points to the underlying pattern of later, medieval Islamic tales of initiation, notably those by Avicenna which set the model for others in his civilization. Indeed, the Hymn's images and plot yield essential keys to understanding all medieval higher narrative Islamic literature – and above all, the works of Nezâmî.

The Hymn, as studied in depth by Hans Jonas and Charles-Henri Puech, recounts the story of a Parthian Prince sent by his royal parents to recover, beyond the shore of Egypt (the lower world), a precious pearl (the soul) swallowed up by a dragon in the all-encompassing sea (darkness). Travelling by stages, the Prince quits his royal garb and in Egypt disguises himself under a native cloak which allays local suspicion. Unfortunately, by dint of conforming to outward Egyptian customs, he forgets his own Eastern (solar) origin and the purpose of his mission. A message from his sire (the God of Light) reminds him of his task. The Prince reduces the dragon to sleep, recovers the pearl, doffs his Egyptian cloak and returns by ascending stages to the East, where he is welcomed back to his parents' court now clad in his original princely Cloak of Light: "As I now beheld the robe, it seemed to me suddenly to become a mirror-image of myself: myself entire I saw in it, and it entire I saw in myself, that we were two in separateness, and yet one again in sameness of our forms." (H. Jonas tr.)

Further elaboration on this Gnostic theme of the Robe of Light in later, medieval Islamic Persia sought to link its symbolism to that of the Seven Colours. Indeed, this is the key to Nezâmî's image of the seven caftans successively worn by Bahrâm. According to the Sufi perception of Gnostic teachings, the soul, on its return ascent to its divine principle, passes through Seven Stages: it is in turn "carnal", "self-critical", "inspired", "pacified", "God-satisfied", "God-satisfying" and finally "perfect". These stages correspond to Seven Colours, that is, to Seven spiritual levels (also represented by the Seven Prophets), so that the soul becomes successively tinted by the Seven Colours, each hue being invested with its own particular set of mystical associations, as if the soul were successively clad in Seven Robes, ending in a final Robe of Light corresponding to one's utterly purified, heavenly self. The order of, and precise allegorical value attributed to, the Seven Colours of the soul's transformation may vary, however, from one Sufi author to another.

Nezâmî's ascending scale of colours differs, for example, from the chromatic scheme devised by the 14th-century Persian divine, Semnânî. Where Semnânî sets the highest colour as Green, Nezâmî substitutes White; Bahrâm's soul thus passes from the Black of mourning, through the Yellow, Green, Red, Blue and Sandalwood-coloured intermediate spiritual stages listed above, to the undifferentiated White of union with the divine principle.

In Manichaean Gnosticism, which absorbed here a Persian mythological theme, the vision of the Robe of Light, as emblem of the purified Self, was further coupled with a second image, that of the Celestial Bride. Such a Bride was also held to be emblematic of the soul freed from gross terrestrial matter – hence the notion of a spiritual wedding of the two facets of the soul as it were reconciled within itself. According to the traditional Persian eschatology adopted by Manichaeism, the soul after death wended its way towards the Other World across a bridge as sharp as the edge of a sword to meet its spiritual Double. A damned soul met with the Demonic figure that reflected its own true face, and fell into the abyss; a hallowed soul crossed the bridge to be united with its Bride of Light. Medieval Islam took over this imagery fully: the sword-bridge, the damned fall and the hallowed union of the soul with its "houris" or heavenly Brides.

Before the rise of Islam, Judaism itself – although it had come under direct attack by the Gnostics who branded the Old Testament God an evil Demiurge – struggled to incorporate the Gnostics' eschatological drama for the purposes of its own monotheistic vision. According to the Hebraized version of Gnosticism known as "Throne Mysticism", the ascending soul, armed with a magic seal graven with incantations, passes through the awesome curtains of water and fire drawn by the "Wardens of the Seven Gates", the Angel-Archons of the planets. On reaching the very threshold of the Throne, the victorious soul apprehends a Divinity, always veiled, however, by the fiery curtain of Its own Majesty.

The genius of medieval Islamic speculation lay in its intellectual feat of harmonizing such contradictory trends in its antique heritage – Judaic, Persian, Neo-Platonic and Gnostic – within a unified vision of a universe at once single and multiple – hence the challenge of traditional Islamic philosophy (which modern "Islamism" of course simply ignores). The contradictions of the universe are only apparent. The many facets of Reality mirror a single Reality: God's twin aspects of Grace and

Wrath weld into One the two contending divinities of Gnosis. The multiplicity of His facets throws the soul off course, for their opposition may be resolved only within the Godhead. For those obtuse souls incapable of perceiving the Seven Spheres as so many mirrors of the One, then these same Seven Spheres immediately turn into so many malignant Gnostic "revetments of ambiguity" (*eltebâs*) or opaque Curtains – the Seven Ramparts which defend or shut off the Higher Heavens, or the Seven Folds of the Cosmic Dragon – while their celestial wardens at once shift their appearance from that of Seven Archangels of Beauty to that of Seven Archons of Fear – Islam calls them the *Zobâniyeh* – who bar access to the Throne.

For once converted, the various Near Eastern peoples by no means renounced the powerful Gnostic myth of the soul's Heavenly Ascent, but instead attributed the visionary opening of its celestial path to the Prophet of Islam himself. The Islamization of the "Ascent", or *Mi'râj* in Arabic, whose imagery we know to have indirectly influenced Dante through medieval Spanish-Latin channels, drew its justification from a brief, enigmatic Koranic allusion (17:1): "Glory unto Him who took His servant by night from the Holy Mosque to the Farthest Mosque whose surroundings We blessed so as to show him Our signs!" Rich folklore with many variants going back to ancient Near Eastern motifs developed around this Scriptural kernel. The Archangel Gabriel was said to have appeared before the Prophet Mohammad asleep in Mecca, "the Holy Mosque". Escorted by Angels, the Prophet mounted a wonderful winged mare with the head of a beautiful young woman, *Al-Burâq* (a transfiguration of Assyrian sphinxes; pronounced in Persian, *Borâq*). Guided by the Archangel, the Prophet thus mounted flew over Jerusalem, "the Farthest Mosque". Here he met with his predecessors, the Prophets of the past. Then began his Ascent through the Seven Spheres, each wrought of subtle matter in successive ramparts of iron, copper, silver, gold, pearl, emerald and ruby. First appeared Archons under the distracting guise of handsome youths and maidens to waylay the Prophet from his mission, then sad Angels with eyes like glowing coals who ruled over Death and guarded Hell. Then came the Archangels of glory. At each celestial stage, under each of the seven astral Pavilions, the Prophet held discourse with the souls that dwelt there. Before the ultimate stage rose the Cosmic Tree, "The Lote-Tree of the End", *Sidrat al-Muntahâ* (Koran 53:14), whose shoots branched forth throughout the entire universe and even as far as the reverse mirror of Hell where they formed in turn a bitter tree, Zaqqûm, loaded with demon-headed fruits (37:61–66). The Throne remained veiled by 70,000 curtains of fire, but Prophetic vision passed through these to within "two bow-shots or nigher still" (53:9). After Initiation came full Knowledge for the mounted visionary guided by the Archangel through all the mansions of Heaven and Hell until his return below. Yet the entire otherworldly journey lasted only the space of a thought, a blink, the lapse of time it took for an upset jug to spill its liquid on the ground.

Nezâmî places his *Brides of the Seven Climes,* and indeed all his poetic works, under the explicit invocation of the *Mi'râj.* Each of his "Five Treasures" is prefaced with verses to the glory of the Prophet's Ascent, and these rank among the most beautiful Gnostic hymns in all Islamic literature. Despite traditional iconoclasm, Nezâmî's Ascent-Hymns were also abundantly illustrated in royal libraries, with this usual precaution: the Prophet's countenance was depicted veiled, for its refulgence or *tajallî* might otherwise prove beyond bearing for human eyes.

As an overture to *The Brides of the Seven Climes,* the Prophet's celestial ride from Star to Star, and Colour to Colour, prefigures Shâh Bahrâm's own initiation in the course of the work, with Nezâmî's wonderful allusion to the silvering hand of the tilemaster who transforms lead-powder in his kiln to heavenly blue with which to sheathe the Dome of Mercury. The poet makes a no less surprising reference, undoubtedly drawn from some Arabic translation of a Greek astronomical work, to the cephalgia of Jupiter whence Minerva was born – and which Nezâmî cures through application of Sandalwood, as in his Thursday tale:

When Mohammad through the dance of the Borâq's hooves
Wrote upon the pages of the Book:
The Gate of the Way of the World he opened,
And all distance from the cycle of the World removed!
He cut through the heavenly stages
By royal wing, an angel's royal way

To the Moon! through the orbit of its sword-belt
He granted Verdant radiance through his own bounty;

And unto Mercury by his silvering hand,
The Colour (Blue) he sealed, from the lead-maker's kiln;

Over Venus from the splendour of his moonship
He drew a quick-Silver veil;

And cantering his way, Turk-raider of the spheres,
A Golden crown he placed upon the Sun;

Robed in the dusk-sky's Green like a caliph of Damascus
He cloaked Bahrâm-Mars altogether in Red;

To Jupiter split from crown to base
The brainpan ached, he saw: with Sandalwood anointed it;

When he rode over Saturn's crown, it kissed his foot,
In the Blackness of its ambergris he planted his banner;
Thus he rode like the dawn-wind that carries off the night
Upon a mount like a demon, harnessed in chains! ...

When he reached to the pillar of the most High Throne
A rope-ladder he cast with the noose of his love
To raise his head from above the Throne of Light
Unto the Siege Perilous of the Secret of "Glory-be-to-Me"!

His ecstasy courted the peril,
Mercy came, took his bridle
Within Two Bow-shots of Him
Nigh; and unto Him went nigher.
As he tore through the Veil of a Thousand Lights
His eye reached unto the Unveiled Light.

Shâh Bahrâm, as the model king to whom the poem's message is addressed, follows in turn Mohammad's Astral Ascent, insofar as it behoved every medieval believer to internalize the Prophet's *Mi'râj* as the path of individual initiation for each soul. Thus the King weds Seven Brides in succession as he moves through the Seven Astral Domes. Who, truly, are his Brides? The final key to this riddle lies

mainly in the Arabic-language tales of initiation by the philosopher Ibn Sînâ of Bokhârâ (980–1037), the "Avicenna" of the medieval Latin translations by the 12th-century Toledo schoolmen. In his tale of *Hayy ibn Yaqzân,* "The Living One, son of He Who Keeps Watch", Avicenna had harmonized his Aristotelian- and Neo-Platonic-derived physics and metaphysics with a Gnostic-type narrative whose outcome was a *Mi'râj.* A fallen soul, cast into the West of Material Darkness, returns to the Luminous East in the course of an Astral Ascent, led from Sphere to Sphere by the guiding figure of its own Archangelic Intelligence.

According to Avicenna's own reading of the Neo-Platonized Ptolemaic astral system common to all medieval culture – this same system is central to Dante and lingers down to Donne – the Divine One becomes Multiple by intellection of His own prodigious Self-contemplation. The fit of vertigo produced by such meditation spawns a procession of Ten Intelligences, whence emanate the Ten Spheres: the Empyrean, the Fixed Stars, the Seven Revolving Bodies, and the Sub-Lunary World. Down to the Sphere of the Moon, each Planet constitutes a Soul, which revolves in endless loving desire around its own Intellectual principle. And from such a desire is spawned a Sphere.

The intellection of the hierarchy's last and Tenth emanated Intelligence, however, that which presides over our own lower world, spawns no longer a single Soul and Sphere but a multitude of souls: ours. And these our souls are likewise impelled by desire to move towards our own intellectual principle, which is just this Tenth Intelligence, termed the "Active Intelligence". It is this Tenth, "Active" Intelligence that thinks the forms of our world into existence, brings them forth out of Matter, sheds light upon our souls and grants us our capacity for abstract reasoning. Union of our souls to our own Active Intelligence is perceived as a reception of mental light and constitutes a mystical experience.

In terms of Scripture, the Ten Intelligences manifest themselves in the form of Archangels. The Tenth Intelligence corresponds to Gabriel, the Holy

Spirit that led the Prophet through his Ascent. But an Archangelic Intelligence, in the privileged guiding relation which it enjoys with each individual soul, may also take upon itself the individualized feminized aspect of a Celestial Bride to which our soul is then wedded. Through the course of the Ascent, a soul may be further illuminated by each successive Intelligence in the seven- or ten-tiered hierarchy and so become wedded to each.

In Nezâmî's multi-layered symbolism, Shâh Bahrâm's Seven Brides, who initiate him to wisdom beneath their successive Seven Astral Domes, undoubtedly correspond to the Seven Archangelic Intelligences of the Spheres, whom he weds as his Celestial Brides. They are no less depicted as voluptuous, loving and very earthly Princesses for all that. Later interpretations of Nezâmî's poem tended to simplify and reduce his amazingly complex symbolism to the celestial plane alone. A late 16th-century Moghol illustration to the Indo-Persian adaptation of Nezâmî's work made by the poet Amîr Khosrô of Delhi (1265–1325) thus gives the symbolism away at a stroke, as it were, by outright depiction of the Seven Princesses as Winged Archangels. But in Nezâmî's poem, each of the Seven Brides, in her own good time, lifts only a small corner of her Neo-Platonic veil in the gradual procession of the tales. Nezâmî moreover shifts their Archangelic astral hierarchy – traditionally, from below to above, in the order of Moon, Mercury, Venus, Sun, Mars, Jupiter and Saturn – to follow the rhythm of the days of the week. We have further modified Nezâmî's own order in this book by setting each Princess within her respective homeland. Suggested interpretations to the tales follow in the original sequence in which they appeared in Nezâmî's own book.

THE INDIAN PRINCESS BENEATH THE BLACK DOME
Saturday, day of Saturn
As the Seventh Star revolving upon the farthest limit of the Lower Sky, this was the planet traditionally associated with melancholy – and Lead. The 2nd-century AD Graeco-Egyptian *Tetrabiblos* of Ptolemy of Alexandria assigned to Saturn, in conjunction with Capricorn, sovereignty over India, Gedrosia (present southwest Pakistan) and Ariana (the land of Herât). According to the Astral Ascent described in Avicenna's *Hayy ibn Yaqzân* (I use here Henry Corbin's 1954 Tehran edition of the Arabic text with its medieval Persian glosses), Saturn might assume an ambiguous aspect, pivoting between evil and good, since its Sphere also constituted the threshold to the Higher Sky: "A kingdom wherein dwells a people with thoughts abstruse, and inclined to evil; but should they tend towards good, then they do so most assuredly to the utmost."

The symbolism of Nezâmî's "Indian" tale is erotic on the surface – and Gnostic beneath. Souls imprisoned in the darkness of this world wear nostalgic mourning for those higher spiritual realities – figured as Heavenly Brides – for which they yearn but which are only vouchsafed to them in this life in glimpses through dreams. Paradise is offered only after death. Mankind's painful lot until then must be one of rigid self-control. Saturn's Warden, or "Archon", only consents intermittent access through her threshold with malicious ambiguity – and the soul, when hurled back, falls into blackest melancholia.

A key to the tale is yielded by Nezâmî's curious allusion to the Moorish city of "Kairouan" (*Qayrawân*). A holy city to Tunisians, to medieval Eastern Muslims Kairouan's name rather evoked the distant, little-known West. To East Arab and Persianate ears, indeed, *Qayrawân* in various literary works was made to sound like a sinister pun on the word for "pitch" (*qîr*), the colour of Hell. "By *Qayrawân*", we are informed in a traditional 17th-century Indo-Persian lexicon, "is understood the utmost limit of the earth." In the Arabic-language mystical and philosophical parable known as "The Tale of the Western Exile", by the late 12th-century divine Sohrawardî of Marâgheh in Iranian Azerbaijan (hence by a fellow countryman and younger contemporary of Nezâmî), *Qayrawân* is made to stand for the City of Darkness. It signifies this lower, dusk-like "Western" World of Matter, wherein the imprisoned soul has been suffered to fall from its far-off "Eastern" homeland of Light. Earthly escape from such a "Kairouan" is possible only through the visions afforded by dreams. Hence Sohrawardî's city has no real geographical location, but lies anywhere: it is the earthly prison of the Gnostic.

While resorting to a motif extant in Far Eastern fables (failure to curb one's lust results in loss of immortality), Nezâmî's narrative also shows interesting resemblance to three stories found in the Arabic-language *Thousand and One Nights:* The Tale of the Third Calandar Prince (fallen from Faerie-Land); The Second Voyage of Sindbâd the Sailor (borne by the Bird Rokh); and the Tale of Is'hâq of Mossoul (likewise hoisted in a basket to the Princesses of Faerie-Land).

THE BYZANTINE PRINCESS beneath the YELLOW DOME
Sunday, day of the Sun

This, the fourth astral sphere, was associated with Gold. Avicenna, in his description of the Gnostic Ascent, warns not to pass too close to the Sun, whose qualities are "of great benefit to those who hold their distance", but "whose immediate neighbourhood is disastrous". Ptolemy assigned to the Sun, in the sign of Leo, Italy itself as the seat of Rome. *Rûm* signifies for Nezâmî, however, the land of the Eastern Romans or Byzantines. These pertain to Yellow, in the poet's eyes, for two reasons: on account of their imperial splendour, hence solar gold; and because, according to the conventional perception of classical Arabic poetry, Greeks were held to be tinged with a sickly, yellowish pallor as the supposed descendants of one *Al-Asfar,* "the Livid".

The tale that Nezâmî attributes to the daughter of the Emperor of Constantinople is a complex inlay-work of narrative motifs ultimately stemming from Hindu and rabbinical lore as well as from the Greeks. The story deals with love between spouses and stresses the loyalty and honesty that they owe one another. The outstanding character in the tale is, however, that of the sly old Crone who acts as go-between among lovers, always intriguing to inveigle foolish young women into vice and entice brainless young men to their perdition. For Persian writers of Nezâmî's day, this stock figure of the Crone was held to typify the evil temptations of the illusory Lower World. Her ultimate literary prototype goes back to classical Hindu narrative: she is the redoubtable Pûrnâ of the Sanskrit *Tales of the Parrot.* Through Islamized versions of the Sanskrit, the character passed into medieval European folklore by means of the usual adaptations from the Arabic by Spanish Jews. In Castilian she thus appears under various names: Trotaconventos ("Trot-'twixt-Convents") in the Archpriest of Hita's classic 14th-century *Libro de Buen Amor,* or as the Jewish *converso* Fernando de Rojas's immortal Celestina at the close of the 15th century, whence finally – through the Italian *novelle* – she re-emerges as Juliet's Nurse in Shakespeare.

THE CHORASMIAN PRINCESS beneath the GREEN DOME
Monday, day of the Moon

This is the sphere closest to Earth. The Moon, characterized by "slender body and rapid movements" according to Avicenna, was traditionally associated with Silver; but she is also a Green-tinted sign, both on account of her own hue and by virtue of her celestial setting at dusk: "The green field of the sky saw I – and therein the new moon's sickle," as classical Persian poetry came to express it in a famous line by the 14th-century writer Hâfez. Nezâmî sets under the sign of the Moon the people of Khwârazm, ancient Chorasmia, probably because they stand for the Central Asian Turks in his own eyes (the area corresponds to present-day Turkmenistan). The beauty of the East Turkish type was much admired in medieval Persianate lands where handsome Turkish faces were compared to "full moons". Bithynia, Phrygia, Colchis, Carthage and Numidia had been the lands assigned by Ptolemy to the Moon in the sign of Cancer.

The tale of the Chorasmian Princess is a transparent allegory, wherein Nezâmî draws a contrast between the virtuous piety of the believer content with good works and due worship of the

Creator and the rationalistic mania of the philosopher who thinks to pierce the secrets of the universe through syllogisms. Despite pitfalls along the way, virtuous simplicity attains its supreme object of yearning, the contemplation of Divine Beauty; while mere reason is led astray by a mirage and sinks to its doom.

In Nezâmî's harsh medieval Islamic view, the unfortunate philosopher Malîkhâ represents Judaism, and Bashr, the godfearing pilgrim, Christianity – since the poet clearly designates Bashr as a "Rûmî" or "Byzantine" at the beginning of his tale. According to orthodox Muslim teaching, Judaism is first superseded by Christianity and then finally by Islam in the sequence of increasingly perfect unfoldings of the Divine message. In the original sequence of the narratives, this tale of the Green Dome thus follows pointedly upon that of the Yellow. In his conclusion to this tale of the Green Dome, where he describes the wedding of Bashr to Malîkhâ's widow "of the Moon-like face", Nezâmî indulges in word-play on the association of Yellow with Judaism in medieval Islam (which imposed the wearing of a yellow turban and sash on Jewish minorities) with the added connotation that such a colour here yields its place to Green, the hue of Islam.

THE SLAV PRINCESS BENEATH THE RED DOME
Tuesday, day of Mars

Revolving in the fifth sphere and associated with Iron, the war-god's planet was assigned jurisdiction by Ptolemy over far northern Europe, Britannia and Germania – and over fog-bound Thrace by the Latin poet Statius. Well into medieval Islamic times, Avicenna remained aware of enough Hellenic mythology to refer to "the ruddy fellow keen on harm and killing and blows" – but who, for all that, was in love with Venus: "He is enthralled, as the story-tellers report, with the Queen whom we have mentioned before, and struck with infatuation."

The tale of the Red Princess, possibly with that of the Turquoise Princess, stands out as the masterpiece of the collection – if not, indeed, as one of the great fairy-tales of world literature.

The Red planet set within the heart of the Persian week (which begins on Saturday) is further associated, by Nezâmî, with the appellation of ancient Persian mythology's own war-god: Bahrâm. Now, Bahrâm is already the name of the romance's royal protagonist. Shâh Bahrâm thus appears doubly clothed in the attributes of the war-god: by bearing his name he assumes his prowess; and in Tuesday's Reddening dawn he dons the planet's appropriate Red-coloured caftan, to ride forth towards the Red Dome, "With Red on Red adorned".

Something more than homing poetic intuition may have caused Nezâmî further to attribute the war-god's hue to a Princess of Russia, whose language, as it happens, has always associated Red (*Krasnyi*) not only with blood, but also with beauty, splendour and majesty. No doubt because he dwelt in northern Azerbaijan, on the far northern edge of classical Islamic civilization, Nezâmî appears to have been the only medieval Persian poet truly to sense the immensity, and threat, of the Russian steppe stretching just beyond his cultural horizon. In his Alexander Romance, he further describes demon-like, barbaric hordes of Slavic raiders who harry the fringes of the civilized world, whence the Conqueror flings them back.

The image of an Iron Citadel, which the poet here imagines towering upon the Caucasian summits of the Russian frontier, is identified in his verse with the celebrated Brazen Hold of pre-Islamic Persian mythology. The *Avesta* attributed to the ruler of the demons of Darkness, Afrâsyâb, an underground castle wrought all of Brass in a mysterious northern land that Iranian tradition called *Tûrân*. According to the medieval version of the myth rendered in Ferdawsî's epic, the Persian hero Esfandyâr had delivered his captive sisters from this metal castle. But the Brazen Hold's escarpments go down much further, to the very bedrock of the most ancient known Near Eastern and Mediterranean literatures. Walls variously described as made of "copper", "iron" or "brass" initially corresponded, in Sumerian, Akkadian and Hebraic usage, to a metaphor expressive of extreme, indeed impenetrable hardness. But mythology transmuted such metaphorical walls into a designation for the impregnable ramparts of the Kingdom of the Other World. The imagery ranges from Hinduism – the demon Maya Vishvakarman's citadel is so wrought – to Greek and Roman lore: Hesiod's Tartarus is walled in brass and Virgil's Hades in adamant with towers of iron – whence Dante's description. Statius (indirectly followed by Chaucer in the *Knight's Tale* from reading Boccaccio's *Teseida*) specifically points to Mars as the warden of an iron-walled shrine in the Thracian North.

The metallic stronghold of Persian lore was not necessarily Satanic, however, but more ambiguously stood for the iron or brazen battlements of the Other World: blank hard walls beyond which mortal eyes could not see. In the 6th century AD, in Sasanian Persia, when the heroic usurper Bahrâm Chôbîn was overthrown and fled into exile, his followers refused to believe in his death but maintained that he dwelt in mystic occultation in the Brazen Hold – far off, somewhere in "China" or "Tûrân" – whence he would messianically return to save his people. In the 8th century AD, now under the caliphs, messianic Persian movements preached that the Brazen Hold was also secret home to the Mahdî – the Saviour to come in Islamic lore. The Brazen Hold moreover figures in the *Thousand and One Nights* – transported to distant Spain. Reflections of this Metal Castle, as refracted through Spanish-Arab lore, glimmer in European knightly romance from Chrétien de Troyes through the prose *Lancelot* down to Ariosto and Spenser.

While Nezâmî's Castle no longer rises in a vague Tûrân but in a specified Slavic North, it remains a symbol for the Other World. The unworthy who make so bold as to storm it forfeit their lives. The heroic prototype of Nezâmî's Prince is of course the ancient Persian hero Esfandyâr, who, in saving his sisters from the Hold, symbolized the deliverance of human souls. But Nezâmî's Lady of the Castle is a far more complex typification: She

ambiguously manifests the principles either of Life or of Death, according to the spiritual capacity of Her lovers.

The Lady's iron walls, Her trenchant talismans, and Her magic spells weave around Her a "revetment of ambiguity", or *eltebâs*. She lurks invisible within Her otherworldly Brazen Hold which mere mortals cannot breach. But She also chooses to manifest Herself to Her lovers, whom She irresistibly attracts, albeit to their doom, by displaying Her painted image – Her reflection – over a portal. The image arouses the longing of Her beholders, but also waylays them by confusing their sight: for behind Her multiple attributes depicted upon the image hides Her secret, single Essence. The Essence remains masked and unseen upon the highest, most isolated summit. The true path leading to the gate of Her citadel is the narrowest, precisely because it is the mystical median way. For the lover must behold his Divinity both in Her visible, earthly manifestation and in Her occult Essence. Only a supreme spiritual master, consulted by Nezâmî's princely hero in the course of the tale, guides him away from error.

For the lover to swerve too far on either side of the median path is to fall grievously: either into the sin of idolatry by not recognizing the One beneath the Many; or into a false monotheism which is actually a disguised dualism, by mistakenly isolating the Divinity from the Creation which mirrors Her, as if the two were ontologically distinct. The talismans that guard the Castle mercilessly cut down those who go astray. While the Divinity may show most gracious welcome, She is also cruel: to deserve union with Her, a lover must be willing to lay down his head, suffer martyrdom, wear a robe of Red and drown in blood.

Only then will the secret gate to Her castle be opened, the riddle of brief earthly life be solved and the symbol of the two equal pearls made manifest. Like the drop of water merged back into the sea from which it originates, and whose distinct existence is thereby ended, the soul at last "God-satisfying" and "pacified" so fully reflects the lustre of the Divine from which it emanates that duality no longer remains between Creator and Creature and is resolved in the One. The word "pearl" in both Arabic and Persian (*jawhar* or *gôhar*) also signifies a mystical Essence. The fusion between Lover and Beloved – now no longer distinguished – is a hierogamy, or holy wedding.

From the mystic summit to which Nezâmî carried this tale, narrative tradition surrounding the cruel Princess of the North sank back into mere folklore. A late Persian prose adaptation of Nezâmî's story, now lost, shifted the Lady's Brazen Hold once again to its more traditional Iranian mythological "location", Tûrân. Hence the name of the Lady in this version: *Tûrân-Dokht,* "Daughter of Tûrân".

However inferior as literature or in symbolic terms, this late Persian prose text was the version of the story first translated between 1710 and 1712 by the pioneering Orientalist, François Pétis de la Croix. "Tourandocte", princess of "China", thus made her European début strangely garbed in the coolly restrained classical French prose of the twilight age of Louis XIV. Carlo Gozzi, in Venice, in turn adapted the plot of *Turandotte* for the stage in 1761. Yet the sternness of the original Persian fable still managed to preserve something of its cutting edge even beneath Gozzi's make-believe rococo "Chinese" setting and despite the fact that minor characters – Pantalone, Brighella, Truffaldino, and the rest – were drawn from the stock figures of the *Commedia dell'Arte.* Gozzi's 18th-century Venetian fantasy was adapted again, in German, by Schiller in 1802; but it took Giacomo Puccini's opera in 1924 to restore to Princess Turandot, in Europe at least, a hint of Nezâmî's original seriousness and grandeur (even though the composer knew nothing of Nezâmî's own version). Puccini's fierce "Princess of Ice, Princess of Death" may be a musical incarnation of masculine fears of the *vagina dentata,* but certainly was not intended to manifest anything like the original Persian tale's awesome feminized Godhead, so dangerously Immanent and Transcendent at

once. Yet the Lady of the opera does at least resume her queenly status as an ambiguous symbol of Love – one dispensing both Death and Life.

THE MOORISH PRINCESS
BENEATH THE TURQUOISE DOME
Wednesday, day of Mercury

Mercury in the second sphere was associated with the quicksilver of alchemy, the "Hermetic" art. For Hellenistic tradition chose to identify the planet's namesake, Mercury or Hermes, with the Egyptian scribe-god, Thoth, lord of magic. The Islamized Archangelic Intelligence who holds wardenship over this sphere still perpetuates, in Avicenna's medieval treatise, all of Thoth-Hermes's scribal character: for those born under Mercury's sign "are fond of the scribal art, of star-gazing, of necromancy and of talismans". Ptolemy assigned to Mercury, in the sign of Gemini, regency over Lower Egypt and Cyrenaica: that is, the Western Desert. Nezâmî draws on such lore to weave the tale in his collection most closely patterned on the Gnostic archetype of the Hymn of the Pearl, as transmitted to him through such Arabic and Persian renditions as those by Avicenna himself and also, perhaps, by Nezâmî's own younger contemporary Sohrawardî (1155–91), whose *Tale of the Western Exile* and *Tale of the Crimson Archangelic Intelligence* offer perhaps the most striking analogies.

There is no mystery to the meaning of the colour Blue which dominates this tale: it is the hue of mourning. Sufis often donned a blue mantle as a sign of mourning for their souls fallen from the World of Light.

The Gnostic drama of the "Pearl" unfolds in the story of Mâhân who has fallen, like a lost soul, into the "Egypt" of this illusory Lower World. The plot and imagery of Mâhân's wanderings through the Western Desert, the land of darkness and demons, closely parallel those of Avicenna and Sohrawardî, which were written to illustrate the teachings of their own school of *Ishrâq*: the mysticism of the so-called "Orient of Light". According to Avicenna's and Sohrawardî's Gnostic-type tales, the soul plunges from its Divine Principle, compared to an "Eastern Dawn", into the desert sands of Matter in the Lower World, assimilated to a "Western Dusk". The sorely tried soul must travel forth to the very edge of the Western Desert, typified by the shore of the Atlantic or "Ocean of Darkness", which symbolizes the dissolution of all earthly forms in death. Only on this distant shore will the pilgrim be permitted, if worthy, to drink of the Fount of Eternal Life and so return to his Heavenly "Eastern" origin.

By dwelling on this Fount at the end of his tale, Nezâmî alludes to a narrative theme that medieval Islam associated with the mythified adventures of Alexander the Great. The Alexander figure was rendered sacred in Muslim eyes by the mention in sûra 18 of the Koran – and Nezâmî further dealt with the mythic Conqueror in his own monumental Alexander Romance. According to medieval Islamic lore, *Eskandar,* or "Alexander", when lost in the Desert of Darkness, failed to discover the Fount of Life, which was instead found by his two mysterious prophetic companions, Elijah (*Eliyâs*) and "The Evergreen One" (Arabic *Al-Khadir,* in Persian *Khezr*). These two saints by God-ordained chance dropped two dried fish from their provisions-basket into this Fount, and when they saw them resuscitated, bathed in it in turn and so gained Eternal Life. But Alexander, conqueror only over this Lower World, was left to weep over his own inevitable death.

This episode from the medieval Islamic Alexander Romance ultimately stems from the Akkadian and Sumerian Epic of Gilgamesh – which Near Eastern civilization never forgot, although it eventually transferred the name and deeds of its protagonist to the figure of Alexander. After a fruitless search through the Darkness, Gilgamesh was also forced to renounce finding the Fount – despite his matchless human strength – and be resigned to his mortal lot. The Fount and its gift of Immortality were vouchsafed only to another hero, Utnapishtim, the prototype of the medieval Islamic "Khezr". This Mesopotamian lore was blended in Hellenistic times with another adventure which also rapidly assumed legendary status: Alexander's search for the oasis of the god Ammon in Egypt's Western Desert.

In Islamized Gnosticism, however, the contrasted names of "Alexander" and "Khezr" came to typify twinned successive stages of the mystic quest within a single soul. Every soul is an "Alexander" when it must subjugate its own lower passions while exploring all the knowledge this world has to offer. But the soul's "Alexander" must die so that it may turn into a "Khezr", and so save itself by drinking of the Fount of Life. This is the meaning of the close of Nezâmî's tale: Mâhân reaches the edge of the Western Desert, drinks and sees not only the Prophet Khezr to guide him by the hand, but his own transfigured earthly shape in the form of this "Khezr". So Sohrawardî concludes his own initiatory *Tale of the Crimson Archangelic Intelligence:* "If you are Khezr, you too may pass."

However Gnostic and mystical Nezâmî's higher purpose, the poet also enjoyed casting his poor protagonist among delightfully depicted grotesque monsters, symbols of the lower passions demonized, over whom the Devil himself rules as master of the garden of illusions of this Lower World.

THE CHINESE PRINCESS
BENEATH THE SANDALWOOD-COLOURED DOME
Thursday, day of Jupiter

The sixth sphere is associated with Tin. Ptolemy had assigned rule over Arabia Felix to Jupiter in the sign of Sagittarius. Nezâmî, however, transfers the planet's domain to China – perhaps in memory of the "saying" ascribed to the Prophet: "Seek you wisdom, even in China." Alert to the planet's traditional association with wisdom, Avicenna attributes to its guardian Archangel a wise, majestic character which ought not to have displeased the ancient monarch of the gods: "temperance, justice, sagacity, piety"; those who come under Jupiter's sway "seek to provide all manner of good to all sectors of the world".

By placing his tale under the colour of the medicinal sandalwood tree, believed to have originated in China, Nezâmî meditates upon the symbolism of the Tree of Life. As envisioned in the *Shajarat al-Kawn* (The Tree of Being), Islam's central treatise on the subject by Nezâmî's younger contemporary, the Spanish mystic Ibn 'Arabî (who fled his homeland to teach in Anatolia and Syria at the turn of the 13th century), the Cosmos could be depicted as an immense tree figuring the manifestation of the Divinity throughout the entire Universe, while enfolding a hidden but unifying Divine Sap which flowed through all things. Each leaf bears a written Name, signifying one or another aspect of the Universe. One's spiritual capacity determines what Name, or Names, one may read thereon. In fact, the Names one reads are precisely those one bears oneself, those that serve to designate and typify oneself. Only the Perfect, Prototypical Men – the line of Prophets and their saintly successors – may read all Names and so apprehend the reality of the entire Tree with its twin aspects of Grace and Wrath. Lesser men, good but limited in wisdom, may read only those leaves written with the Names of Good and remain blind to the Names of Evil. Evil men, conversely, read only those leaves stamped with their own Names of Wrath and Damnation and are even more blind to the rest. The Devil's very name in Islamic languages, *Iblîs* or *Eblîs* (actually an Arabization of the Greek *diabolos*), was believed to derive from *eltebâs*, the "revetment of ambiguity" which prevented him from discerning the entire Tree. He and his followers are usually described as blind in one eye, or otherwise suffering from optical deficiency, in Islamic symbolism.

The two protagonists of Nezâmî's tale are also defined by their very names, Khayr (Good) and Sharr (Evil). Moreover, the poet puns on the various Arabic and Persian words – *'ayn* and *jawhar* – which may mean, according to context, "eye", "essence" or "gem". Though Khayr the "Good" is innocent, yet he is made to suffer because he remains blind to Sharr the "Evil".

Khayr the Good can only have his two "eyes" –

and "gems" – restored by the leaves of the Tree of Life through the ministrations of the Kurdish chief and his daughter. Indeed, the Kurdish chief remains an indispensable helpmate to Khayr the Good, who, without him, cannot see the whole Tree with its "evil" side because he is constrained by his own defining Name. Even when king, Khayr still cannot see the Evil in Sharr, and the Kurdish chief, as executor of God's Wrath, must be the one to slay him. But the Kurd's daughter is one of Nezâmî's exemplary feminine figures, an initiator to Grace – which alone may restore sight.

In the *Thousand and One Nights,* the tale of the good Abû-Sîr and the evil Abû-Qîr shows the closest analogy to Nezâmî's story.

THE PERSIAN PRINCESS BENEATH THE WHITE DOME
Friday, day of Venus

Venus lies in the third sphere; she is associated with Copper; Ptolemy's own authority assigned her regency over Persia, in the sign of Taurus. Avicenna does not forget that she was the goddess of Love. Those who dwell in her kingdom "are of strikingly handsome countenance, They are inclined to good fellowship, keen on music and merry-making, free of care, excellent instrumentalists in many modes. A Lady rules over them as Queen. They follow after things comely and good. And if evil is mentioned to them, they turn away with a shudder."

For the last of his seven tales, Nezâmî merrily passes, Chaucer-like, from the sublime to the burlesque and back again. In this book addressed not to dervishes but to a king, carnal sensuality lies in the order of things, so long as properly indulged with due respect for Holy Law and sanctioned wedlock. It behoves the temporal ruler, lord of all below, and free to enjoy whatever he finds in his garden-kingdom, to curb his own lust, and obey higher Law : the final stage for a ruler now fully initiated into all a king should know of the matters of this world.

He may now move on to realities higher still, while the seven-tiered skies open before him in the last and purest radiance of all: White.

The Initiate of the Seven Tales has become an accomplished ruler. On reaching the age of sixty ("a cypress turned jasmine"), he prepares to pass into the Other World. For the last time, he rides forth into the desert for the chase. His sobriquet of Bahrâm-Gûr, "Bahrâm of the Onager", now reveals its grim pun: *gûr* in Persian also means "tomb". The hero-archetype of terrestrial rule is fated to meet with his last onager. This onager appears and lures the Shâh behind him at a gallop into a dark cave – into the depths of which the ruler plunges, never to reappear before human eyes again. The Queen Mother orders her guards to search the cave – to no avail: the chasm preserves its secret. Just as God would do for the Prophet Mohammad by veiling him in a cave beneath the spider's web (along with his select companion Abû-Bakr), so does He now call back Shâh Bahrâm to Himself as still another Companion of the Cave, as the voice of an Angel makes known to the Queen Mother:

> Unto the Shâh the Grotto spun its curtain-web
> And hugged him to the bosom of the Grotto's Friend.

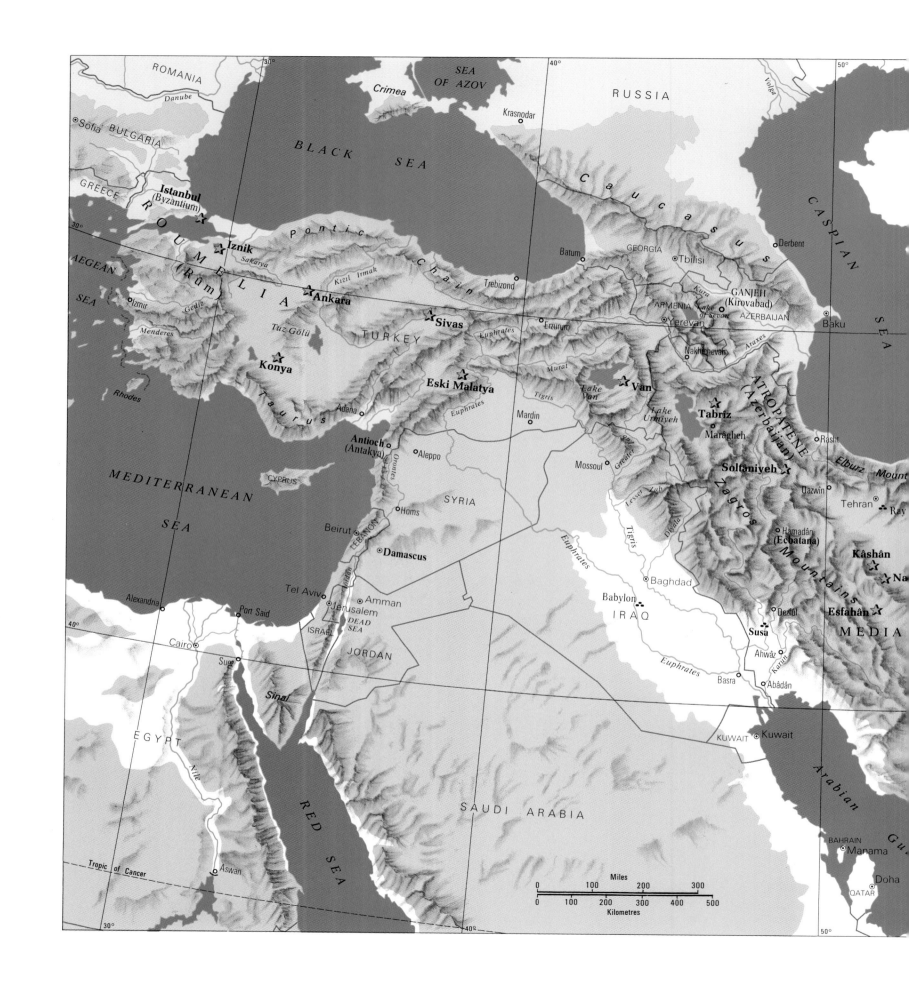

ROMANIA

Danube

Sofia BULGARIA

GREECE

Istanbul
(Byzàntium)

R O U M E L I A
(Rûm)

AEGEAN
SEA

Izmir

Menderes

Gediz

Rhodes

Crimea

SEA
OF AZOV

B L A C K   S E A

Krasnodar

RUSSIA

Volga

☆ **Iznik**

Sakarya

Kızıl Irmak

P o n t i c

☆ **Ankara**

Tuz Gölü

☆ **Sivas**

☆ **Konya**

T U R K E Y

Trebizond

C h a i n

CAUCASUS

Batum

GEORGIA

Tbilisi

Derbent

CASPIAN

Kura

ARMENIA Lake
of Sevan

GANJEH
(Kirovabad)

AZERBAIJAN

Yerevan

Nakhichevan

Araxes

Baku

SEA

☆ **Eski Malatya**

Taurus

Adana

Euphrates

Euphrates

Murat

Tigris

Lake
Van

☆ **Van**

Lake
Urmiyeh

☆ **Tabriz**

Marágheh

ATROPATENE
(Azerbaijan)

Rasht

Elburz Mount

MEDITERRANEAN

SEA

CYPRUS

Antioch
(Antakya)

Aleppo

Homs

Beirut

LEBANON

Orontes

Mardin

SYRIA

Mossoul

Greater Zab

Lesser Zab

Soltâniyeh ☆

Z a g r o s

Qazwin

Tehran

Ray

Kâshân
☆

M
o
u
n
t
a
i
n
s

Na

MEDIA

Alexandria

Port Said

Cairo

Suez

Damascus

Tel Aviv

ISRAEL

Jerusalem

DEAD
SEA

Amman

JORDAN

Jordan

Euphrates

Tigris

Baghdad

Babylon ▪▪

I R A Q

Diyala

Hamadân
(Ecbatana)

Dezfûl

Susa ☆

Esfahân ☆

Ahwâz

Karun

Basra

Abâdân

E G Y P T

Nile

Sinai

RED

SEA

J O R D A N

S A U D I   A R A B I A

KUWAIT

Kuwait

Arabian
Gu

Tropic of Cancer

Aswan

Miles
0   100   200   300
0   100   200   300   400   500
Kilometres

BAHRAIN
Manama

QATAR

Doha

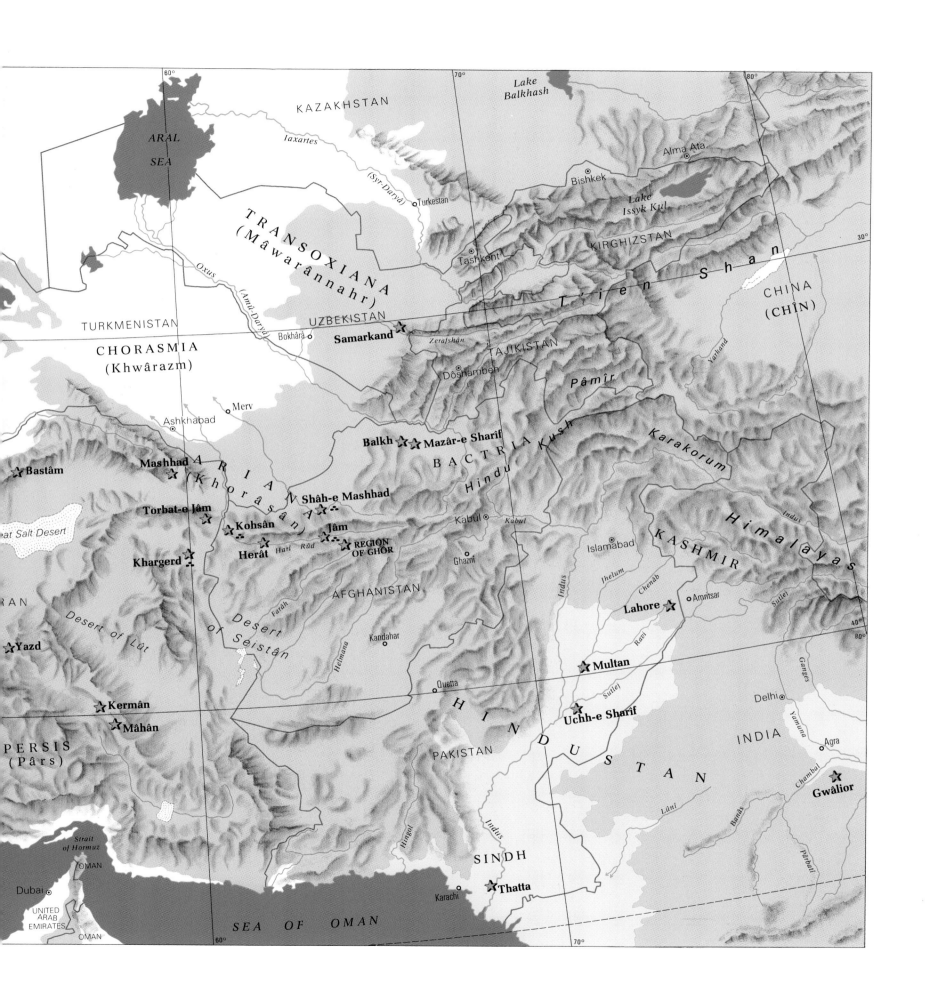

Descriptive Index of the Monuments Illustrated

Central Asia

AFGHANISTAN

BALKH. Balkh, the ancient *Baktra* or Bactria as it was known to the Greeks, 18 km (11 miles) to the west of Mazâr-e Sharîf, is one of the oldest cities in the world. Zoroaster preached within its walls. Alexander conquered it in 329 BC and married its princess, Roxana (*Rôshanag*). After the Conqueror's death, the city remained the *mêtropolis* of the Greek kings of Bactria for nearly two centuries. The Graeco-Bactrian kings ultimately converted to Buddhism: pilgrims came from as far afield as China to admire the Bactrian kingdom's famous statues of the Buddha. When the Arabs became overlords of "Balkh" in the 8th century AD, they also translated into their own language its old Greek title of *mêtropolis* (mother of cities). One of medieval Islam's greatest Persian-language mystic poets, Jalâloddîn Rûmî, was born here in 1207. Destroyed by the Mongols in 1220, Balkh still lay in ruins when it was seen by Marco Polo in 1275 and by the Moroccan traveller Ibn Battûta in 1333. It has remained only a small country town ever since.

Mosque of Khwâjeh Mohammad Pârsâ, 1460.
p. 69: This shrine, also known as the Green Mosque, was built in Tîmûrid times to commemorate a local Sufi saint. Although it has suffered from weather (and pigeons), it still preserves admirable 15th-century tiles.
p. 65: Entrance-portal with spiralled "Tree of Life" column.

JAM. *Minaret, late 12th century.*
p. 52: The minaret of Jâm rises 65 metres (213 feet) into the air in a lonely gorge by the bank of the Harî Rûd, or "Herât River", 200 km (124 miles) east of Herât city. The tower's kufic calligraphy, carved in stucco and highlighted with turquoise ceramics, reproduces the Koranic sûra of Mary, mother of Jesus "unto whom We bestowed Wisdom even when he was a child" (19:12).
p. 53: Detail of the minaret's stucco adornment.
pp. 54–55: The minaret's ring of turquoise calligraphy surrounds the shaft at mid-height.

HERÂT.

The Castle, 1416.
pp. 70-71: Traditionally believed to have been founded by Alexander, Herât's stronghold has dominated the cityscape for the last 23 centuries. This panoramic view, composed of two assembled photographs, suggests the scale of the fortress's walls and towers (*borj*). In 1416, the emperor Shâh Rokh had them all sheathed in tiles – as shown in the illumination by Behzâd reproduced on page 17 – but only fragments survive on a single corner tower.

The Friday Mosque, 1200, 1498, 1996.
The Friday Mosque, the city's most revered monument, was miraculously spared during more than a decade of Soviet warfare in Afghanistan, after having previously survived in some shape or other through eight centuries of successive invasions, sieges, reigns and architectural resurrections. In 1964, large-scale restoration of its tilework was undertaken through a special local tax on sugar, levied by the municipal authorities with the full agreement of Herât's population.
p. 37: Tileworkers in Herât's Friday Mosque in 1964.
p. 46: Detail of a Ghôrid panel in carved stucco with turquoise ceramic knobs. Turn of the 13th century.
p. 47: Beneath the Ghôrid Old Portal, where a Tîmûrid spandrel bears witness to the renovation carried out in 1498, a modern Herâtî tileworker in 1964 paints a calligraphic motif to be fired onto a tile, according to the underglaze *Haft Rang* or "Seven Colours" technique.

Mausoleum of Gôhar Shâd, before 1447.
Empress Gôhar Shâd, consort to Tîmûr's son Shâh Rokh, commissioned the most important architectural complex in Herât. When Robert Byron saw what was left in 1937, he was moved to write that "every tile, every flower, every petal of mosaic contributes its genius to the whole. … If the mosaic on the rest of the Musalla surpassed or even equalled what survives today, there was never such a mosque before or since."
p. 66: Gôhar Shâd's mausoleum is crowned by a ribbed dome whose remaining blue tiling, even today, sparkles with flecks of pure gold. The photograph shows the monument as it stood before

further damage by shelling in 1984.
p. 67: Detail of the pre-1984 dome, with stalactite corbelling (*moqarnas*) and underglaze-painted calligraphic frieze.

Shrine of Shâhzâdeh 'Abdollâh, 1487.
Raised in the 15th century over the tomb of one of the earlier missionaries of Islam to Herât, the 8th-century Arab prince (Persian *shâhzâdeh*) 'Abd Allâh ibn Ja'far of the royal Umayyad line, the shrine preserves fine examples of Tîmûrid mosaic.
p. 80: Detail of floral panel with symmetrical wreaths.
p. 81: Corner of the frieze on the same panel.

HERÂT, GÂZOR-GÂH.

Shrine of 'Abdollâh Ansârî, 1428.
Lying in a fold of hills 5 km (3 miles) to the northeast of Herât, this highly frequented pilgrimage site was built around the tomb of an 11th-century mystic teacher and poet who composed not only in classical Arabic but also in Herât's own Persian dialect, and became the city's patron saint. Ansârî wrote of Herât that it had "a noble heart" and that, "while the Sun rises yonder, here shines its ray: who ever saw the Sun's ray separated from its orb?"
pp. 72 and 73: Panels of geometrical calligraphy in kufic style line the inner walls and îwân of the courtyard.
p. 74: Gateway to the shrine. *Bannâ'î* or "masonwrought" brickwork, under the blind ogees on either side of the portal, yields a stylized pattern figuring the Perfect Man, made up of the consonants of the Prophet's name (see page 24).
p. 75: Detail of a mosaic panel with floral and geometric stellar patterns, and calligraphic designs entwining within each lozenge-medallion the name of GOD (*Allâh*) repeated twice.
p. 79: Detail of a mosaic panel with *shamseh* or "sunburst" motif.

KOHSÂN. This village lies 105 km (65 miles) west of Herât.

Tomb of the Princess Tômân Âghâ, 1440.
Tradition attributes the commissioning of this

mausoleum to Empress Gôhar Shâd. Its walls exhibited a pattern of bare and enamelled bricks according to the *bannâ'î* or "masonwrought" technique, while mosaic work adorned the stalactite corbelling around the drum of its dome.

p. 77: State of the building before it was bombed in 1984.

MAZÂR-E SHARÎF. The main city of Afghan Turkestan.

Mosque and mausoleum of the caliph 'Alî, 1480, 1963.
Mazâr-e Sharîf, "The Noble Shrine", is locally believed to shelter the tomb of the Prophet's son-in-law.

p. 8: Afghan masons restoring the shrine in 1963. Previous restorations were carried out in the 17th and 19th centuries.

p. 44: One of the mosque's few original 15th-century decorative elements (possibly restored in the 17th): a turret with ribbed cupola.

pp. 58–59: Local tradition avers that every pigeon settling around the shrine turns white within 40 days.

SHÂH-E MASHHAD. *Madraseh, 1165–66.*

p. 32. The Ghôrid ruins of Shâh-e Mashhad, discovered in 1970, crown an isolated butte overlooking the Morghâb river, flowing here through a wild gorge near the village of Jawand, some 60 km (37 miles) north of the minaret of Jâm. Its adornment testifies to the virtuosity of medieval Muslim craftsmen in playing with light and shadow by means of brickwork and carved stucco.

p. 48: The gateway, whose arch collapsed in the 1980s.

p. 49: Detail of the now vanished geometric-patterned stucco work under the arch.

HIGHLANDS OF GHÔR.

pp. 50–51. Two Afghan horsemen cross the endless, treeless, undulating yellow clay hills of Ghôr, spiked with thorns – "alone with God and the sky," observed the photographers. But out of this unprepossessing desert clay, medieval Central Asian architects shaped shrines and castles to be sheathed in blue tiling.

SEISTAN DESERT.

pp. 226–27. The haunting 12th-century sun-baked ramparts of the *Shahr-e Gholgholeh* or "City of Lamentations", one of several Central Asian sites so named, crumble into the shapeless sand dunes out of which they were first moulded, and so into oblivion, in Afghanistan's far southwestern Seistan (Saystân) Desert, also known as the *Dasht-e Marg*, or "Desert of Death".

IRAN (Eastern: Province of Khorâsân)

BASTÂM. Halfway along the road skirting the Great Salt Desert and leading from modern Tehran towards Mashhad in Khorâsân, the little town of Bastâm is famed for its shrine raised by Iran's 14th-century Mongol rulers over the tomb of its local saint, Shaykh Bâyezîd, a key figure in the history of Sufism.

Shrine of Shaykh Bâyezîd, 1313.
This 9th-century Sufi saint, grandson of a Zoroastrian convert to Islam, preached a form of pantheism so extreme that he once proclaimed "Glory be to Me!", thereby signifying the utter absorption of his soul into the Godhead.

pp. 45, 56 and 57: Details of the revetment within the entrance portal.

KHARGERD. A small town some 300 km (186 miles) southeast of Mashhad.

Madraseh, 1445.
This theological school was completed under the rule of the Tîmûrid Emperor of Herât, Shâh Rokh.

p. 76: Detail of a panel in *bannâ'î* or "masonwrought" work of alternating bare and enamelled brick, forming a central Seal of Solomon, with the name of GOD written in geometric kufic within lozenge-medallions.

MASHHAD. The main city of Iranian Central Asia lies at a height of 1000 metres (3280 feet), 800 km (500 miles) east of Tehran. Meaning "the place where one bears witness", Mashhad was built around the tomb of the 9th-century imâm Rezâ, eighth in the succession of Shî'î imâms.

Mosque of Gôhar Shâd, 1418 and 20th century.
The Empress had the mosque which bears her name erected to the south of the imâm's tomb.

pp. 92–93: The walls of the vast courtyard, with its four îwân ogee gateways, are covered with a large variety of tiles, both medieval and modern restorations, assembled in mosaic, in underglaze-painting of the "Seven Colours" or *Haft Rang* and in alternating enamelled and bare brickwork in the *bannâ'î* or "masonwrought" style. Flanked by twin minarets, the southern îwân leads to the mihrâb-hall, crowned with a blue-tiled dome.

p. 97: Two Shî'î mullahs beneath one of the mosque's minarets.

pp. 98–99: Details of calligraphic and floral decoration.

pp. 100–1: View of the Mashhad shrines in winter. The blue-domed mosque of Gôhar Shâd appears on the left, and, to the right, the gilded dome to Imâm Rezâ's tomb.

TORBAT-E JÂM. The small locality of Torbat-e Jâm, 185 km (115 miles) southeast of Mashhad, boasts

an imposing shrine raised over the tomb of a local Sufi saint, Shaykh Ahmad ibn Abi-l-Hasan (1049–1142).

Shrine of Shaykh Ahmad ibn Abi-l-Hasan, 13th–15th centuries. Built in the 13th century, the shrine was tiled between 1440 and 1443.

pp. 102–3: Details of a large mosaic panel within the main entrance portal; the traditionally Islamic floral design includes a motif directly derived from Chinese ceramics, a waterfowl in flight (see also text and illustration on page 269).

UZBEKISTAN

SAMARKAND.

The Cathedral Mosque, also known as "Bîbî-Khânom", or "My Lady's", 1399–1404.
Built at far too great speed under the prodding of an impatient Tîmûr, the mosque began to deteriorate rapidly, and would be no more than an immense ruined hulk today but for centuries of constant restoration work. Its dome, 18.5 metres (61 feet) in diameter, soars 37 metres (121 feet) into the air.

pp. 82–83: So imposing was the mosque when it was first built that a contemporary chronicler wrote: "Its dome might be unique – were it not for the sky; its arch might be unique – were it not for the Milky Way."

The Gûr-e Mîr, 15th and 20th centuries.
This mausoleum, known as the "Tomb of the Emir", shelters a crypt which holds the tombs of Tîmûr, his grandson Ulugh Beg and other Tîmûrid princes. Originally, Tîmûr apparently commissioned the building to honour the resting-place of his favourite grandson Mohammad-Soltân, whom he had appointed heir-apparent but who died on campaign in 1403. Work on the funerary monument began immediately, but Tîmûr died the following year and was himself buried beneath the dome.

p. 95: The dome after heavy-handed Soviet restoration. The crowning tiles, still visible in this photograph taken in the late 1960s, had already flaked off by the 1980s.

The burial-ground of Shâh-e Zendeh.
Rising on the outskirts of medieval Samarkand, the necropolis of the "Living King" (*Shâh-e Zendeh*) was made up of funerary monuments built around the tomb of Quthâm ibn 'Abbâs, a nephew of the Prophet who was allegedly cut down by his sabre-wielding enemies at this spot towards the end of the 7th century AD. (According to legend, like the martyred Saint Denis of France, the "Living King" picked up his head with his own hands.) The monuments, lining both sides of a narrow causeway, bear magnificent witness to the evolution of architectural adornment in 14th- and 15th-century Central Asia.

Tomb of Tômân Âghâ, 1405.
Raised by order of Tômân Âghâ herself, one of Tîmûr's consorts.
p. 88: Floral mosaic on a pillar.

Tomb of Shîrîn Bîbî Âghâ, 1385.
The resting-place of one of Tîmûr's sisters.
p. 89: Geometric pattern with inset floral motifs.

Tomb of the Amîr-Zâdeh, 1386.
"The Emir's Son": The resting-place of a son of the Tîmûrid lord Toghloq-Tekîn.
p. 108: Chinese-inspired lotus flowers, in relief.

Tomb of Shâd-e Molk Âghâ, 1371.
Tîmûr's sister, the Lady Torkân Âghâ, commissioned this mausoleum for her daughter, "Lady Joy of the Kingdom".
pp. 109, 114, 115, 118 and 119: Variations in tile

decoration on the façade, partly inspired by Chinese floral motifs.

Tomb of an Unknown Princess, 1360.
p. 113: Ceramic in relief moulded in eight-pointed "Seals of Solomon", with central knob or "bezel".

Tomb of Ostâd 'Alî (or 'Alîm), about 1385.
p. 117: Detail of the façade. Woven around a chain of "Seals of Solomon", calligraphic virtuosity in the kufic style has made these inscriptions almost impossible to read – unless successive restorations have blurred their original sense. The result, in any case, is an exercise in pure abstract art.

The Rêgestân Square.
Around the *Rêgestân*, or "Place of Sand", stand the finest Central Asian architectural façades of the 15th and 17th centuries, corresponding to the

Tîmûrids' imperial heyday and to the political zenith of their Uzbek successor-state. The three *madraseh*-s or theological schools facing the square are, on the west, the college raised by the Tîmûrid prince Ulugh Beg, and on the east and north respectively, the Shêr-Dâr and Tila-Kârî colleges built by the Uzbek khâns.

Madraseh "of the Goldsmiths" (Tilâ-Kârî), 1647.
p. 120: The madraseh's façade. The ogee openings of the two storeys correspond to the students' cells. The tiling of the arches is "masonwrought" (*bannâ'î*), while that of the façade is underglaze-painted.

Madraseh "of the Lions" (Shêr-Dâr), 1619–36.
p. 121: One of its two ribbed domes, sheathed in mosaic.

Western Persia and Azerbaijan

IRAN (Central and Western)

ESFAHÂN.

The Royal Mosque, 1612–38.
The Royal Mosque – with the Royal Square which it dominates, the most ambitious complex of urban planning in traditional Islamic architecture – was an imperial showpiece for the Safavid ruler, Shâh 'Abbâs (1587–1629).
pp. 174–75: The layout of Esfahân's imperial urban centre, seen from a helicopter in late afternoon in winter.
pp. 150–51: Horizontal view of Esfahân's imperial urban centre. From left to right, the dome and portal of the Royal Mosque; to the centre-left, the cream-coloured dome of the Lotfollâh Mosque; on the right, Esfahân's own "Sublime Porte" or *'Alî Qâpt*, a pavilion with a wooden-colonnaded terrace where Safavid royalty entertained, and whence it could watch polo-playing in the square below.
p. 177: The great entrance-portal to the Royal Mosque dominates the southern face of the square, laid out according to the cardinal directions. Hence the mosque beyond the portal is orientated at a different angle – the corridor leading from gateway to prayer-hall marks a sharp 45-degree bend – in order to point towards Mecca, which lies to the southwest of Esfahân. Titus Burckhardt comments that this corridor is like "a passage from the outer to the inner world, a sharp reorientation of the soul" (*L'art de l'Islam*, p. 252). Framed in bands of cursive calligraphy, the portal's *Haft Rang* floral adornment closely parallels the style of contemporary Safavid royal carpets. Kufic calligraphy reproduces more Koranic verses in spirals around the minarets.
p. 178: Snow and light in a side-courtyard within the Royal Mosque.

p. 181: The Royal Mosque's winter prayer-hall.
p. 183: The Royal Mosque's dome, under snow.

Friday Mosque, 11th, 15th, 18th and 20th centuries.
Within the urban maze of Esfahân's Old City, the Friday Mosque, a far more ancient construction, reflects successive centuries of Eastern Islamic architecture and decoration.
pp. 166–67: Helicopter view of the Friday Mosque. To the right, the southern îwân is framed by a pair of minarets; while the western îwân, in the lower centre, is topped by a small pavilion known as a *goldasteh*, or "spray of flowers", whence the call to prayer might also be chanted.
p. 153: The 15th-century southern îwân, with its Tudor-like depressed ogee arch and complex corbelling, is the finest of the four portals facing the Friday Mosque's inner courtyard.
p. 169: Detail of the corbelling of the western îwân; the inscribed date of the restored tiling (*anno hegirae* 1112) corresponds to the turn of the 18th century AD.
pp. 162 and 163: Three small mosaic panels dated 1475.

Mosque and madraseh of the Mother of the Shâh, 1706–14.
This charming theological college, the architectural swansong of the Safavid age, provided 150 cells for divinity students on two levels around a central courtyard shaded by plane-trees.

Mosque of 'Alî, 1521.
This mosque, which boasts a famous, 48-metre high (157 feet) minaret, otherwise conforms to the classical architectural pattern of four îwân gateways around a central courtyard.
p. 172: Detail of a mosaic panel, with tendrils and geometric calligraphic compositions.

Tomb of Bâbâ Qâsem, 1340–41.
To the immediate north of the Friday Mosque, this little shrine, dating back to Esfahân's older Sunnî period, shelters the grave of an orthodox theologian under a pyramidal roof.
p. 152: Brick vaulting of the shrine's inner dome, forming an eight-pointed Seal of Solomon.

Shrine of Hârûn Welâyat, 1513.
pp. 154–55: Dating from the earlier years of Safavid rule, the adornment of this shrine still reflects the flamboyance of later 15th-century Turcoman taste.
p. 161: Tendril ornament in mosaic on a spandrel.
p. 164: Endless ramifications of the Tree of Life, in mosaic.
p. 173: Brilliant, difficult geometric calligraphic maze-compositions, for meditation, including the name 'ALÎ (lower right) and ALLÂHU AKBAR ("God Supreme": lower centre).

Shrine of Darb-e Imâm, 1453.
Built under the rule of Jahân Shâh, sultan of the Turcoman clan of the Black Sheep, this small mausoleum, with the Turcomans' Blue Mosque in Tabrîz, displays the finest tile ornamentation in Iran. Throughout the Persianate world, whether in Iran proper or in neighbouring Afghanistan and Uzbekistan, the 15th century is the high water mark of this art form.
p. 165: Detail of tendrils in mosaic.
pp. 170–71: Interconnected motifs in refined mosaic: a Seal of Solomon holding an inner Tree of Life radiates into a *shamseh* or "sunburst" amidst a field of sparks and stars.

KÂSHÂN. Lying 260 km (162 miles) south of modern Tehran, the city of Kâshân with its rich neighbouring deposits of fine white clay gave its name in Persian to the art of ceramic tiles: *kâshî-kârî*, "Kâshân work". Large sections of the little treatise dedicated to this art form, written in 1301 by Master Abo-l-Qâsem of Kâshân, appear throughout this book (see here especially pages 265–67 and 301).

Domes of the bazaar.
p. 132: The dried mud-brick architecture of the city, typical of the Persianate world, seen from a helicopter. The covered bazaars are marked by strings of domes, which shade the city's commercial lanes from an angry sun. Yarns of dyed wool – raw material for the city's famous carpets – dry on the flat rooftops.

Mosque of Maydân-e Fayz, 1462, 1711, 1827.
p. 133: The mosaic work of this stalactite corbelling or *moqarnas* dates from the great century of the art form, the 15th.

KERMÂN. This oasis-city lies 400 km (250 miles) southeast of Yazd at a height of 1800 metres (5906 feet) above sea-level.
pp. 140–41: Its location on the high desert plateau, surrounded by mountains, tempers the heat and yields clear skies – except when obscured by dust-storms.

The Friday Mosque, 1349, 1559.
p. 139: The 16th-century mosaic work expresses traditional Islamic cosmology – from the inscribed Seals of Solomon in a starry geometric sky, on the left, to the spiral on the right implying the emanation of all things from, and return to, the Divine Principle in an endless flux-and-reflux: a concept going back to the Neo-Platonism of Plotinus, medieval Islam's acknowledged *Shaykh Yûnânî*, the "Greek Master".

MÂHÂN. Found 42 km (26 miles) to the southeast of Kermân, is the shrine of a 15th-century master of a Sufi Order, Shâh Ne'matollâh Walî.

Shrine of Shâh Ne'matollâh Walî.
pp. 146–47: Within the star-motifs of the dome restored under Shâh 'Abbâs in the early 17th century, the brickwork appears to form a deliberate spiderweb pattern in a mystical allusion to the Web across the Prophet's Cave.

NATANZ. This small oasis, 75 km (47 miles) southeast of Kâshân, holds several important 14th-century monuments, including a mosque, a Sufi saint's mausoleum and a *khânqâh* or dervish convent.

The Khânqâh, 1316–17.
pp. 122–23: Early tiling from the Mongol age: kufic and cursive calligraphy (left); sky of stars (right).
pp. 124–25: Detail from a mosaic panel on the façade.
pp. 126–27: The mihrâb or prayer-niche, mixing stucco and tiling, with a fine calligraphic band in floriated kufic.

SOLTÂNIYEH. Lying at a height of 1800 metres (5806 feet) on a desert plateau midway between Tabrîz and modern Tehran, this was a favourite residence of Iran's Mongol rulers, the Îl-Khâns.

Mausoleum of the Îl-Khân Oljâytû, 1307–13.
With its many remaining wall-tiles, this monument was identified by Wilber as the earliest surviving model of the classical Persianate ceramic-sheathed mausoleum.
p. 128: Detail of the dome's revetment in "masonwrought" kufic calligraphy, combining the names of GOD, MOHAMMAD and 'ALÎ.
p. 129: Detail of a spandrel to one of the four îwâns, thickly enmeshed with tilebands across the exposed brickwork.

TABRÎZ. "Tauris" as it used to be known to Europeans, and now – save for its matchless mosque

– a mostly featureless Iranian provincial city, but once the capital of the 13th- and 14th-century Mongol Îl-Khâns, 15th-century Turcoman sultans and early 16th-century Safavid shâhs – themselves called the "Sophi" kings by Europeans, as in Milton's "Bactrian Sophi, from the horns / Of Turkish crescent, leaves all waste beyond / The realm of Aladule in his retreat / To Tauris."

The Blue Mosque (Masjed-e Kabûd), 1465.
Although damaged by earthquake, the cathedral mosque of the Turcoman sultans still displays the Persianate world's supreme achievement in ceramic wall-adorment.
pp. 142–43: Mosaic work within the portal, of unsurpassed subtlety of colour.
p. 145: Detail of a floral medallion, masterfully set into, and contrasted with, honey-coloured brick.

YAZD. Lying in the very heart of Iran, in the solitude of the Desert of Lût at the foot of a 4000-metre high (13,123 feet) mountain range, the sand-coloured baked-brick oasis of Yazd, once an important caravan centre, still boasts a major mosque and most of Persia's surviving Zoroastrian minority.

The Friday Mosque, 14th, 15th, 17th and 20th centuries.
pp. 136–37: The dome and soaring ogee portal of the mosque dominate a traditional roofscape marked by "chimneys", actually "wind-catchers" (*bâdgîr*) serving to ventilate and cool old-fashioned Iranian homes.
pp. 134–35: Three details of a 15th-century mosaic panel.

Chaqmaq Mosque, 1437.
p. 138: Star pattern in stucco and tiling.
p. 162: Tendril and geometrical calligraphic panel.

Anatolia

TURKEY

ANKARA. Turkey's austere modern capital still contains older sections of considerable historical interest.

Arslanhane (Lion-dwelling) Mosque, 1289.
This is Ankara's oldest and largest mosque, at the foot of the citadel.
p. 190: Stalactite corbelling or *moqarnas* in the prayer niche.

ESKI MALATYA. From the heart of Anatolia, modern Malatya exports dried apricots to Europe. Old Malatya (*Eski Malatya*), 20 km (12 miles) to the northeast, is now only a village, but with an interesting 13th-century mosque.

The Great Mosque (Ulu Camii), 1225–70.
pp. 184–85: Details of inset tile-bands.
pp. 188–89: The spiralling "masonwrought" tiling of the dome evokes the circling flux-and-reflux of Divine Emanation, which the poet and mystic teacher Rûmî, in Konya, stylized into a dance observed by the dervishes of his Order.

ISTANBUL.

Mosque of Sokollu Mehmet Paşa, 1572.
The famed Ottoman architect Sinân built this richly tiled mosque, now situated deep within one of the city's most traditional quarters with old wooden houses, for a vizier of Bosnian origin.
p. 207: The calligraphy of this underglaze-painted

tiling contains within its circle the entirety of *sûra* 112, one of the shortest in the Koran but significantly stressing God's unity: "In the name of God Merciful, Compassionate. Say: He is God, One! God, Eternal! He hath not begotten, nor been begotten! He is only One!" Below: "I bear witness that Mohammad is His Servant and Prophet."

Mosque of Rüstem Paşa, 1557.

Also built by Sinân, the interior of this little mosque, accessible by steep stairs from the Street of the Matmakers below in the old commercial quarter near the Golden Horn, is richly lined with Iznik tiles.

pp. 211, 214 and 215: Hyacinths, carnations, pomegranate blossoms and fruits, with thick applications of brilliant red from "Armenian bole".

Topkapı Palace.
p. 217: 16th-century Iznik tiles: tulips, carnations and eglantine stems.

IZNIK. Now a sleepy little lakeside Anatolian town some 230 km (143 miles) southeast of Istanbul, Iznik was ancient Nicaea, where Orthodox Christianity defined its creed in council in the year 325. In Ottoman times, down to the 18th century, it was a major centre for ceramic production. After his victory over Safavid Persia in 1514, Sultan Selim I settled Iranian master potters to work and teach in the town.

15th and 16th-century tiles: Musée des Arts Décoratifs, Paris.
p. 208: Hyacinth and eglantine around a cypress, on cobalt-blue ground.
p. 209: "The Four Flowers": tulip, hyacinth, carnation and eglantine.

KONYA. Ancient Iconium, the capital of the Seljuk sultans of Rûm in the 12th and 13th centuries, preserves important monuments from their rule.

MOROCCO

FEZ. Since the loss of Cordova and Granada to Castile, Moroccan Fez has remained the great traditional cultural centre of the Islamic West.

PAKISTAN

LAHORE.

The Fort, 1565–1631.
The city's traditional stronghold was restored to fresh splendour under its 16th- and 17th-century Moghol Emperors, from Akbar to Aurangzêb.
pp. 240–41: Details of the Fort's "Picture Wall". Begun under the Emperor Jahângîr in 1624, the wall was completed under Shâh Jahân in 1631. To its traditional abstract Islamic decorative patterns were added figural motifs of humans and animals, some of them ultimately drawn from the works of famous painters, such as the interlocked fighting camels, which derive from a prototype created by Behzâd.

MULTAN. A harsh old Persian proverb affirms that this city in the Punjab has nothing to recommend it but "heat, dust, tombs and beggars". The architectural magnificence of its tombs, however, does serve to redeem Multan.
Shrine of Roknoddîn, 1310.
Toghloq Shâh, sultan of Delhi, had destined this

The great mystic poet and teacher from Central Asia, Jalâloddîn Rûmî (1207–73), founded his dervish Order here, making Konya a hallowed ground for Sufism.
"Tiled" (Sirçali) Medrese, 1242.
pp. 192–93: Detail of early tilework on the îwân.

Büyük Karatay Medrese, 1251.
Within its marble portal carved with stalactite corbelling, the interior of this theological school boasts the richest collection of early 13th-century tiling in the Islamic world.
p. 196: Two geometric panels.
p. 197: Ornamental cursive and geometric calligraphy. The vertical kufic bands, extreme stylizations of the four Arabic consonants making up the name of Mohammad, are so difficult to read that they virtually constitute purely abstract ornament.
p. 199: Squinch in brickwork with tiling.
pp. 200–1: Horizons of calligraphic bands in knotted and floriated kufic, surmounted with what are rising "sunbursts", whose thorny spikes have, however, evoked in the eyes of many modern

Barbary

Medersa Bû 'Inâniya, 1351–58.
Raised by Sultan Abû 'Inân of the Marînid dynasty, this is the largest and most sumptuously decorated *medersa* (in Moroccan dialect for classical *madrasa* or "theological college") in Fez.
p. 219: Moorish-style cursive calligraphy and star-patterned *zulayj*-tiling in the inner courtyard.

Hindustan

mausoleum for his own resting-place, but his son and successor preferred to dedicate the white-domed octagonal building, with its slightly inward-sloping reddish walls and corner turrets, to a local Muslim saint.
pp. 234–35: Decorative band around the dome's drum, contrasting blue-and-white enamelled bricks against the reddish ground of the building. The carved calligraphy in the blind ogees attests the Islamic profession of faith: "There is no god but God and Mohammad is the Prophet of God."

UCHH-E SHARÎF. This small, remote but "noble" (*sharîf*) oasis in the southern Punjab preserves a few tomb-shrines dedicated to local 13th-century Sufi saints.
Mausoleum of Bîbî Jâwandî, 1498.
pp. 232–33: Although partly ruined, this female saint's tomb has kept much of its revetment in blue-and-white tiling.

THATTA. An oasis in Sindh lying 100 km (62 miles) east of Karachi, Thatta has lost its former importance but preserves a magnificent mosque

visitors the thistles of the arid Anatolian highlands.

SIVAS. This major stronghold of the Anatolian Seljuks preserves its 13th-century Gök (Blue) Medrese, and a hospital complex founded by Sultan Keykavus I.
Hospital and tomb of Sultan Keykavus I, 1217.
p. 187: Detail of main portal to the mausoleum, within the hospital courtyard.

Gök Medrese (Blue Medrese), 1271–72.
p. 191: Detail of star-patterned geometric ornament.

SHORES OF LAKE VAN.
Islamic ruins at the foot of the citadel of Van.
pp. 194–95: Overshadowed by an old fort and surrounded with the scattered ruins of mosques and tombs (*türbe*), the ancient lakeside city of Van lies under a rim of spent volcanoes at the eastern edge of the Anatolian plateau, not far from the modern Iranian border. Its hard blue sky and adamant-hard steppe signal a traveller's approach to Inner Asia.

Medersa el-'Attârîn, 1323–25.
While earlier and smaller than the Bû 'Inâniya, the theological school "of the Scent-Merchants" is considered the most exquisite in Morocco.
p. 229: From the ground upwards, *zulayj*-tiling, carved stucco and cedarwood combine in perfect harmony.

commissioned by Shâh Jahân.
Mosque of Shâh Jahân, 1647.
Begun by Shâh Jahân, but only completed under his son and successor (who overthrew him in 1659), Aurangzêb, the Thatta Mosque has recently been restored. The 93 domes, which crown the courtyard's enclosing galleries, echo and amplify the prayer-leader's voice throughout the building.
p. 245: Covered gallery of the mosque.

INDIA

GWÂLIOR.

The Fort, 1486–1516.
The mighty stronghold of Gwâlior still reflects the pride of medieval Râjput chivalry.
p. 247: Persianate tiling over the main gate lightens the general tone of the castle's imposing austerity.
p. 246: A stylized elephant adds a merry, dancing touch to the southern wall.
pp. 248–49: The Fort's ramparts crown 3 km (2 miles) of cliffs, 100 metres (328 feet) above the Indian plain.

A MEDIEVAL CERAMIST AND HIS CRAFT

Extract from *The Book of Those Brides That Are Gems and Scents* by Abo-l-Qâsem

And concerning the art of the city of Kâshân (*kâshî-garî*) which they call "faïence" (*ghazâreh*, literally "the abundance"), it is a craft which in truth is a sort of Alchemy (*eksîr* = "elixir"), and it is of three kinds: the first concerns the knowledge of its instruments and means and ingredients and what is necessary thereto; second is the knowledge of the solution of these elements; and third is the knowledge of their composition.

[THE TWELVE ELEMENTS]

The instruments and means and ingredients pertaining to this matter are many:

1. First is the *mahâ* stone (quartz) which in Arabic they call *hasât*, and in the expression of the craftsmen "sugar of stone" (*shakar-e sang*). It is a stone that is white, pure, sparkling, less so than crystal, but far whiter and purer than marble, hard to an extreme, and many sparks fly forth when it is stricken with the flintstone. Its quarries are in many places, and the virtue (*fâ'îdeh*) of the *hasât* stone is the same as that of crystal, save that crystal is rarer and less of it may be found, therefore they do not use it.

2. And like unto quartz (*mahâ*) are other stones. One sort they call *sâ ashkanâ* (Arabic-Persian hybrid for *'asâ eshkaneh* = "stickbreaking" = lime- or chalk-stone). It comes in large pieces, but its purity and lustre ("gem-essence") are less than that of the "sugar of stone", although it is found in more places than that stone.

3. The third stone is a grey-white powder which arises in the hills of the village of Fìn in the area of Kâshân: it is the colour of lime, which the craftsmen call *batâneh* ("the lining of clothes"). And this is the prime matter (*mâdeh-ye asl*) for vessels made by means of the "Two Fires". (R. Winderlich suggests translating this ingredient by "feldspath".)

4. The fourth stone is the *Qamsarî*, thus known from a village [also in the area of Kâshân]. This they bake and crush into powder like unto white sugar [and this stone is used in the composition of turquoise colours]. (Winderlich: "borax?")

5. The fifth is potassium (*shakhâr*) which they also call *qeliyeh* (*qelî*), and it grows in the manner of the *oshnân* (saltwort) to an extreme of perfection. This they burn pure without mixing it with *shôreh* (saltpetre). And the best potassium is that which, when ground, yields in its midst a red colour giving forth a sharp smell. [Saltwort may be found in all places, and potassium's virtue is that it may enter into composition with other stones.]

6. The sixth stone is the stone of azure (*lâjward*), which the craftsmen in their expression call the "Solomonic" (*Solaymânî*). Its mine is at the village of Qamsar in the hills visible from Kâshân, and in their view it was from thence that it was extracted by Solomon the Prophet, upon whom be peace! And it is like unto the silver of *Talqam* [white] sparkling, in a matrix of [hard] black stone. From thence proceed the colour of celestial Azure (*lâjward-e âbgîneh*) and other colours (= cobalt oxide, according to Winderlich). And another sort they bring from the land of the Franks, ashen and soft (cobalt-manganese in Winderlich's view, asbolane in J.W. Allen's). And there is a sort of a red colour, in the mine it is exuded from the surface of the rocks. It is like unto the red shell of the pistachio. It is of great power, but a deadly poison and a killing venom. [And the virtue of the Solomonic Stone is its azure colour, which they use for Aleppo glass vessels and blue beads of India.]

7. And the seventh stone [like pitch] is black and dark to an extreme like unto kohl or eye-ointment; even in fire its blackness flashes like lightning; its mines are in the regions of Khorâsân amongst the hills of Jâjarm, where there they call it "chain-mail" (*mozarrad* = graphite). And its virtue lies in its black colour with which they paint vessels.

8. The eighth is marcassite (*marqashîthâ*), gold or silver; and magnesium (*maghnîsiyâ*) male or female (= hard or soft); and yellow vitriol (*zâj-e zard*, pyrite mixed with its own gradual oxidization); and [yellow and red] arsenic (*zarnîkh* = orpiment, arsenic sulphite); and litharge (*mardâ-sang*); and antimony (*sormeh*); and tutty (*tûtiyâ* or zinc); and lead (*osrob*). Each enters into its proper place.

9. The ninth is a clay (*gel*), white and clinging, and of great virtue (Winderlich: kaolin). While it may be found everywhere, the white is rarer, and that of Kâshân is the most white, and of perfect virtue. And the craftsmen call it *Warkânî* and *Lûrî*, for it pertains to a village of the Lûr people. And thereof is a sort like unto white snow; its mine lies in the hills of Nâ'în, in the neighbourhood of Esfahân; this they mix with plaster, and therewith whitewash houses. [And its virtue, in the craft, lies in its body and gem-essence, *jawhar*.]

10. The tenth of the stones is that born of the Seven Metals. And one is the gem-essence of tin, *qal'î*, which they call (in Arabic) *rasâs*. [And its mines may be found in many famous places, and the first of these is] the land of the Franks where it is moulded in the form of a snake and stamped with a seal [against admixture]. And divers sorts are brought from the land of China, in large plaques, and others from the marches of the land of the Bulgars (= southern Russia), thinner, like pieces of paper folded above one another, and such is the best sort of tin.

11. The eleventh is the gem-essence of lead (*osrob*), found in many places such as Kermân and Yazd and Byzantium (*Rûm;* possibly Turkish Anatolia is meant) and the land of the Bulgars where its occurs in pieces. The best of the sorts of lead is that whose gem-essence is white to an extreme, and the poorest are all those from Byzantium (or Anatolia). And from thence the painters derive, for their use, litharge (*mardâ-sang*), red and yellow vermilion (or cinnaber: *esrenj-e sorkh-ô zard*), and white lead (*safêdâb*). [And the virtue of tin and lead is the sealing of the colour turquoise, and the virtue of lead lies in the sorts of blue-enamel, *mînâ-hâ*, it yields.]

12. The twelfth is baked copper (*nohâs-e moharraq*), and copper hammer-flakes (*tûbâl-e mes*). [Its mines are in Rûm and at Dezh-Mâr – Snake Castle – in Azerbaijan.] And the best is of a greenish-red (*sorkh-e sabzfâm*), a most pliable sort (*narm-âhang*). From it is born the colour green. And likewise from hammer-flakes of baked iron the colour yellow arises in the fire.

BUT CONCERNING THEIR SOLUTION *(tahlîl)*

One must smash and crush these matters (gem-essences) like unto atoms of eye-ointment, by pounding them and grinding them and so pulverizing them and sifting them and screening them. And some of these matters must be struck with an iron mallet until they are like unto chick-peas, and crushed in a mill – and if by means of a hand-mill, so much the better and the more virtue: so for the "sugar of stone" and the "stickbreaker" and the "lining of clothes" and the divers sorts of the Seven Metals, I mean tin and lead and copper and iron and stone of azure and "chain-mail" and the other kinds of gem-essences, to be ground upon the long mortarstone which they use.

From Persian MS Aya Sofya 3614 (Istanbul) dated 1301; additions in square brackets from MS Aya Sofya 3613 dated 1583. Published with German tr. by Ritter, Ruska, Sarre and Winderlich, Istanbul 1935.

Descriptive Index of the Miniatures Reproduced

p. 9: *The Building of Castle Khawarnaq*, by Behzâd; Herât, 1494; British Library, Or. 6810, f. 154v. Photograph: R. and S. Michaud.

At the command of the Arabian prince No'mân of Hîra, and under the direction of his Byzantine architect-magician Semnâr, workers raise the most beautiful castle in the world. This illustration to a manuscript of Nezâmî's *Khamseh* or "Quintet", copied for the Tîmûrid lord 'Alî Fârsî Barlâs (one of the grandees around Sultan Hosayn Mîrzâ Bâyqarâ), reflects the quintessence of the Herât school of painting's cool, restrained, academic style as exemplified by its master artist, Behzâd. Tiny, colourful, doll-like figures, but with subtly individualized features, dance across and so enliven a severely balanced (owing to the scaffolding) geometrical composition.

p. 17: *Alexander Visits a Holy Man*, by Behzâd; Herât, 1494; British Library, Or. 6810, f. 237r. Photograph: R. and S. Michaud.

This illustration to Nezâmî's rendition of the Alexander Romance represents the Conqueror humbly asking a holy man how best to take the fort lying on the horizon. Behzâd depicted his Eskandar figure with the features of his ruling sultan, Hosayn Mîrzâ Bâyqarâ (r. 1469–1506), and the fort is Herât's Royal Castle itself, sparkling with tile-mosaics.

p. 21: *King Khosrô Nôsherwân and his Vizier Listen to the Owls in a Ruined Building*, by Âghâ-Mîrak, assisted according to S.C. Welch by Mîr Sayyed 'Alî; Tabrîz, 1539–43; British Library, Or. 2265. Photograph reproduced by permission of the British Library.

This illustration to Nezâmî's "Treasury of Secrets" (*Makhzan-ol-Asrâr*) adorns the most sumptuous manuscript of the poet's collected works ever copied – that for the Safavid Shî'î Emperor, Shâh Tahmâsp, whose artistic taste was formed in Herât where he grew up. Painters from both Herât and Tabrîz collaborated in producing this particular manuscript, which perfectly synthesizes the contribution of both schools and indeed represents the crowning achievement of the medieval Islamic Persianate tradition in figurative art. By 1545, like his symbolic model King Nôsherwân, Shâh Tahmâsp himself became seized with religious scruples and turned away from patronage of the figurative arts. Book-painting's aesthetic level thereafter dropped steeply in Iran itself, but won a new lease of creative life in Moghol India, whither

artists like Mîr Sayyed 'Alî himself departed to teach. Beneath the scribe Shâh-Mahmûd of Nîshâpûr's exquisite calligraphy (the swanlike necks of the horse and mule seem to echo the curves of his penmanship), Âghâ-Mîrak of Tabrîz and Mîr Sayyed 'Alî poignantly evoke the melancholy of fragile, animal-haunted desert buildings with flaking tiles lying shattered on the ground, leaving blank brick walls further disfigured by woodcutters' campfires. The disintegrating revetments with their tendrils and Prophetic Seals were designed with the surety of touch of master ceramists to convey a sense of brittleness and ruin. Another major artist of the period, Mîr Sayyed 'Alî's own father, Mîr Mosawwer of Herât, traced in a very fine hand the barely decipherable inscription on the whitewashed wall (near the gazelles): "The edifice of your ruined heart, in (illegible: 'piety'?') secure it in joy; no edifice is better in this lower world of ruin: Mîr Mosawwer wrote this in the year 946 (= AD 1538/1539)."

p. 43: *Bahrâm-Gûr Discovers the Effigies of his Future Seven Brides in the Secret Hall of Castle Khawarnaq*; Shîrâz, 1410; anonymous illumination to an anthology of poems for the Tîmûrid prince Eskandar; L.A. 161 f. 66v; Lisbon, Calouste Gulbenkian Foundation (state of the painting before recent deterioration). Photograph: Calouste Gulbenkian Foundation.

As governor of Shîrâz, Prince Eskandar, grandson to Tîmûr, gathered together the most talented painters in the Middle East to create a true Fine Arts Academy at his court and so sponsored the birth of the 15th-century Tîmûrid classical style. The failure of his rising in 1414 against his own father and overlord, the emperor Shâh Rokh, doomed the rash Prince to the penalty of blinding with hot irons – so putting an end both to his political career and to his sponsorship of the arts. Shâh Rokh took Eskandar's painters back with him to Herât, which thus became the Persianate world's new centre of the arts.

p. 60: *The Princess of Khwârazm beneath the Green Dome*, attributed to the painter Shaykhî; Tabrîz, 1481; illustration to a *Khamseh* (Quintet) of Nezâmî; Istanbul, Topkapı, H. 762/K. 412, f. 180v. Photograph: Topkapı Palace Museum Library.

In this painting, Bahrâm-Gûr betrays the features of the manuscript's sponsor, the youthful Turcoman sultan Ya'qûb of the White Sheep clan, draped over cushions in languid royal pose with concubines to

entertain him and massage his feet, but still wearing his archer's thumb-ring to remind the beholder of his warrior status as well. Shaykhî's exuberant handling of a spring landscape with twisted trees and tormented rocks in the Chinese manner – through which irrelevant hunters chase various beasts (as in the contemporary canvases of Paolo Uccello) – is an outstanding example of the romantic taste in painting prevalent at the 15th-century Tabrîz court, the former capital of the Western Mongols with its rich library of Chinese scrolls.

p. 84: *The Slav Princess beneath the Red Dome*, f. 212r.

p. 202: *The Byzantine Princess beneath the Yellow Dome*, f. 205v. Anonymous illustrations to a *Khamseh* of Nezâmî; Shîrâz, 1543; St Petersburg Institute of Oriental Studies, D-212. Photographs: R. and S. Michaud.

Reduced to provincial status after the fall of Prince Eskandar, Shîrâz nevertheless remained an important centre for the illumination of fine, although somewhat stereotyped, manuscripts for aristocratic patrons under Tîmûrid, Turcoman and Safavid rule. The painter here again depicts his Bahrâm-Gûr with the (stylized) features – round face, moustache, shaved chin – of his own ruling sovereign, Shâh Tahmâsp (r. 1524–76), represented in the Sasanian royal sitting pose, cup of sovereignty in hand. The red skullcap of the Shâh's turban is prolonged by a long, slender baton known as a *tâj* or "crown". This particular headgear was worn as an identifying sign by Shî'î partisans of Safavid rule in the earlier half of the 16th century (whence their Turkish nickname, *qizilbâsh* or "red-heads").

p. 96: *Building Tîmûr's Cathedral (Bîbî Khânom) Mosque in Samarkand*, by Behzâd; Herât; manuscript dated 1467, illustration added about 1480 to a *Zafar-Nâmeh* or "Book of Victories" by Sharafoddîn Yazdî: f. 359v; Baltimore, Johns Hopkins University, Milton S. Eisenhower Library, John Work Garrett Collection. Photograph: Johns Hopkins University.

Behzâd's illustration, for an epic in praise of the founder of the Tîmûrid dynasty, accurately mirrors the sort of architecture and building activity that the painter saw all around him in his native Herât and in neighbouring Mashhad – whose type of minaret studded with lozenge-medallions is very recognizable in this picture. The Castilian envoy to Tîmûr's court, Clavijo, testifies to the use of elephants for construction work in Samarkand; Behzâd sketched this animal from life in Sultan Hosayn Mîrzâ Bâyqarâ's own menagerie.

p. 104: *The Chinese Princess beneath the Sandalwood-coloured Dome*, f. 52v.

p. 220: *The Moorish Princess of the Moors beneath the Turquoise Dome*, f. 47r. Anonymous illuminations to the Turkish-language adaptation of Nezâmî's poem entitled *Sab'eh Sayyâreh* (The Seven Stars) by the vizier Mîr 'Alî Shêr Nawâ'î of Herât (1440–1501); Bokhârâ, 1553; Bodleian Library, Oxford, Elliot 318. Photograph: The Bodleian Library, University of Oxford.

Bahrâm-Gûr appears here with the mature, bearded features of the Uzbek emir, Yâr-Mohammad Khân (r. 1550–57). As conservative Sunnîs and stubborn opponents to the Shî'î Safavids of Iran, whom they regarded as heretics, the Uzbek emirs fought hard to wrest from the Safavids sovereignty of Herât, whose political and cultural legacy they also claimed. Many painters from Herât, who elected to remain Sunnî during the Persianate world's own bitter 16th-century Wars of Religion, sought shelter in Uzbek Bokhârâ, where they perpetuated the Tîmûrid style in a nostalgic and increasingly formalistic and repetitive manner – as here – until their generation died out.

p. 156: *The Persian Princess beneath the White Dome*, by Soltân-Mohammad; Tabrîz, about 1505; illustration to a *Khamseh* of Nezâmî; Istanbul, Topkapı, H. 762/K. 412, f. 196r. Photograph: Topkapı Palace Museum Library.

This painting belongs to the same manuscript as the depiction of the Princess of the Green Dome described above. The manuscript, still unfinished, fell as booty into the hands of the young Shî'î leader, Esmâ'îl, when he overthrew the White Sheep Turcomans and seized power as the first Safavid ruler in Tabrîz in 1501. This added illustration shows Esmâ'îl himself as successor to Bahrâm-Gûr and as Persia's new imperial ruler in the wake of the Turcoman sultans – right down to the same cup of sovereignty and royal foot-massage. The new Shâh, however, wears the *tâj* or baton-turban of his Shî'î partisans. The painter, Soltân-Mohammad, one of the very greatest masters of the Tabrîz school, here perpetuates the expressionist romantic manner enjoyed by his former Turcoman sponsors for his new royal patron – tortured Chinese-style rocks and clouds, wind-blown spring vegetation and boldly spiralled pool.

p. 236: *The Indian Princess beneath the Black Dome*; Herât, 1427; anonymous illustration, now detached, to a *Khamseh* of Nezâmî copied for the Tîmûrid prince Bâysonghor; Metropolitan Museum of Art, New York, Gift of Alexander Smith Cochrane, 1913 (13.228.13).

Beneath a Sasanian-style portal carved with angels, Bahrâm-Gûr is impersonated here by the young prince Bâysonghor (with faintly incipient moustache), brother to the unfortunate prince Eskandar. As the favourite son of Shâh Rokh and his consort Gôhar Shâd, Bâysonghor, "Royal Falcon", himself a gifted calligrapher, took the group of painters gathered in Shîrâz by Eskandar

under his own protection, and so sponsored and launched the classic school of Herât painting. But Bâysonghor never ruled. A sot like many of his house, he died prematurely of cirrhosis of the liver in 1434.

p. 276: *Nezâmî in the Magic Garden of the Poets*, by Qâsem 'Alî; Herât, 1485; frontispiece to the *Sadd-e Eskandar* (The Wall of Alexander), a Turkish-language adaptation of Nezâmî's *Alexander Romance* by Herât's vizier Mîr 'Alî Shêr Nawâ'î (1441–1501); Bodleian Library, Oxford, Elliot 340, f. 95v.

The vizier and Turkish-language poet Mîr 'Alî Shêr Nawâ'î is transported in a dream-vision to the magic garden of the great Persian poets of the past, whither he is guided by his older friend and literary mentor, Jâmî (1414–92), considered the greatest poet in Persian in his own day. The two living writers are welcomed on the same mat by the benevolent shade of Nezâmî, long-bearded and dignified, sitting near his scribal tools in the centre of the august assembly as the supreme master of narrative verse. By Nezâmî's left side also kneels the shade of his main Indo-Persian adaptor, Amîr Khosrô of Delhi (1253–1325). The living poet-vizier, in a standard gesture of respect, bows and hides his hands in his caftan sleeves, while Jâmî introduces him to Nezâmî as a disciple who, though a writer in Turkish, is not unworthy to be welcomed in such a gathering. The spirit of this painting very much recalls the atmosphere of Canto IV of the *Inferno*, where in similar fashion Virgil introduces Dante, poet in a new language, to the shades of the great Greek and Latin writers.

Chronology

ARAB PERIOD (622–1055)

622: Mohammad becomes ruler of Medina. Beginning of Islamic era.

632: Death of the Prophet.

635–37: Arab conquest of Byzantine Syria. Sasanian Persians defeated by Arabs at Battle of Qâdesiyeh (Iraq).

661: Umayyad caliphs set up their capital at Damascus. IN ART: Damascus Mosque; Dome of the Rock in Jerusalem; influence of Roman-Byzantine mosaics.

711: Muslims conquer Spain.

750: Umayyads overthrown by 'Abbâsids.

756: Independent Umayyad emirate of Cordova.

762: Capital of 'Abbâsid caliphate transferred to Baghdad.

786–809: Reign of Caliph Hârûn ar-Rashîd. Zenith of 'Abbâsid power.

875: Autonomous Iranian emirate of Sâmânids in Bokhârâ (Uzbekistan).
IN ART: Stucco revetment; resurgence of Sasanian influences in Eastern Islam; faïence technique developed.

911: Rise of Shî'î Fâtimids in Tunisia, torn from caliph's rule.

929: Cordova proclaims herself a (Sunnî) caliphate in the Islamic West.

969: Fâtimids take Egypt, found Cairo and create Shî'î counter-caliphate.

997–1030: Rule of East Turkish (Sunnî) sultan Mahmûd in Ghaznî (Afghanistan): Islamic conquests in northwest India. Persian regains linguistic parity with Arabic in the administration throughout Eastern Islam.

1030: In the West, fall and division of the caliphate of Cordova between rival Andalusian emirates. Rise of Berber powers in North Africa.

1055: Seljuk Turks enter Baghdad as "protectors" and emerge as Sunnî overlords of the Levant. Beginning of nearly nine centuries of Turkish sway throughout Eastern Islam. Strengthening of Persian linguistic and cultural influence.

MEDIEVAL TURCO-MONGOL PERIOD (1055–1501)

1071: Battle of Manzikert: Seljuk Turks break through Byzantine lines and conquer Anatolia, or "Rûm".

1085: Toledo falls to Castilian knights.

1099: Jerusalem falls to Frankish Crusaders.

1156: Death of Sultan Sanjar in Merv (Turkmenistan); break-up of Seljuk Empire which survives only in Anatolia.

1171: The Kurdish sultan Salâh ad-Dîn (Saladin) overthrows Fâtimids and restores rule of Sunnî orthodoxy in Cairo.

1187: Saladin recaptures Jerusalem from Crusaders.

1192: The Ghôrids of Herât (Afghanistan) conquer Delhi. IN ART: Tomb of Seljuk sultan Sanjar at Merv: first known dome sheathed in blue tiles (now disappeared). Appearance of blue tiles on Ghôrid monuments. Persian poetry of Nezâmî in Azerbaijan (1141–1209). In West, zenith of Moorish style in architecture in Morocco and Andalusia under Berber Almohad caliphs; rise of mystical school of Ibn 'Arabî, who departs to teach in Eastern Islam (Syria, Anatolia) after 1198.

1206: Founding of Sultanate of Delhi. Rise of Indo-Islamic architecture in red sandstone (Qutb Minar).

1212: In the West, Almohad caliphs crushed by Castilian forces at Battle of Las Navas de Tolosa: collapse of Islamic Spain. Only emirate of Granada survives by end of century.

1220: Beginning of Mongol invasions in Eastern Islam.

1243: Mongols reduce Seljuk Sultanate of Rûm (Anatolia) to vassalage, but spare the region, which comes to shelter much of 13th-century Eastern Islam's cultural creativity. Rise of use of architectural tiling at Konya. Poetry of Rûmî.

1258: Mongols destroy Baghdad.

1260: Battle of 'Ayn-Jalût (Palestine): Mamlûk rulers of Egypt block further Mongol expansion. Carved stone architecture in Egyptian capital.

1295: The Mongol Îl-Khân, Ghazan, converts to Islam in his capital at Tabrîz (Iran). Persianate cultural renaissance. Strong Chinese artistic influences. In Anatolia, Seljuk Sultanate disintegrates among contending Turkish emirates. Rise of Ottoman emirate.

1313: Tomb of the Îl-Khân Oljâytû at Soltâniyeh (Iran): rise of the classic Persian-type mausoleum, with blue-tiled dome.

1335: Break-up of Mongol rule in Eastern Islam.

1346–48: Black Death. In Islamic West, sunset glow of Moorish architectural style: Alhambra in Granada, theological colleges of Fez: stucco with tiled dadoes (*azulejos*).

1357: Ottoman Turks, at Gallipoli, cross over into Europe.

1370–1405: Tîmûr-e Lang or Tamerlane, Turco-Mongol emir of Samarkand, attempts to restore Mongol Empire. Raids as far as Anatolia and India. Samarkand embellished. Triumph of tiled architecture.

1405–1506: Rule of Tîmûr's successors, the Tîmûrids, at Herât, now centre of "Tîmûrid Renaissance" in Eastern Islam. Flourishing of the poet Jâmî and the painter Behzâd.

1447: Turcomans of the clan of the Black Sheep establish power in Tabrîz and Western Iran, now lost to Tîmûrids.

1453: Ottoman Turks conquer Constantinople.

1492: Fall of Granada, end of Islamic Spain.

1498: Vasco da Gama reaches Calicut: Portuguese now outflank Islamic landmass by sea. Islamic states fail fully to perceive naval and other technical implications, scorn invention of the printing press, but adopt gunpowder.

1501: Uzbek Turks take Samarkand from the Tîmûrids (Herât falls to them in 1507).
In Art: Golden Age of classical Persianate manuscript illumination, architecture and tiling, as at Samarkand (Mausoleum of Tîmûr, 1405), Herât (Mausoleum of Gôhar Shâd, 1447) and Tabrîz (Blue Mosque, 1465).

PERIOD OF THE NEO-CLASSICAL EMPIRES (1501–1722)

1501: Esmâ'îl, first Safavid ruler, imposes Shî'ism in Tabrîz.

1510: Safavids spread Shî'ism as far as Herât.

1514: Battle of Châlderân: Ottomans block western expansion of Shî'î political power and restrict it to Iranian plateau, where it is further hemmed in, to the East, by Sunnî Uzbeks.

1516–17: Ottomans annex Syria and Egypt.

1526: Ottomans in Hungary and outside Vienna. Creation of "Moghol" Empire of India by the Tîmûrid prince Bâber of Kabul. Islamic landmass now mainly split between three empires, two of them Sunnî (the Ottoman and the Moghol), separated by an Iranian Shî'î enclave (the Safavid).

1552: Muscovites take emirate of Kazan; beginning of Russian expansion into Islamic Asia.

1557: Zenith of Ottoman architecture. Tiling restricted to interiors. Appearance of "Iznik red" on tiles of Istanbul's Süleymâniye Mosque, built by master architect Sinân.

1571: Battle of Lepanto: Venice and Spain break Ottoman naval power in Mediterranean, after Portuguese naval supremacy already ensured over Islamic fleets in Indian Ocean at battle of Diu (1509).

1598: Esfahân becomes capital of Safavids. Final flowering of neo-classical Persian architecture. Complete sheathing in tiles of Lotfollâh Mosque (1601–28) and Royal Mosque (1612–38) on Esfahân's Royal Square.

1628–58: In India, rule of Shâh Jahân; zenith of Moghol architecture. After completion of the "Picture Wall" (1631) and the Wazîr Khân Mosque (1634) in Lahore, tiling progressively abandoned in favour of red sandstone (Delhi Fort, 1639–48) and marble (Tâj Mahal in Agra, 1630–48).

1699: Treaty of Karlowitz: permanent retreat of Ottoman power in the Balkans before Austrian forces.

1706–17: Mosque of the Mother of the Shâh, last Safavid monument in Esfahân. In the West, first appearance of French translation of the *Thousand and One Nights*.

1707: Decline of Moghol Empire, weakened by Hindu revolts. British supremacy in subcontinent as of 1757.

1722: Sack of Esfahân by insurgent Sunnî Afghans. Fall of Safavid Empire. Russian forces reach Caucasus.

Glossary

"Persianate" (*Pârsîwân*) best designates that part of Eastern Islamic civilization between the Bosphorus and the Ganges where Persian, rather than Arabic (save in ritual), increasingly served as the main cultural and administrative language from the 11th century onwards. By the 16th century, written Persian was being wielded with equal facility by Ottoman Bosnians like the literary critic Sûdî and by Brahmins at the Moghol court – such as Emperor Akbar's pundits who translated the Sanskrit classics into what had become the universal court language of the subcontinent. In India, chancery Persian declined only when replaced in 1836 by English. Today, official use of Persian has contracted to Iran, Afghanistan and Tajikistan. The cultural relation of Persian to Arabic rather resembles that of Japanese to Chinese – same borrowed script, followed by a vast stock of borrowed words, but radically modified pronunciation and, of course, completely different linguistic family.

Transcriptions here reflect Persian rather than Arabic forms. The Persian standard used is that of the city of Herât, which much better than Tehran upholds to this day the high classical or *darî* pronunciation. Accented vowels are lengthened. *W* may be read with an English or German value, depending on district; *r* is trilled as in Spanish; *kh* corresponds to Spanish "j" or final German "ch"; *gh* represents the throaty French "r" of Paris; *q* normally designates a hard "k" pronounced deep in the throat (as observed in conservative Herât), but Tehran slurs it into a "gh" and modern Western Turks render it as a simple "k" – so the English reader can afford to do likewise. Many English ceramic terms are Iberian, reflecting medieval Spain's transmission of Islamic techniques to the West.

ALICATADO (Spanish): Mosaic faïence.

ALICERES (Spanish): The individual monochrome pieces making up mosaic faïence.

ARISTA (DE) (Spanish): Bands moulded in relief to separate fields of colour when baked in the kiln.

"ARMENIAN BOLE": From Greek *bôlos*, "clay" or "earth". An Anatolian clay rich in iron oxide, valued in medieval times for its supposed medical properties, and from which mid-16th-century Ottoman ceramists learned to secure a brilliant red.

AVESTIC: From *Avesta*, the Zoroastrian Scriptures: the oldest known form of the Persian language, related to Sanskrit; transcribed in cuneiform characters under the Achaemenids.

AZULEJO (Spanish and Portuguese): "Ceramic tile". Resemblance to Spanish "azul" or "azure" is coincidental, since the etymology is classical Arabic *az-zulayj*, "the tile" (*ez-zelîj* in Moroccan patois). Here as elsewhere, conservative softer Portuguese pronunciation ("z" and "j" as in French) better points to an original underlying Arabic word than harsher post-medieval Castilian usage. For the

Islamic etymology of Spanish "azul", whence English "azure" (through French *azur*), see LÂJWARD.

BÂDANJÂN (Persian): The eggplant – whence English "aubergine" (through French). Medieval Persian potters used this name to designate a brownish purple.

BANNÂ'Î (Arabic): "Masonwrought" or, literally, "what pertains to the mason (*bannâ*)"; in medieval Persian, designated patterned wall-surfaces of alternating bare and enamelled bricks.

CHÎN, CHÎNÎ (Persian): "China" and "Chinese". The origin of this name, whence European forms, goes back to the 3rd-century BC Ch'in Dynasty, which built the Great Wall. In medieval Persian, the epithet could also designate tile revetment itself (compare English "china"), as well as decorative motifs of acknowledged Chinese origin, like the lotus. GEL-E CHÎNÎ = "Chinese clay" = kaolin. ÎZÂR-E CHÎNÎ = "Chinese casing" = i.e. an internal tiled dado. See also KHATÂ, KHATÂ'Î.

CUERDA SECA (Spanish): "Dry cord": in ceramics, the manganese-based greasy black line drawn to separate fields of colour and prevent them from running into one another in the kiln.

DARÎ: "Court language". The official title of Persian (*Pârsî* or *Fârsî*) as transcribed into Arabic characters, when it recovered full administrative parity with Arabic in the chancery of the Sâmânid emirs of Bokhârâ in the 9th century AD. Today designates the more classical form of Persian still observed in Afghanistan, Tajikistan and northeastern Iran, as opposed to the "modern" accent of Tehran (reminiscent of modern Greek) with its reduced vowel system and slurred consonants.

EBLÎS or IBLÎS (Arabic): The Devil. Originally an Arabization of Greek *diabolos*, but the mystic Al-Hallâj (executed for heresy in Baghdad in 922) explained the name as being derived from the Arabic root *l-b-s*, "clothing", whence the word ELTEBÂS (q.v.): "revetment". The Devil, who here serves God's purposes unawares, is suffered to weave the illusory veil of the lower world and thereby hinders profane vision from apprehending underlying divine unity – whence the mystic expression, *Talbîs Eblîs*, "Devil's Revetment".

EKSÎR (Persian) or AL-IKSÎR (Arabic): The "elixir" (medieval Europe's word entered through Spain) or Philosopher's Stone: one which, if at long last located and so added to the ores and minerals crushed by the craftsman, might finally yield gold when baked in the kiln or retort. In mystic usage, symbolizes the transformation of the soul.

ELTEBÂS or ILTIBÂS (Arabic): "Revetment". In mysticism, the word designates a "revetment of ambiguity" or Veil of phenomenal appearances behind which the Divine remains masked. Corresponds in Islamic thought to the Sanskrit concept of *mâyâ*.

ENSÂN-E KÂMEL (Persian) or AL-INSÂN AL-KÂMIL (Arabic): Prototypical or Perfect Man; Anthropos; a Prophet or Imâm.

'ERFÂN (Persian) or 'IRFÂN (Arabic): Arabization of the Greek word *Gnôsis*, "knowledge" (mystical).

ESLÎMÎ-E BARGÎ (Persian): In adornment, a "wreath of leaves". See also TAWRÎQ (Arabic).

FERANGÎ, FERANGESTÂN (Persian) or FIRANJ (Arabic): "Frank", "Land of the Franks": Eastern Islam so designated Western Christians after the First Crusade.

FUSAYFISA (Arabic): In medieval usage, designated glass-cube mosaics of Roman and Byzantine type.

GOMBAD (Persian): "Dome"; the expressions GOMBAD-E MÎNÂ, "turquoise dome", and GOMBAD-E KHAZRÂ, "green dome", both designate the sky.

GÛR: Onager, or wild ass of the desert; sobriquet of Shâh Bahram, famous for hunting them; homonym: GÛR = tomb, whence innumerable mystic puns and also the GÛR-E MÎR, "Tomb of the Emir" (Tîmûr's mausoleum in Samarkand).

HAFT RANG (Persian): "Seven Colours", polychromy; see RANG.

HAKKÂKÎ (Arabic): "Lapidary"; used by the tilemasters of Herât for inlaid work within an incised surface.

HAZÂR BÂF (Persian): "Thousand Weavings"; a wall-surface patterned in relief with light and shadow play, created solely by the arrangement of its bare bricks.

IMÂM (Arabic) or EMÂM (Persian): He who guides prayer "before", a prayer leader; title of the legitimate successor to the caliph 'Alî in the eyes of the Shî'î faithful.

ÎWÂN (Persian, borrowed by Arabic): High ogee gateway.

JAWHAR (Arabic; also Persian *gôhar*): Gem; pearl; also (in alchemy, and especially in mysticism) the Essence.

KAPI (Western Turkish): A portal or gateway (Topkapı = "Cannon Gate"); in Ottoman and Eastern Turkish, *qâpı*; *'Âlî Qâpı* = "the Sublime Porte".

KÂSHÎ (Persian): Adjective formed from the name of the city of Kâshân, a major ceramic centre from the 12th century on; KÂSHÎ KÂRÎ: "Kâshân work" = ceramics, tilework; medieval Arabic harshens the epithet with an initial guttural: QÂSHÂNÎ.

KAWTHAR (Arabic) or KAWSAR (Persian): Name of a river in Heaven.

KHADRÂ (Arabic) or KHAZRÂ (Persian): Green; GOMBAD-E KHAZRÂ: the "Green Dome" = the sky.

KHÂN (Turco-Mongol): "Lord"; title adopted throughout Persianate Islam. ÎL-KHÂN – "Vassal Lord" – title of the Mongol rulers of Iran, vassals to the Great Khân in Peking, in the 13th and early 14th centuries.

KHÂNEH (Persian): Dwelling, home, house.

KHATÂ, KHATÂ'Î: One of the Persian names and epithets for China, Chinese – whence Marco Polo's "Cathay". KHATÂ'Î may designate a decorative motif of Chinese origin. See also CHÎN, CHÎNÎ.

KHATT, KHATTÂT (Arabic): Calligraphy; calligrapher.

KHEZR (Persian; Arabic al-Khadir, the "Evergreen One"): A mysterious holy man, companion to Eskandar (Alexander), who won immortality by bathing in the Fountain of Life. The ultimate origin of this figure goes back to the character of Utnapishtim in the Sumerian Epic of Gilgamesh. In medieval Islamic writings, Khezr typifies both the initiator of the mystic path and the immortal aspect of each soul itself.

KOSHTEH (Persian): "Slain"; designates heated or baked metal in the language of the Herât tilemasters.

KUFIC (Arabic: *Kûfî*): From the name of the city of Kûfa in Iraq; designates an archaic, highly geometric and right-angled form of Arabic script. Much used in architectural adornment or for monumental inscriptions in stylized variations ranging from geometric mazes to "floriated". It is often exceedingly difficult to read – when it is meant to be read at all. Persianate KÛFÎ GONG, or "mute kufic", means precisely that: letter-shapes devoid of sense and used solely for abstract decoration.

LÂJWARD (Persian, borrowed by Arabic): "Lapis lazuli" (itself the medieval Spanish Latin rendering for "stone of lâjward" or "stone of azure"): originally the name of a village near famous mines of the stone in what is now the northeast Afghan province of Badakhshan; ended by designating first the stone, then its colour, in Persian and Arabic, whence Spanish *azul* and finally English "azure"; really a misnomer, since etymologically "azure" should signify a dark or ultramarine blue.

MA'DAN, MA'DANI (Arabic): Mine; mineral.

MADRASA (classical Arabic form): "Place of study", institution for higher religious education. Such schools were created in the Near East in the 11th century under the Seljuk sultans by their vizier Nezâm-ol-Molk to spread Sunnî doctrine and counteract Shî'î influence; ironically, the Shî'î hierarchy adopted the institution for their own purposes. Regional forms: *madraseh* (Persian); *medrese* (Turkish); *medersa* (Moroccan Arabic).

MALANG (Persian): A dervish, or wandering and begging Muslim mystic devotee, as known in Afghanistan, Pakistan and India.

MASJID (Arabic) or MASJED (Persian): "Place for prostration"; pronounced in various West Arabic dialects *mesgid*, whence Spanish *mezquita*, and ultimately English "mosque".

MAWLÂ, MAWLÂNÂ (Arabic; Turkish pronunciation: *Mevlânâ*): "Lord", "Our Lord", title of respect for religious dignitaries (hence the famous 13th-century poet and divine, Mawlânâ or Mevlânâ

Jalâloddîn Rumî). This title was corrupted in Persian and Indo-Persian usage into *mollâ*, whence English "mullah".

MIHRÂB (Arabic) or MEHRÂB (Persian): Blind niche in the far wall of a mosque, indicating the direction of Mecca.

MÎNÂ, MÎNÂ'Î (Arabic and Persian): Name and epithet for glazing, enamel and a deep turquoise blue; MÎNÂ'Î also designates a 12th- and 13th-century Persianate school of figurative underglaze painting on ceramics, where such blue was much used; GOMBAD-E MÎNÂ, "the turquoise dome", is the sky.

MINÂR (Arabic), MENÂR (Persian), MINÂRE (Turkish): "Minaret". Etymologically, a "fire-tower" or "light-house", but adopted in Islam for the call to prayer: whence ultimately the English name for a mosque-tower.

MI'RÂJ (Arabic) or ME'RÂJ (Persian): "Ascent", especially the ecstatic, visionary otherworldly ascent of the Prophet.

MITHQÂL (Arabic): Variable medieval measure of weight (about 4.5 grams).

MO'ARRAQ (Arabic): "Inlaid"; designates mosaic faïence in the language of the tilemasters of Herât.

MOQARNAS (Arabic): On squinches or under the vaulting of ogee gateways, a typically Islamic form of decoration basically carved in wood or plaster, then painted, gilt or tiled, to form complex honeycombed corbellings suggestive of stalactites.

MOSALLÂ (Arabic): "Place of prayer". Several celebrated devotional architectural complexes in the Persianate world have been so called, notably in Shîrâz and Herât.

NAQQÂSH (Arabic): Painter, manuscript illuminator. NAQQÂSH-KHÂNEH (Persian) or NAKKAŞ-HANE (Turkish): "Painters' house": the Ottoman court workshop.

NASKH (Arabic): Ordinary Arabic cursive script.

NASTA'LÎQ (Persian): A compound of the two Arabic words *naskh* (cursive script) and *ta'lîq* (suspension) to designate the typical Persian form of elegant penmanship, "suspended cursive", invented by the master scribe Mîr 'Alî Tabrîzî at the end of the 14th century; it was at once adopted for the best manuscripts in Persian, then Turkish and more recently Urdu; its use is relatively rare for Arabic. All the 15th- and 16th-century manuscript illuminations reproduced in this book feature this script.

PAHLAVÎ: Original form of the name "Parthian"; also designates Middle Persian, the form of the language spoken before the rise of Islam under the Parthian and Sasanian dynasties.

PARWÂNEH (Persian; Turkish pronunciation: *Pervanê*): Literally, "moth" or "butterfly"; the strange title borne by the prime ministers to the 13th-century Anatolian Seljuk sultans, in a poetic allusion to "moths" circling the royal flame.

PIETRA DURA (Italian): Marquetry of semi-precious "hard stones" inlaid in marble; technique invented in Renaissance Florence and adopted in 17th-

century Moghol Indian architecture through the influence of European artisans in Moghol court service.

QÂSHÂNÎ (Arabic): Ceramic tiling. See KÂSHÎ.

RANG (Persian): Colour; HAFT RANG = "Seven Colours", polychromy (said of a brick fired in several colours at once); RANG-E DÔ ÂTESHÎ = "Colour of Twin Fires", lustring; TAGHYÎR-E RANG = "Change of colour".

RÛM, RÛMÎ: "Rome" and "Roman". In medieval Arabic and Persian, first designated the Eastern Roman Empire and its subjects, and mainly Anatolia; then, once Anatolia was brought under Seljuk Turkish domination, the term RÛM continued to be applied to this territory – whence the sobriquet of the poet Rûmî, "the Anatolian". In Islamic art terminology, RÛMÎ also designated decorative motifs of manifest Graeco-Roman origin: for example, the GEREH-E RÛMÎ or "Roman knot", our "Greek frieze".

SANDALÎ (Arabic): "Pertaining to Sandalwood"; the poet Nezâmî used this term to describe a rich reddish-brown.

SANG (Persian): "Stone"; SANG-E SOLAYMÂNÎ = "Stone of Solomon", the magic seal of this Prophet. In the language of the medieval Persian tilemasters, the "Stone of Solomon" is false lapis lazuli, that is, cobalt, which alone yielded ultramarine or "azure" in the kiln. SANG-E ÂTESH-BARQ: the "fire-stone", or flintstone.

SÂZ (Persian): "Fashion" or "manner"; in Ottoman Turkey, designated a painting style of floral-type ornaments.

SHAJARA, SHAJARAT AL-KAWN (Arabic): "Tree" and "Tree of Being" or "Tree of Life". Title of a mystic treatise by Ibn 'Arabî (1160–1240). The root form *sh-j-r* yields the Arabic name for a key element in ornament: *tashjîr*, "that which is arboreal".

SHÂKHÛRÂ (Persian): Medieval kiln, for lustring.

SÛFÎ (Arabic): A mystic, whence English "Sufism" to designate Islamic mysticism (in Arabic and Persian, *tasawwof*). Popular Islamic tradition would have the name derive from Arabic *sûf*, the "pure white wool" which the first Muslim mystics were supposed to have worn; but the etymology suggested by the learned 11th-century polymath Al-Bêrûnî of Khwârazm, from Greek *sophos* or "wise man", makes far more sense.

TASHJÎR (Arabic): In ornament, "that which is arboreal". See SHAJARA.

TAWRÎQ (Arabic): In ornament, "leaf tendril" – from the Arabic root *w-r-q*, "a leaf". See also ESLÎMÎ-E BARGÎ (Persian).

THULUTH (Arabic) or SOLOS (Persian): A cursive Arabic script, slightly inclined to the left.

TÜLBEND (Turkish: from Persian *tûl-band*, "long band"): The "turban", in Ottoman usage, also served to designate the tulip, literally considered the "turban-flower"; English "turban" and "tulip" thus both derive from Turkish *tülbend*.

WAZÎR (Arabic and Persian; Turkish pronunciation: *vezîr*): Minister, "vizier"; the European forms derive from the Turkish.

Further Reading

ISLAMIC FINE ARTS
IN THEIR HISTORICAL CONTEXT

Greek sources

BERTHELOT, M.: *Collection des alchimistes grecs*, Paris 1887–88 (with original Greek texts).

CTESIAS in DIODORUS SICULUS, bk II, Loeb text (C.H. Oldfather).

"Hermes Trismegistus": *Corpus Hermeticum*, Greek text ed. by A.D. Nock and A.J. Festugière, Fr. tr. by A.J. Festugière, Paris 1954–60.

HERODOTUS: *Histories*, bk I, Loeb text (A.D. Godley).

PTOLEMY OF ALEXANDRIA: *Tetrabiblos*, Greek text ed. with Italian tr. by Simonetta Feraboli, Fondazione Lorenzo Valla/Mondadori 1985.

Islamic sources pertaining to tilework, painting and alchemy

ABO-L-QÂSEM 'Abdollâh ebn-e 'Alî ebn-e Mohammad ebn-e Tâher of Kâshân, *fl. anno hegirae* 700 (AD 1301): *Ketâb-e Jawâher al-'Arâ'es wa Atâyeb an-Nafâ'es* (Book of Those Brides That Are Gems and Scents); Persian text ed. from Istanbul MSS. with German intr. and tr. by H. Ritter, J. Ruska, F. Sarre and R. Winderlich, *Orientalische Steinbücher und Persische Fayencetechnik*, Istanbuler Mitteilungen, Istanbul, 1935. Engl. version by J.W. Allan, "Abu'l-Qasim's Treatise on Ceramics", *Iran* 11 (1973), pp. 111–20.

ABU-L-QÂSIM Muhammad al-'Irâqî (13th cent.): *Zirâ'at adh-Dhahab* (The Cultivation of Gold), Arabic text ed. with Engl. intr. and tr. by A.J. Holmyard, Paris 1923.

AL-BÊRÛNÎ (11th cent.): *Kitâb al-Jamâhir* (Book of Gems), Arabic text ed. by F. Krenkow, Hyderabad (India) 1936; *Kitâb al-Athâr al-Bâqiya* (Book of Remaining Traces)/*Chronology of Ancient Nations*, Arabic text ed. with Engl. intr. and tr. by E. Sachau, London 1879.

DÔST MOHAMMAD of Herât (16th cent.): So-called "Book of Painters and Calligraphers" (introductory epistle to an album of paintings collected for the Safavid prince Bahrâm Mîrzâ, Topkapı MS. H. 2154); Persian text ed. by Mohammad 'Abdollâh Chaghatâ'î, Lahore 1936, and Fekrî Saljûqî, Kabul 1970; Engl. tr. in *A Century of Princes: Sources on Timurid History and Art* (translations with commentaries from Persian and Turkish), by W.M. Thackston, Cambridge (Mass.) 1989.

MOHAMMAD ebn-e Mansûr (*fl.* AD 1450): *Dar Lâjward* (On lapis lazuli): Persian text ed. with German intr. and tr. in Ritter, Ruska, Sarre and Winderlich, 1935.

QÂZÎ AHMAD QOMÎ (16th cent.): *Golestân-e Honar* (Garden of Arts); Persian text ed. by A.S. Sohaylî, Tehran 1973; Engl. tr. by V. Minorsky, *Calligraphers and Painters*, Washington DC 1959.

BERTHELOT, M.: *La chimie au Moyen Âge* (collection of Arabic and Medieval Latin texts), Paris 1893.

KRAUS, P.: *Jâbir ibn Hayyân* (with Arabic texts), Cairo 1942–43.

RUSKA, J.: *Das Steinbuch des Aristoteles*, Heidelberg 1912; *Arabische Alchemisten*, Heidelberg 1924; *Tabula Smaragdina*, Heidelberg 1926 (with Greek, Arabic and Medieval Latin texts).

Selected modern studies pertaining to Islamic architecture, its decoration and general aesthetics

ALBARN, K., with J.M. SMITH, S. STEELE and D. WALKER: *The Language of Pattern*, London 1974.

ALLEN, T.: *A Catalogue of Monuments and Toponyms of Tîmûrid Herât*, Cambridge (Mass.) 1981.

ATASOY, N., and J. RABY: *Iznik: The Pottery of Ottoman Turkey*, London 1989.

ATIL, E.: "The Royal Kilns", in *The Age of Sultan Sûleyman the Magnificent*, ed. by J.M. ROGERS and M. WARD, New York 1987/London 1988.

AUBIN, J.: "Le mécénat tîmoûride à Chiraz", *Studia Islamica*, (1957); "Comment Tamerlan prenait les villes", ibid. (1963).

BERNUS-TAYLOR, M.: *Les arts de l'Islam*, Louvre, Réunion des Musées nationaux, Paris 1994; with M. CHARITAT and J. GUILLERMINA: "Céramique de l'Orient musulman", *Cahiers, Musée d'art et d'essai*, 1 (Dec. 1979).

BLAIR, S., and J. BLOOM: *The Art and Architecture of Islam, 1250–1800*, London 1995.

BREND, B.: *Islamic Art*, London 1991.

BRUNO, A.: *Restoration of Monuments in Herât*, UNESCO 1981.

BYRON, R.: *The Road to Oxiana*, London 1937.

CARSWELL, J.: "Ceramics", in *Tulips, Arabesques and Turbans: Decorative Arts from the Ottoman Empire*, ed. by Y. Petsopoulos, London 1982.

CENTLIVRES, M.: *Une communauté de potiers en Iran*, Wiesbaden 1971.

ETTINGHAUSEN, R.: *Arab Painting*, Skira/Geneva 1962; with O. GRABAR: *The Art and Architecture of Islam, 650–1250*, Harmondsworth 1987.

GHIRSHMAN, R.: *Parthes et Sassanides*, Paris 1962; *Iran ancien*, Paris 1964.

GLATZER, B., with M. CASIMIR: "Šâh-i Mašhad, a Recently Discovered Madrasah of the Ghûrid Period in Garǧistân (Afghanistan)", *East and West* n.s. vol. 211–2 (March–June 1971), Istituto per il Medio Oriente, Via Merulana 248, Rome; "Das Mausoleum und die Moschee des Ghôriden Ghiyât ud-Dîn in Herât", *Afghanistan Journal* 7/1 (1980), pp. 6–22.

GOLOMBEK, L., and D. WILBER: *The Timurid Architecture of Iran and Turan*, 2 vols, Princeton 1988.

GRABAR, O. (D. HILL, photographer): *Islamic Architecture and its Decoration*, London 1967.

KEHREN, L.: "Une brique émaillée de la Grande Mosquée de Samarkand", *Journal asiatique* (1967).

LANE, A.: *Early Islamic Pottery*, London 1947; *Later Islamic Pottery*, London 1957; *Victoria and Albert Museum: A Guide to the Collection of Tiles*, London 1960.

LENTZ, G., and G.D. LOWRY: *Timur and the Princely Vision*, Los Angeles/Washington DC 1989.

McCHESNEY, R.D.: *Waqf in Central Asia: Four Hundred Years of the History of a Muslim Shrine, 1480–1889* (= Mazâr-e Sharîf), Princeton 1991.

MELIKIAN-CHIRVANI, A.S.: "Eastern Iranian Architecture: Apropos of the Ghûrid Parts of the Great Mosque of Harât", *Bulletin of the School of Oriental and African Studies* 33/2 (1970), pp. 322–27.

O'KANE, B.: *Timurid Architecture in Khurasan*, Costa Mesa (California) 1987.

OTTO-DORN, K.: *Türkische Keramik*, Ankara 1957.

PACCARD, A.: *Le Maroc et l'artisanat traditionnel dans l'architecture islamique*, 2 vols, 1979.

PARROT, A.: *Sumer*, Paris 1960; *Assur*, Paris 1961.

PINDER WILSON, R.: *Islamic Art*, New York 1957.

POPE, A.U.: *A Survey of Persian Art*, 6 vols, London and New York 1938–39; new ed. 1964; *Persian Architecture*, London 1965.

PORTER, V.: *Islamic Tiles*, London 1995.

POUGATCHENKOVA, G.: *Chefs-d'oeuvre de l'architecture de l'Asie Centrale, XIVe–XVe siècles*, Paris 1981.

QURAESHI, S., with A. SCHIMMEL: *Lahore: The City Within*, Singapore 1988.

ROGERS, J.M.: *Islamic Art and Design, 1500–1700*, London 1983.

SAMIZAY, R.: *Islamic Architecture in Herât: A Study towards Conservation*, Seattle 1981.

SOUDAVAR, A.: *Art of the Persian Courts*, New York 1992.

SOURDEL-THOMINE, J., and D. SCHLUMBERGER: "Lashkarî Bâzâr: une résidence royale ghaznévide et ghôride", *Mémoires de la Délégation Archéologique Française en Afghanistan (DAFA)* 18 (1978).

STIERLIN, H.: *L'Alhambra*, Paris 1989.

TALBOT RICE, T.: *The Seljuks*, New York 1961.

TORRES BALBAS, L.: "Arte califal", in *Historia de España*, ed. by R. Menéndez Pidal, vol. 5: *España musulmana hasta la caída del califato de Córdoba*, new ed., Madrid 1990.

VOGEL, J. Ph.: *The Tile Mosaics of Lahore Fort*, Calcutta 1920.

WATSON, O.: *Persian Lustre Ware*, London 1985; "Islamic Ceramics" in *Treasures of Islam*, Geneva 1985; "Ceramics" in *Islamic Art in the Keir Collection*, London 1988.

WIET, G.: *Le minaret de Djâm*, Paris 1957.

WILBER, D.: "The Development of Mosaic Faïence in Islamic Architecture in Iran", *Ars Islamica* 6/1 (1939), pp. 16–47.

WOLFE, Nancy Hatche (Dupree): *Herât: A Pictorial Guide*, Kabul 1966.

WULFF, H.: *The Traditional Crafts of Persia*, Cambridge (Mass.) 1966.

NEZÂMÎ: TEXTS, TRANSLATIONS, STUDIES, ILLUSTRATIONS

Texts

The poet's five romances in verse, collectively known in Persian as "The Five Treasures" (*Panj Ganj*) or "Quintet" (*Khamseh*), are believed to have been composed in the following order (according to A. Bausani's chronology):

"The Treasury of Secrets" (*Makhzan-ol-Asrâr*), 1176;

"Chosroes and Shîrîn" (*Khosrô-ô Shîrîn*), 1180;

"Laylâ and Majnûn" (*Laylâ-ô Majnûn*), 1188;

"The Alexander Romance" (*Eskandar-Nâmeh*), itself divided into two parts: "The Book of Nobility" (*Sharaf-Nâmeh*), 1191, and "The Book of Good Fortune" (*Eqbâl-Nâmeh*), before 1209;

"The Brides of the Seven Climes", literally "The Seven Effigies" (*Haft Paykar*), dedicated to Sultan 'Alâ-od-Dîn Korb-Arslân of Marâgheh in southern Azerbaijan, in 1197.

For the Persian text of the *Haft Paykar*, three recensions are standard: 1) ed. by H. Ritter and J. Rypka, Prague 1934; 2) ed. by V. Dastgerdî, Tehran 1955; 3) ed. by T.A. Magerramov, Baku/Moscow 1987.

Translations

In the 15th and 16th centuries many Turkish adaptations of Nezâmî appeared, both in Herât (by Mîr 'Alî Shêr Nawâ'î) and in the Ottoman lands (by Ahmedî, Shaykhî and Fuzûlî, among others).

Nezâmî's poetry is extremely difficult to translate into modern Western languages, although "Euphuism" and the English 17th-century Metaphysicals – and better, Italian and Spanish Baroque writers – may suggest some traits he shares with other classical Persian poets. Louis Massignon has described the process of metaphor in traditional Islamic poetry as one often following a descending scale whereby a human being is compared to a noble animal, such an animal to a flower, and this flower to a jewel: thus perceived reality becomes frozen into a garden of gems. In Nezâmî's case, Ritter further suggests that the poet's metaphors turn into almost autonomous images which interact independently of their initial supports. The two European poets to whom Nezâmî comes perhaps the closest – and with whom he certainly ranks in greatness – are Góngora and Mallarmé. Like the Spanish Baroque and French Symbolist masters, Nezâmî often prefers *not to name* an object, but rather to suggest it, by forcing his reader to *guess* its presence through sparkling verbal touches which outline its imaginary contour. He thus leaves in the centre a deliberate *absence* (to borrow Mallarmé's phrase). So difficult, however, might such imagery become when woven around these contrived "absences", even for Persian readers familiar with the poet's cultural conventions, that Nezâmî himself occasionally condescends to yield the key, and inserts the Arabic verb *ya'nî* – "this means" – and *names* his missing object. The translator must take this cue from Nezâmî's own example and supply the missing name where its absence would simply prevent a modern Western reader from grasping the poet's purpose at all. The free verse translation here is designed to suggest the nobility and rhythm, but makes no attempt slavishly (and impossibly) to reproduce the exact cadences of the poem's original metre, *khafîf*.

English translations: Through their living contact with Indo-Persian culture, the British were the first Westerners to perceive Nezâmî's importance. But when James Kritzeck in his classic *Anthology of Islamic Literature* (London 1964) dismissed Nezâmî as "so incredibly ponderous a poet", he passed a terrible verdict, if not on the Persian writer himself, then at least on his three major English translators: James Atkinson (*Laylí Majnún*, 1836: the most poetic); H. Wilberforce Clarke (*Sikandar-Náma*, the first part of the *Alexander Romance*, 1881); and C.H. Wilson (*Haft Paikar*, with a volume of commentary, 1924). All those who would further attempt Nezâmî, be warned.

French: A very accurate, serviceable but also somewhat "ponderous" (again) translation in prose of *Chosroès et Chîrîn* by Henri Massé appeared in 1970.

German: R. Gelpke charmingly paraphrased in prose the central portion of the *Haft Paykar*, in seven tales, in *Die sieben Geschichten der sieben Prinzessinnen*, Zurich 1959.

Italian: Alessandro Bausani's *Le sette principesse*, Bari 1967, is the most accurate European prose translation of the *Haft Paykar*, but given the author's noted sensitivity (his essays on Persian literature in general and on Nezâmî in particular are among the best in any Western language), it falls strangely flat.

Studies

BAUSANI, A.: *Storia della letteratura persiana*, Turin 1960.

BERTHELS, E.: *Velikyi azerbaïdzhanskyi poët Nizâmî*, Baku 1940; *Roman ob Aleksandre i yevo glavnye versii po vostoke*, Moscow 1948; art. "Nizâmî" in *Encyclopaedia of Islam*, 2nd edn.

DUDA, H.W.: *Ferhâd und Schîrîn*, Prague 1933.

GRÜNEBAUM, G. VON: *Medieval Islam*, Chicago 1946; short but profound insight on the *Haft Paykar*, pp. 290–92.

MEIER, F.: "Turandot in Persien", in *Zeitschrift der Deutschen Morgenländischen Gesellschaft* N.F., 20 (1941), pp. 1–27.

RITTER, H.: *Über die Bildersprache Nizâmîs*, Berlin/Leipzig 1927.

Illustrations

Nezâmî was the most illustrated of all Persian authors. Study of his illuminations virtually amounts to a scan of the full history of Persianate Islamic painting itself.

BINYON, L: *The Poems of Nizâmî* (study of British Museum MS. Or. 2265), London 1928; with B. GRAY and J. WILKINSON: *Persian Miniature Painting*, London 1933.

BREND, B.: *The Emperor Akbar's Khamsa of Nizâmî*, London 1995.

ROBINSON, B.W.: "Prince Bâysonghor's Nizâmî", *Ars Orientalis* 2 (1957); "The Earliest Illustrated Manuscripts of Nizâmî", *Ars Orientalis* 3 (1957).

STCHOUKINE, I.: "Les peintures de la Khamseh de Nizâmî du British Museum, Or. 6810", *Syria* (1950); "Peintures turcomanes et safavides d'une Khamseh de Nizâmî achevée à Tabrîz en 1481", *Arts asiatiques* (1966); *Les peintures des manuscrits de la Khamseh de Nizâmî au Topkapı Sarayı Müzesi d'Istanbul*, Paris 1977.

WELCH, S.C.: *Persian Painting: Five Royal Safavid Manuscripts of the Sixteenth Century*, New York 1975; with S. CANBY and N. TITLEY: *Wonders of the Age: Masterpieces of Early Safavid Painting, 1501–1576*, Fogg Art Museum, Harvard University 1979.

Acknowledgments

Roland and Sabrina Michaud wish to join Michael Barry in expressing their thanks to Masters 'Abd-ol-Ahad Ahmadî, Abû-Bakr and Habîbollâh, tilemasters of Herât's Friday Mosque, and to Masters Sharîfî, Bahareh and Najîmî, superintendents to Herât's archaeological inheritance, for their hospitality and welcome, for the generosity with which they shared their secrets and for their stubborn success in preserving and perpetuating things of supreme beauty through the darkest hours of their country's agony.

Index